MARKINGS
ON A
LONG JOURNEY

MARKINGS
ON A
LONG JOURNEY
WRITINGS OF JOHN J. TIMMERMAN

Rodney J. Mulder & John H. Timmerman, Editors

BAKER BOOK HOUSE
Grand Rapids, Michigan 49506

Copyright 1982 by
Baker Book House Company

ISBN: 0-8010-6146-6

Printed in the United States of America

Contents

Preface

Professor John J. Timmerman is best remembered, respected, and loved as a teacher. Thousands of his former students have keen recollections of their classes with him. They may not remember the lectures delivered or the notes taken, but they all vividly recall Dr. Timmerman as a person, his inimitable teaching style, what he stood for or against, and what moved him to laughter, admiration, or sadness.

For more than forty years John J. Timmerman poured his heart and soul into his teaching. He loved his profession. However, he was not blind to the perils and pitfalls in teaching, and perhaps that is why he was so successful in it.

To collect and organize selections from the many writings of Professor Timmerman has been a rare pleasure. Recorded in them one finds moving and eloquent witness not only to his personal joys or sorrows but also to those which delineate the spirit of Christian people of all times. These selections represent the rarest kind of writing, that which at once entertains and instructs. They are, in the words of one of Dr. Timmerman's favorite teaching subjects, Geoffrey Chaucer, "tales of best sentence and moost solaas" — tales of highest meaning and most consolation.

These samples of Professor Timmerman's many writings are divided into chapters according to subject areas. Within most chapters the selections are arranged chronologically, a few thematically. Two selections are original essays, appearing in print for the first time. "The Muse in Harness" is a reminiscence of the English Department of Calvin College during Professor Timmerman's tenure. "Memories of Grundy College" is a brief history of that short-lived institution, shedding light on Midwestern culture in the early twenties.

With appreciation we acknowledge the permission of the following periodicals to reprint articles authored by Professor Timmerman: *The Banner, Calvin Forum, The Calvin Spark, College Composition, Dialogue, The Outlook*, and *The Reformed Journal.*

Professor John J. Timmerman

Professor John J. Timmerman

CHRONOLOGY

1908	November 2	Born in Iowa City, Iowa
1909	June	Adopted by the Reverend Mr. and Mrs. John Timmerman
1914-1916		Attended Orange City, Iowa, Christian School
1916		Moved to Grundy Center, Iowa, where Rev. Timmerman was appointed Professor of Theology and German at the Grundy Center Seminary and College
1916-1920		Attended Grundy Center Public School
1920		Moved to Paterson, New Jersey, where Rev. Timmerman became the pastor of Fourth Christian Reformed Church
1920-1922		Attended Riverside Christian School
1922-1926		Attended Eastern Academy
1927-1931		Attended Calvin College
1931-1932		Attended University of Michigan, with University of Michigan State Colleges Fellowship. Received M.A.
1932-1934		Taught English, German, and Philosophy at Grundy Center Junior College
1934-1935		Graduate Student Assistant in English at Calvin College
1935		Scholarship at the University of Virginia
1935-1937		Graduate Fellowships in English at Northwestern University
1937		Graduate Assistantship in English at Northwestern University declined because of temporary ill health
1937-1938		Taught German and Latin at Eastern Academy

1938	August 5	Married Carolyn Jane Hager
1938-1945		Taught English at Grand Rapids Christian High School
1941	September 24	Birth of daughter, Lucarol M., now married to Rodney J. Mulder
1945	January 19	Birth of son, John H., now married to Patricia L. Knoll
1945		Appointed to English Department, Calvin College
1948		Received Ph.D from Northwestern University
1950	February 9	Birth of daughter, Miriam Shelley, now married to Steven Robert Lilley
1956	May 17	Birth of son, Luverne Carlyle, now married to Velda Kay Graham
1963-1964		Fulbright Senior Lectureship in American Literature, Free University, Amsterdam
1975		Retired from Calvin College as Professor of English, Emeritus

John J. Timmerman

A REMINISCENCE

Richard R. Tiemersma

Although the collection of essays in this anthology clearly demonstrates John J. Timmerman's eminence as a Christian scholar, it shows only one side of him — and, perhaps, not the most important side. For, while there can be no doubt that the articles, reviews, and addresses were a salutary influence in and on the community that he served, Dr. Timmerman was, in the first place, a master teacher who left his indelible imprint on the thousands of students who came under his tutelage during a long and distinguished academic career.

"Tim" began teaching even before he had completed his own undergraduate education, when, as a senior English major at Calvin College, he taught a course in German, a language that, by virtue of his home upbringing as well as his formal studies, he was well equipped to teach. When, in 1932, he began looking for a full-time teaching position, the vocational scene could hardly have been less propitious. The Great Depression that afflicted the entire Western world had wreaked havoc with the job market for teachers, and many school boards were rather more interested in cheap labor, however unqualified, than in quality education of the sort that a young man with a Master's degree from the University of Michigan had to offer. Consequently, when a position in the short-lived Grundy Junior College in Grundy Center, Iowa, offered itself, Tim was faced with something of a Hobson's choice, and, like Hobson's clientele, he accepted.

When Grundy Junior closed its doors after an eighteen-year struggle, Tim returned to Calvin College for a year, which he devoted to teaching one section of freshman English while earning his state certification to teach in secondary schools. Highly "over-qualified" by then for the few teaching positions available, he resumed his graduate studies, this time at Northwestern University, where during the academic years 1935 to 1937 he completed all but the dissertation requirements for the Doctor's degree. From Northwestern he went to Eastern Academy in Paterson, New Jersey, to teach for a year before returning to Grand Rapids. There, for the next seven years, he taught in the Christian High School, occupying his summers as an instructor in the Calvin College summer sessions.

Tim joined the Calvin staff as a full-fledged faculty member in 1945 and spent the rest of his teaching career at his alma mater. During the thirty years before his retirement from full-time teaching in 1975, he prepared, taught, and generously relinquished to junior colleagues an array of courses that few in modern times would have thought possible for one person to master. In addition to the ubiquitous freshman composition courses — which in themselves constituted perhaps a dozen different courses as the program underwent constant revision — he taught virtually the whole range of English and American literature from the medieval to the immediately contemporary: Chaucer, Shakespeare, Seventeenth-Century, Eighteenth-Century, Romantic, Victorian Poetry, English Novel, Literary Criticism, American Literature (a two-semester course), besides Principles of Teaching English. In addition, after his retirement he returned to teach a specially prepared course, American Western Writers.

His devotion to teaching did not reward him handsomely in material returns. He entered the profession during some of the darkest days of the Depression, and he left before a professor's salary at Calvin compared especially favorably with that of a Detroit assembly-line worker. Nor was his tenure at the college the sinecure that it is sometimes imagined by the laity to be. Always teaching a full load, with overflowing classes and only an occasional concession to the burdens of the department chairmanship, he was not one to seize every opportunity to avoid the classroom. Indeed, he was absent from the campus during those thirty years on only two widely separated occasions — once for the spring semester of 1947 to complete his doctoral dissertation, and, a second time, during the 1963-1964 academic year, when he accepted a Fulbright lectureship at the Free University in Amsterdam, a venture that, notwithstanding some modest college assistance, was at least partially underwritten by himself. He could not, therefore, be said to be like the village preacher of Goldsmith's "Deserted Village" — "passing rich with forty pounds a year." The numerous articles that comprise this collection are, further, only a highly selective representation of his total scholarly production, as a glance at the "Bibliography of Published Works" will attest. It is to his unending credit that, without the threat of "publish or perish" that has for years hung over much of academe, he published voluminously — but never at the expense of what he considered his primary calling, that of teaching the students entrusted to his care. His "jewels," like Cornelia's children, are his students, rough-cut though some of us may have turned out to be in spite of his best efforts to polish us.

When he retired from full-time teaching in 1975, I had the pleasant duty of compiling the numerous expressions of good will that poured into the English Department from these students. The felicitations came from all parts of the country and from all walks of life. Many of them were from persons who were themselves now teachers and who professed their indebtedness to him as a model. Others were from members of distinguished, non-academic professions — medicine, law, the ministry. Still others — and these were, perhaps, the most telling of all — were from men and women who made no pretense to professional achievement but whose personal lives, and those of their children and even grandchildren, had been enriched because of the influence of a master teacher, a genuine scholar, and, above all, a practicing as well as professing Christian.

Running like a *leitmotif* through these letters was the comparison of Dr. Timmerman to the very characters that he had taught his classes over the years. And, indeed, my own recollections take a similar turn. I think of the Canterbury pilgrims whom Chaucer described in his *Tales:* of the Knight, who "nevere yet no vilenye ne sayde/In al his lyf unto no manner wight"; of the genial and generous Franklin in whose house "It snewed . . . of mete and drynke" '; of the Parson, who "though he hooly were and vertuous/ . . . was noght to synful men despitous,/ Ne of his speche daungerous ne digne." But, above all — and it came as no surprise to see how many of his former students cited the passage — I think of that accolade of accolades, as applicable to Dr. Timmerman as it was to the Oxford Clerk: "And gladly wolde he lerne and gladly teche." For Tim belongs to that same company to whom Matthew Arnold paid tribute in *Culture and Anarchy*: men

> . . . who have had a passion for diffusing, for making prevail, for carrying from one end of society to the other, the best knowledge, the best ideas of their time: who have laboured to divest knowledge of all

that was harsh, uncouth, difficult, abstract, professional, exclusive, to humanize it, to make it efficient outside the clique of the cultivated and learned. . . .

My personal contact with Tim began in 1947 when, as an under-graduate junior, I enrolled in his Eighteenth-Century Literature course. I was one of the horde of ex-servicemen whose return threatened to engulf the current teaching staff and whose numbers — and sometimes mores — rather markedly changed the nature of the Calvin student body. By that time Tim had already established a reputation for ex-cellent teaching, and I considered myself fortunate to get into one of his classes, since an almost semi-annual complaint was that those classes were over-subscribed.

It was a memorable course, as were all of his courses. Men whose names meant little or nothing to me came alive as Tim introduced us to their works and illuminated their lives by anecdotes gleaned from his voracious reading of biographies. One *saw* the spidery little Pope antagonizing his friends, satirizing his times, and instructing his peers in the art of writing and evaluating poetry. One *heard* the august Dr. Johnson making his pronouncements, as it were *ex cathedra*, from his throne in the coffee shop or his place of honor at Mrs. Thrale's table. One cringed with embarrassment for Boswell as he played the sycophant, and chuckled over his Machiavellian maneuvering to bring Johnson and the radical John Wilkes together at Edward Dilly's dinner table.

It was in this Eighteenth-Century course, too, that I became aware of one of the qualities that distinguished Tim as a teacher and as a public speaker — his prodigious capacity for memorization. To be sure, he used notes to guide him in his lectures, but I have never seen him use a note in a public address. In class, as well, he enlivened his discussions of the current works by appropriate — and often wryly humorous — quotations from other works. I recall, for example, his telling a class in Victorian poetry about the Tennysons' frustrating, decades-long postponement of marriage because of poverty. "Chill penury," he observed, quoting from Gray's "Elegy," "repress'd their noble rage."

Realizing, as he did, the inestimable value of memorizing signifi-cant passages of literature, he assigned twelve couplets from Pope — we were allowed to choose our own — for the final examination. He did not demand them at examination time, as I recall, but the threat of being held accountable was incentive enough for most of us. As a result, I can still quote most of the lines that I learned, and I have used many of them to advantage, time and again, in my own courses.

One thing more makes that course stand out in my memory. Several of the former students who wrote on the occasion of Tim's retirement observed that his was the first — and perhaps only — professor's home to which they had been invited. In the current academic climate, in which students are sometimes overwhelmed with personalized attention from whole bureaus of "support services," such direct contact with professors is more or less taken for granted; in any event, each entering student is assigned a professional counselor, departmental majors have their major programs tailor-made, and faculty offices and time are at the disposal of any student who chooses to avail himself of them. In the late forties, and, in fact, well beyond that era, however, there were no faculty offices on campus, and professors typically went to their private studies when their classes were finished for the day. (As Tim has observed — in *Promises to Keep,* I believe — "In those days, if you had a problem, you had a problem.") Consequently, it was a rare experience for us students in that Eighteenth-Century course to be invited to the Timmermans for afternoon tea, where our mentor played the role of genial, if somewhat diffident, host and most of us for the first time met his exuberant and superlatively hospitable wife. "Most of us," I say, because the occasion was a mixed pleasure for one of the young ladies in the class. I learned later that, a few weeks before, Mrs. Timmerman had been sitting, unrecognized, on a public bus behind two Calvin coeds who were animatedly discussing their professors. Arriving at her stop, Mrs. Timmerman, I am told, leaned forward and said, "I'm Mrs. Timmerman, and I can't tell you how much I've enjoyed your conversation, girls. I'm just sorry that you didn't get around to *my* husband." Whereupon she got off, leaving the coeds on the verge of catalepsy.

One has to remember the awe that professors inspired in the typical student of those less democratic days. Prominent among the opening sentences of the annual catalog was the statement "Attendance at Calvin is a privilege, not a right," a pronouncement that most of us took at face value. In such an atmosphere the Faculty Room on the old Franklin Street campus was roughly analogous to the Inner Temple of the ancient Israelites. None but the priestly caste and such acolytes as custodians and mail clerks would have dreamed of entering the sanctum when it was likely to be occupied. The more fastidious among us would even avert our eyes if, on occasion, the door opened while we were stooping over the adjacent drinking fountain. I, myself, would have expected lightning to leap from the doorknob if ever it were touched by a profane hand.

Consider, then, the terrible dilemma of this classmate of ours when we were invited to tea at the Timmermans' home. To forgo the inestimable privilege of sitting at the feet of the master in his own private citadel was unthinkable. On the other hand, to go to the tea entailed being recognized by Mrs. Timmerman as one of the conversationalists on the bus.

In the end, adulation triumphed over terror, but at what cost could be seen as we lined up to be presented to our hostess. One by one we stepped forward to acknowledge the introductions, the culprit lagging behind until there was no way to further postpone the ordeal. When, finally, Tim made the introduction, all the poor girl could do was stammer tremulously, "I'm afraid we've already met!" It is a mark of the Timmermans' sense of humor and magnanimity that both the young lady and the man she married, also one of Tim's students, became fast personal friends of the family and remain, to this day, two of Tim's most ardent admirers.

As was true of all of Tim's courses, the lectures in his Eighteenth-Century course were distinguished by the finely turned phrase, the apt word, the wry understatement, the polysyllabic juxtapositions — language that, appropriately enough, epitomized Pope's definition of true wit: ". . . nature to advantage dressed,/What oft was thought, but ne'er so well expressed." Oliver Goldsmith's undistinguished college career, for instance, was described as "a perfect example of unrivaled economy of effort." When, a year or so later in another course, a lackluster paper of my own came back from Tim with almost the exact comment on it (he had deleted the "perfect" and had inserted the word "hitherto" before "unrivaled"), I derived some small comfort from ranking, in at least one respect, with the likes of Goldsmith.

Compared with a typical Timmerman class, that Eighteenth-Century class was a relatively small one, consisting for the most part of serious upper-class English majors. Consequently, Tim was spared the irritation that he occasionally encountered in courses that attracted less dedicated students — those who, needing a literature course for graduation or to fulfill a particular cognate requirement for their programs, came as much to be entertained as to be instructed. The two courses in American Literature that I took with Tim seem, in retrospect, to have had more than their just proportion of such students and, if I am not mistaken, prompted one of Tim's many memorable observations on the academic climate: "We ought to confer a Calvin A.B. on all Christian Reformed infants at baptism, and then only those who want to be educated would have to go to the trouble of coming to college."

One rather well-defined group appeared to be obsessed with any author's "view of the after-life," and indicated that, if it was not strictly orthodox by their lights, there was little point in hearing anything else he might have to say. Their moment came toward the end of the second semester when we studied Edwin Arlington Robinson's "Ben Jonson Entertains a Man from Stratford," in which the poet, using Jonson as the persona in a dramatic monologue, depicts Shakespeare as an out-and-out naturalist whose chief source of comfort was "that House — /The best you ever saw," from which the bard would reign in Stratford as the hometown boy who had made good in the big city. When asked what the poem was "about," one of this group, in an almost Pavlovian response, volunteered, "The after-life!" If most of us were surprised, Tim was positively astounded at this ingenious exegesis. Searching for a clue, or perhaps hoping to penetrate the labyrinthine ways of the student's mind, he asked, "What gave you that impression?" " 'That House,' " answered the student. "*What* 'house'?" asked the increasingly mystified Timmerman. "The house not made with hands," came the response!

Barely concealing his exasperation, Tim explained that the "House" was a material house, quite assuredly made with someone's hands, and that Robinson had capitalized the word only to suggest how important a status symbol it was for Shakespeare. It was apparent to most of us that the limit had almost been reached; and, when one of the student's cronies had the effrontery to ask how a non-major could be expected to see this, Tim almost exploded. He restrained himself, however, though with obvious effort, and merely wondered aloud whether one had to be an English major to know what a "house" is.

I doubt that the student realized how close to annihilation he came, but another student in the same course (though possibly not in the same semester) was less fortunate. Tim had the gentleman's abhorrence of direct confrontation and often went out of his way to respond charitably, or at worst with satiric humor often missed by the intended recipient, to inanities or affronts that exasperated him. On very rare occasions, a head of steam that had been slowly building up for weeks would erupt in a Vesuvian release that would inundate some hapless creature who had pulled the plug.

When that occurred, Tim's wrath could assume Titanic proportions, as when a student, at the next class after a blue book, entered the room, asked — unreasonably enough, considering the forty-odd students who had written the test — whether the blue books would be

Spring, 1939

Coach, Grand Rapids
Christian High School,
1941

Registration, 1954

Calvin Essay Contest Award to
Betty Duimstra

With Donald Bouma, 1954

Portrait, 1953

returned that day, and then brazenly sauntered out again when told that they would not. As though this original act of lese majesty were not enough, the student spent the next class session copying his seat-mate's notes on the lecture that he had missed — with the inevitable result that he missed taking notes on the current lecture. Almost every-one in the class could see that the student was not listening to the lecture. We could also sense that Tim was aware of what was going on and was becoming increasingly annoyed. The storm signals were clearly flying, and several of us warned the scapegrace after class that he was sailing dangerously close to the wind. He was apparently a slow learner, however, and the next session was a repeat of the note-copying routine. Halfway through the session, Tim stopped in mid paragraph, demanded to know what was "going on back there," fired a barrage that shriveled even those sitting in the direct line of fire, and summarily ordered the student out of the room. Tim was livid, shaking with anger, and embarrassed at having made the rest of the class participants in this deviation from his customary equanimity. He turned his back on the class and, for what must have been, per-haps, thirty seconds but seemed an hour to us, struggled to regain his composure. For the rest of the period he almost certainly had the most attentive audience that he has ever had.

Such reactions, however, were very rare, and the more memorable because of their rarity. For the most part, Tim suffered fools, if not gladly, at least with restraint. His perspective can perhaps best be summed up in his answer when I once asked why he had not given an egregiously bad book a more thorough castigation in one of his numerous book reviews: "You don't use artillery to kill a bedbug!"

Not that he considered his students bedbugs (though I have heard him describe a select few in other, similarly uncomplimentary, terms), but generally his response to student ineptitude was of a piece with the irenic tone of that review. He had no difficulty in recognizing stupidity when he saw it, but in public he usually tried to call it by some less opprobrious name. Among the letters from former students when Tim retired was one from a man who has since earned a repu-tation of his own as a teacher and scholar. "I still remember," he wrote, "your mercy in overlooking my terrible slovenliness in some sophomore papers in order to give me all possible credit for what I had done well." That, in a sentence, was Tim's preferred way of doing business — generous in his praise of even minor accomplishments, whether of students or colleagues, and conciliatory even when he had to criticize adversely.

Part of his technique in this respect was owing to the quality of his mirth. He loved a good joke, though he often complained that he had difficulty in remembering anecdotes that were not related to his literary figures. But I cannot say that, in all the years that I have known him, I have ever heard him really laugh; neither his humor nor his reaction to the humor of others was of the boisterous sort. What emerged when Tim's funny bone was tickled was something between a titter and a giggle, sometimes so uncontrolled that tears would run down his cheeks, and so infectious that the class would shake with merriment long after the original sally had lost its own effect.

The first page of the class notes that I took in Tim's Victorian Poetry course begins with a typically Timmermanian observation: Queen Victoria was preceded by "an idiot [George III], a libertine [George IV], and a fool [William IV]." There follow some three closely written pages on the political, social, economic, and religious climate of the age, into which a thumbnail biography of Victoria herself had been slipped. That, as I remember, was standard procedure for one of Tim's courses. At a time when some of the more extreme "New Critics" were extolling the virtues of dealing only with the work itself, regardless of the age or the author's personal experiences out of which the work had grown, Tim managed to walk the line between ignoring such data and the opposite extreme — that of dealing so extensively in biography that the work was virtually ignored. As a consequence (much as Tim came to hate the word as it was increasingly abused by educationists) his courses had a "relevance" that took the student into the mind of the period by means of what Matthew Arnold termed "the best that has been thought and said."

I did not take Tim's Literary Criticism course — it was not in the curriculum in my day — but every class session in every course that I did take with him was an object lesson in literary criticism. Eschewing both the "historical" and the "personal" estimates that Arnold so thoroughly disparaged, Tim strove, with outstanding success, to present the "real" estimate, the one that took as the final criterion the degree of "high truth and seriousness" that a work contained. He took the connoisseur's delight in well-executed form and would never sanctify a shoddy work on the grounds of its undeniable moral content. At·the same time, he made it abundantly clear that no amount of literary expertise can compensate for a distorted view of life. Nor did he make the mistake of treating every work by a distinguished author as though it were, by virtue of the authorship, a thing to be venerated. With all due respect for Tennyson, he could shake with glee over Swinburne's devastating parody of "The Higher Pantheism." With similar respect for Browning's vehement, if somewhat unorthodox, defense of Christianity, he could also point out that in "The Statue and the Bust" Browning was skating on what was morally very thin ice. Tim was the modern, grown-up equivalent of the *enfant terrible* in "The Emperor's New Clothes"; regardless of popular or critical opinion, if the Emperor was naked, Tim called attention to the fact, and the poetry of the Victorian Age offered, perhaps, as much opportunity for such exposure, either in form or in content, as that of any period in English or American literature.

My notes on that course, like the margins in the text that we used, are studded with Tim's *bon mots*. As he paraphrased the woman in Browning's "The Glove," she urged her suitor: "You're willing to die for me? All right; here's your chance," as she flung her glove into the lion pit. At the word "rathe" in Swinburne's "Nephelidia" I have a note saying, " 'He hadda hunt around for *that* one' — Tim." To reread those notes (as I did — *hard* — when first called on to teach some of those works myself) is to be transported back to one of the most consistently enjoyable periods of my formal education. One never knew exactly what to expect, but one could always expect to find in any given lecture the essence of the eighteenth-century ideal for literature: to please and to instruct.

An earlier course in the prose of the Victorian period had predisposed me to concentrating in that era, and Tim's handling of the poetry of Tennyson, Browning, Arnold, *et al.* persuaded me. When George Harper and I went to Northwestern to begin our work under Frederick Faverty, the man who had directed Tim's dissertation, we went with Tim's blessing, his generous recommendation, and his scholarly reputation to smooth our way but also to constitute a standard by which our own performances would be measured. Dr. Faverty rarely let us forget, in that first harrowing year, that we were, in a way, intellectual descendants of his; and whom Faverty loved, he chastened. Our Calvin training in Victorian literature, however, was proof against the best, or the worst, that he threw our way, though I suspect that our being the protégés of one of his own protégés occasionally caused him to overlook some of our foibles. In short, the name *Timmerman* proved to be an "open sesame" in Northwestern's English Department during our residence, and it continued to be for a number of years thereafter.

The qualities that characterized Tim as a mentor also marked him as a colleague. His gracious acceptance of junior members of the department did much to make those first difficult years bearable for us. A staunch defender of departmental integrity and of academic freedom within the bounds of Christian responsibility, he did not always see eye to eye with the administration's policies regarding the department

Caricature of John J. Timmerman by
Jack Harkema, 1974

and its members. During the numerous years that he served as department chairman, he campaigned tirelessly for recognition of the onerous burdens borne by the teachers of freshman English, and the concession of limited enrollment in freshman classes owed much to his persistence. As chairman he was the most democratic of leaders, *primus inter pares*, and guided the department through some traumatic months during the radical change from the semester to the "four-one-four" curriculum.

Course after course that he had worked on for years and had made famous among the students, he relinquished cheerfully, in order to give a junior colleague the pleasure of teaching something other than freshman composition. I think that my own obstreperousness in those early years must have sometimes made him question the wisdom of supporting my appointment; but he never indicated by word or action anything but the warmest concern for my well-being, listening to my gripes, smoothing my frequently ruffled feathers, praising my often bumbling efforts to reform the entire academic world, defending me against well-deserved criticism, and pouring oil on waters that I had troubled. And always, as an integral part of his function in the Calvin English community, there was the justly renowned hospitality of the Timmerman home, where one could let his hair down, speak off the record, and be sumptuously wined and dined while enjoying the kind of conversation that invariably ensued when Tim and Carolyn were part of the group.

Indeed, it was on such informal occasions that Tim was often at his best. A master of colorful description that he kept a careful rein on in class, Tim was an all-faculty favorite at the coffee table or in the faculty room, where he frequently called a spade a spade in mellifluously scathing terms, to the instruction, edification, merriment — and envy — of his less linguistically gifted colleagues.

Something of the same kind of humor, modified to suit the context, to be sure, flavored the faculty minutes with which, during two elected terms as secretary, he regaled the faculty. He had an unerring ear for pomposity and pseudo-intellectualism, and it was a delight to see him deflate a hot-air balloon with a sly pinprick or nudge a sacred cow with a mischievous elbow. As an elected member of the Educational Policy Committee, which for years passed final judgment on proposals for new courses and screened candidates for faculty appointment, he similarly did much, I am told, to enliven the proceedings. Not all the members of that august body, by Tim's own account, were always amused; much depended on the object of his satire. But he generally said what he thought had to be said, and he said it inimitably.

Tim's teaching career headed toward a premature end when in 1972, under the threat of a projected decline in enrollments and urged by the North Central Association's accrediting committee to make room for "new blood" in the faculty, the college lowered the mandatory retirement age from seventy to sixty-five. With little or no forewarning, the faculty was confronted with this decision, and the effects on senior members were, to say the least, unsettling. The edict was made somewhat less draconian for those over sixty at the time; by application of a complicated formula involving the difference between a faculty member's age and seventy years, Tim's tenure was extended for a year beyond the newly prescribed limits. A further proviso was that for the benefit of the college, if the department could demonstrate need, the early retirees would be permitted to teach for a limited time even beyond the extended deadline. It goes without saying that the English Department needed Tim, and so his departure was not as precipitate as it might have been. Still, he "retired" officially a significant number of years before he would have chosen to retire. Partly for economic reasons, surely, but, one suspects, chiefly because he loved doing what he did so outstandingly well — and had done so singlemindedly that he had few extracurricular avocations to take the place of teaching and writing — Tim was noticeably affected by this untoward turn of events.

It is axiomatic that no person is indispensable. But it is equally true that some are less dispensable than others, and Tim very decidedly falls into that latter category. In some forty years as a student and as a teacher I have encountered a comparatively few college and university instructors who, in widely differing ways, could be considered Tim's equal. I think that I am not exaggerating when I profess not to have met his superior. His influence is still felt in the English Department, many of whose current members are his former students. His influence is, perforce, less pronounced in the college as a whole, where the proportion of his former colleagues and students is reduced with every passing year. But what is most to be regretted is that present and future students of Calvin College will not have the privilege of pursuing their education under the guidance and direction of a man who for thirty years exemplified the best that the teaching profession has to offer. For, as one of his former students wrote in 1975, Tim "made a difference."

Professor John J. Timmerman

1

"So Close to Our Dwelling Place"

ESSAYS

*F*irst, Professor Timmerman has adamantly denied the rumor that his youthful pitching arm attracted the attention of Yankee scouts. Second, he readily confesses to a lifelong love for baseball. There are baseball players and baseball games that are great to remember. Those players and games are recollected with evident fondness in the following selections, for Professor Timmerman remembers that behind every superstar among the boys of summer, for every Babe Ruth or Reggie Jackson, there are a few thousand sunburned lads thunking tattered gloves on sandlot diamonds. These are the forgotten boys of summer. And perhaps also Alice would have been forgotten had she not been remembered with evident fondness and immortalized in Professor Timmerman's columns in The Reformed Journal. Alice was no superstar, although she had a talent for attracting attention. But her life is heroic in other ways, and she is as worth remembering as the immortal Babe trotting around the diamond "like a vat on stilts."

Darkness on the Diamond

The Reformed Journal (August, 1977)

Baseball has always attracted writers as well as fans. Unlike football, where the action is often partially hidden under a pile of writhing bodies, baseball's every move, except a sly spitter or two, is open to everybody. The individual player's achievement or failure is obvious. Baseball affords drama, strategy, and statistics. You can always look it up, and the figures are hard, clear, and definitive.

From the beginning, there have been great pulp players like Frank Merriwell mesmerizing the opponents of Yale with his double curve and the ghost written biographies turning history into legend. In recent years the pundit and the perceptive spectator have fused in the writing of Angell and Creamer. Baseball is over a century old, and has always battened on nostalgia. But in recent years one of the major springs of that nostalgia — the fixed traditions of playing the game — is crumbling and many fans are experiencing future shock.

During the last five years baseball has been wrenched by more changes than in its entire previous history. Television has tried to speed up a slow-moving drama with its sudden stirring spurts of action by freely ad-libbing announcers, who inundate viewers with statistics, momentary interviews, occasional humor, and in-depth diagnoses, at which Mr. Cosell is most eager and often arrogantly wrong. During these years the fat cat owners — notably the flamboyant, despotic, and vindictive Mr. Finley — together with the unionized players, who may eventually help wreck the game, have changed its character, rocked its traditions, and offended many fans.

In pursuit of profits they have, together or separately, changed the rules of the game, made a carom board of the infield, introduced the designated hitter and the ten-man team, ballooned the leagues to twenty-six teams, a third of them inept. They have extended the World Series into the chilly nights of October. They have scheduled games intended for green grass and sunlight to be played under artificial light and thereby reduced the number of .300 hitters to a near vanishing point. By trades, free agentry, and annexation they have shuffled line-ups beyond recognition. Who can keep track of Dick Allen as he pouts and prances from club to club?

If this sounds like a case for revolution, it is a futile gesture because profits are the name of the game which will probably take the World Series to Houston, where the stadium is roofed with glass, where it never gets cold, and only loyal fans with plenty of money will be able to attend.

Mr. Roger Angell, a senior fiction editor at the *New Yorker*, occupies an office containing a bookcase devoted to baseball including a solitary shelf devoted to a single, unsigned ball. That baseball is an apt symbol for the book, *Five Seasons* (1977), which is exceedingly knowledgeable about the genius of the game. Despite the cameo and occasionally full-length portraits, the central concern of the book is the playing and analysis of actual games. It will be most appreciated by the type of fan who regards the phrase "baseball trivia" as a defamation of what should be referred to as "little known facts." Even if the reader should regard many of the details as trivia he cannot disregard the electrical quality of the prose. It is well to remind ourselves that scintillating prose need not be wedded to great ideas, that keen senses and an imaginative mind can present relatively unimportant things with captivating skill. One may agree with Melville that one cannot write a great book about a flea, but a gifted writer can really put a flea in orbit.

Five Seasons has many charms. The author has style, the brilliant, hammered *New Yorker* prose. There is not a dead sentence in the book, and there are many memorable passages: Luis Tiant, the Boston pitcher, "stands on hill like a sunstruck archaeologist at Knossos"; Hank Aaron with that "familiar grooved, elegant, iron-wristed, late, *late* swing"; Billy Martin "staring out from under his long-billed cap with a cold and ferrety edginess." Among the arresting digressions are the lengthy analyses of the psychological erosion and inexplicable collapse of pitcher Steve Blass of the Pirates, and the amusing story of the three Detroit fans, one of whom had attended twelve hundred Tiger games, including those of the last five years, thereby establishing, I should judge, a record in willed frustration. Another of the trio, a masterly surgeon, Dr. D. Shapiro, scheduled his operations in hospital rooms "that he knows have an acceptable interior Harwell level."

There is also a touching incident involving Hank Greenberg, Detroit's towering first baseman, who nearly eclipsed Babe Ruth's home run record. Greenberg had said he would autograph baseballs in the neighborhood of a little boy with a broken leg. After the little boy had sobbed himself to sleep with disappointment, he was awakened by the entry of the huge Detroit star, who sat on his bed talking to him for half an hour and autographed his cast before leaving. For the fanciful there is a line-up of all-stars whose names begin with *K*, a team including Kaline, Klein, Kubek, and Kell, with Sandy Koufax as pitcher. I may as well end this paragraph with a few bizarre names in baseball: Alpha Brazle, Bibb Falk, Zach Wheat, Possum Whitted, Hank Arft, and Mordecai Peter Centennial Brown, only two of whom — Falk and Wheat — possessed more than curious names.

In April 1976, Mr. Angell, together with 54,016 other fans, including Joe Dimaggio, Mickey Mantle, and Babe Ruth's widow, attended the opening of the new Yankee Stadium, a house built by New York City instead of George Herman Ruth. It cost New York, a bankrupt city, $100 million. It was built in a decadent, dangerous disaster area. To build a sports palace in an area as seedy as the Bronx, where firebugs flourish and old people slink along the streets, seems like a grotesque and ironical joke. Angell suggests that the vast sums spent on sports are a copout; we thereby delude ourselves that they are worth it.

One can moralize about this, but Americans have overvalued sports for a century. Robert Frost made $200 during his first twenty years as a poet; Catfish Hunter makes more than a thousand times that for pitching thirty games in 1977 and now appears likely to lose half of them. The editorialist in *The Grand Rapids Press* of June 6 remarks:

> There are school systems in Kent County, for example, that will spend $200 to outfit one boy for football but cannot find the same amount to finance a school publication serving more than a dozen young writers.

Sports are entirely out of focus in this country, but that is the fault of greed or deluded people, not the games themselves. Seeing a batter hit a small, hard ball that travels sixty feet from pitcher to catcher in less than half a second and a fielder catching it one-handed deep in centerfield while running away from it is still a thrill which the crass materialism producing that feat cannot attenuate. Sports constitute a peripheral, legitimate, and salutary pleasure, but when they preoccupy a mind they trivialize it.

I agree with Thomas Wolfe that one can't go home again and with Thornton Wilder that one hadn't better, but if one could keep the old time steady and roll the new time back I should like to do this. I should like to board an Erie passenger car in Paterson, puff along with it to Jersey City, board the spray-splashed ferry to cross the windswept Hudson, walk down the raucous streets of New York to the elevated railroad and clatter in the drafty heat and noise to the *old* Yankee Stadium in the Bronx. I would sit in the sun-drenched bleachers overlooking a grassy outfield *and* infield in the mild Indian summer waiting for that open sesame "Play Ball!" I would watch the triple threat of Ruth, Gehrig, and Meusel of the 1927 Yankees pitted against the triple threat of Morgan, Bench, and Perez of the 1977 Cincinnati Reds. I would make no wager on the game except that it would be a game to remember and that great teams do not belong to nostalgia.

Babe Ruth and the National Pastime

The Reformed Journal (July-August, 1975)

During the first quarter of this century baseball was the national pastime in attendance, public interest, and consummate skill. Many think it has been slipping ever since.

The game of sheer strategy, the John McGraw, New York Giants type of game, is as dead as the baseball it was played with. Today a low-scoring game is usually unintentional. The old game of a sharp single, stolen base, well-executed bunt, and sacrifice fly, ensuring a one-run lead which was made to hold up through superb fielding and tricky pitching is almost obsolete. George Herman Ruth, who already as an all-star pitcher with the Red Sox was blasting the dead ball over the longest fences, together with the cork-center ball changed the game permanently in the early 1920s. With the Yankees Ruth hit more and longer home runs in a dozen years than any other player, with accompanying batting averages from .300 to .393. The day of the classic, lean beauty of the old game was over, and after 1920 not only Ruth but most of the batters were swinging for the stands. The old, tricky pitches were outlawed; attendance ballooned; and baseball entered its greatest age.

At the center of the dramatic revolution in the nature of baseball was the raucous, illiterate, and superbly coordinated son of a German saloonkeeper in Baltimore. A troublesome lad, he was at an early age put into the care of St. Mary's Industrial School, where he was saved from a sinister future by Brother Matthias — "THE GREATEST MAN I ever knew," as Ruth said — who transformed the seedy boy from the waterfront into a vividly exciting baseball player. The life of Ruth, gaudy, uninhibited, and often vulgar, moving from indigence and bar-keeping to national prominence, drawing bigger crowds than presidents and glamorous Hollywood stars, exalted into a hero by boyhood America, is a saga in success and snuffed-out sunlight. He was cheered and hooted for twenty years, experiencing unparalleled acclaim and bitter frustration. He was the symbol of a dazzling era even when he stood at home plate in Yankee Stadium — sick, suffering, and near death — to receive a last tumultuous hurrah. Beaten down by cancer, he croakily mumbled thanks from his ravished throat, and then after hobbling to the dugout said to old friend Dugan, "I'm gone, Joe. I'm gone, Joe." A few days later he died. The famous number 3 uniform was retired, and baseball never saw his like again.

Mr. Robert W. Creamer, senior editor of *Sports Illustrated*, in his biography *Babe* (1974) has written a first-rate life about Ruth. It is a popular, unsentimental, and highly skillful narrative. Creamer effectively uses all the resources of biography: the meticulous statistics with which baseball is almost obsessively concerned, newspaper accounts, an enormous range of interviews, substantially accurate conversations, and the physical data of ball parks. In all the multifarious data, we never lose sight of Babe and the sharply etched portrait that is constantly emerging. There is little waste and little pointless repetition. The style is lively, fresh, and easy, and the character of Ruth becomes luminously alive.

Ruth was a character, an extraordinary human being in whom the purely physical reached an excellence and intensity seldom seen. His personality forces an ambivalence from admiration to disgust. At twenty, fame stoked his natural exhibitionism into flame for over a decade. Ruth did things with resonance. Everything about him was gargantuan: his size, which he constantly fueled with prodigious meals, beer, whiskey, and interminable hot dogs; his pursuit of women in every American League port; his grotesque social ineptitude; his madcap driving; his mammoth home runs and the crowd-pleasing élan with which he struck out, even his proneness to injury and the exciting ritual of a dramatic exit from the stadium on a stretcher.

Ruth's salary disputes aroused national interest, and when in 1930 he received $80,000 a year, more than President Hoover, he justified the fact by claiming to be doing a better job. In the World Series with the Cubs, while being unmercifully harassed by the Chicago fans and players, he presumably pointed to center field and, at a count of 3 and 2, hit the longest home run ever seen in that park. Whether he actually pointed to the bleachers and called his shot has been disputed; that he hit the long home run is a fact. Ruth was big, and the record is convincingly big. The man who compiled it loomed high over the world of sport. Some idea of his value to the Yankees in 1930 may be gathered from the fact that the next highest salary on the Yankee team was $17,500. In those days one could support a family in great comfort on $60 a week. Ruth never doubted the public was getting a fair deal.

The fact remains that no player ever did what Ruth did. For three years he was the best pitcher, or at least the best left-handed pitcher, in the American league. In 1916 he won twenty-three games, had nine shutouts, and the lowest earned run average in the league. He won twenty or more games a year for three years, but his overwhelmingly impressive batting turned him into an outfielder in 1920, when he was sold to the New York Yankees, in whose employ he accumulated the most astonishing batting record ever compiled in a similar span of years. It is wholly unlikely that any single player will duplicate his dual achievement.

Ruth's enormous appeal says something about American culture and human nature. He was the epitome of the Horatio Alger hero in his rise from rags to riches through pluck, industry, and ability, although he was no prim moral model as Ragged Dick and the other Alger heroes were. An unruly bartender's son rose from snitching beers to handing out hundred dollar tips to waitresses. He offered vicarious satisfaction to the man tied to a weaver's shuttle hour after hour. He was the daydream come true of a home run in the last of the ninth with two out and the score tied. His uninhibited vulgarity tallied with the freewheeling morality of the era. Ruth meant power and Americans liked power. His geniality and largesse attracted people. He would autograph scorecards long after other players had wearied of it, and he would serve the little kids first; he never forgot St. Mary's Industrial School. He would put a five dollar tip on the table while Lou Gehrig sneaked in a dime. He seemed to justify the whole American inflation of sports. Finally, after the betrayal of the White Sox in the World Series, Ruth restored integrity to the game. Nobody doubted the validity of his swing. Finally, he gave his best to the game even when he was as taped and bruised as Mantle. Ruth never quit; he was mowed down by cancer.

Some are no doubt thinking, "But it's all just a game." Indeed it is, and I am not confusing it with much more important forms of effort and excellence. But what a game it was! A major league park was a happy place years ago with the flags streaming, the vivid green of natural grass, the graceful, geometric design of the diamond, with its precise chalk-white lines, the traditional and exacting ritual of the action. The hum and stir of the big crowd, the sense of steady action punctuated by sudden drama all made for pleasure. Many of us have happy memories of great plays. I have seen Ruth hit his long home runs, and I once saw Lefty Grove shut out the tremendous Yankees of 1928. I saw Detroit play when they had Cochrane, Gehringer, and a major league team. However, the best catch I ever saw occurred in a game at Riverside oval in Paterson, when a centerfielder called Murphy ran at top speed into the farthest reaches of left-center field and caught the ball with his bare right hand. There were no important consequences; it was simply a marvelous piece of judgment and co-ordination as pleasing in its own way as a well-executed sonnet. There is something memorable about excellence wherever it occurs.

Baseball, in my judgment, reached its peak of performance and prestige during the first quarter of the century. There have been superb teams since, but the overall excellence has declined until today. With the disastrous fattening of both leagues, there are teams that would have been consistently beaten by such first class semi-pro teams as the Paterson Silk Sox of the 1920's. If one were to combine the Tigers and White Sox today, one would have a fair second division team of that decade. Three-hundred-hitters have greatly declined; relief pitchers do a great business; the production of extra base hits is waning. Other more popular sports drain off talent. Sandlot baseball, so common in my youth, has greatly declined; the minor leagues are a joke compared to what they were. Baseball in the major leagues will probably continue to flourish, heavily supported by television instead of attending fans, but the pervasive presence of baseball on the American scene is going toward twilight. In the twenties boys like me knew the batting averages better than their catechism; we collected pictured players' cards by the hundreds; and to go to the big park to see Ruth hit a homer was a treat anticipated half a summer and talked about for the rest of it. *Optima dies . . . prima fugit.*

Diamond Greed

The Reformed Journal (July, 1981)

By the time this note appears, the baseball strike may be over. The mutual greed of owners and players may have been accommodated, aggrandized, or moderated. Whatever the outcome, an impeccably Reformed assessment of the matter should be made on this seedy affair.

Put simply, the quarrel between players and owners is about money, a great deal of money. It has nothing to do with sportsmanship; it is a bitter battle between seasonal grabbers, some of whom are superlative athletes, and entrenched, self-serving business men. But everybody is in the act: the designated hitter who bats .247, has fifteen homers a year, and lumbers about the bases like a sprained stallion; the pitcher who wins a fourth of his games; and even Mark Fidrych, who is paid over a hundred thousand dollars a year for losing games in the minor leagues. Neither side wants to lose a dime; so they meet from time to time to glower at each other. If my sympathies lie on any side, they lie on the side of the owners, not because of their case but because it will mean a better deal for the fans. They will get something instead of nothing. If one wants to be very charitable, he will assume that the owners had that in mind.

Technically, the dispute concerns a demand on the part of the owners that they be reimbursed for the loss of a free agent by a player from a designated pool of players. The players oppose this because it will trim both their availability and price. The buying club may not wish to pay so princely a salary if it has to give up a good player in addition.

In 1919, the Chicago White Sox threw the World Series. They were a superlatively good team, and with three untainted superstars, they barely managed to lose. The participants in the fix, even Joe ("Shoeless") Jackson, who was too dumb to know what he was doing, and Buck Weaver, who protested his innocence to the end, were thrown out of baseball. Jackson never got a dime out of the fix; he reported his doubts to the management, but he was drummed out of organized baseball and for years, under assumed names and until uncovered, he amazed sandlot teams by his prowess. The Black Sox deserved expulsion, but they had their reasons. Comiskey was the most tight-fisted, exploitative owner in baseball. They were one of the greatest teams in the game and, except for Eddie Collins, the poorest paid. Comiskey rather than the players was guilty of greed.

George Herman Ruth was the most flamboyant and probably also the best of all baseball players. As John Kieran put it in a bit of doggerel alien to these pages:

> My voice may be loud above the crowd
> And my words a bit uncouth,
> But I'll stand and shout till the last man out:
> "There was never a guy like Ruth."

In baseball there never was. For three years he was the best left-handed pitcher in the American league; then he built Yankee Stadium with the most astonishing batting record ever completed in a similar number of years. He could never steal second base, but then he didn't have to. Despite his ungainly figure, something like a vat on short stilts, he was a very competent outfielder. Allowing for inflation, Dave Winfield, the Yankee outfielder, still makes twice as much as Ruth after hitting thirty home runs with a batting average considerably less than three hundred. Ruth's lifetime average was .331 and his home runs usually ran around fifty. His frequent pre-season holdouts became national drama in the twenties. Colonel Rupert, owner of the Yankees, always capitulated because Ruth had a legitimate cause.

This baseball strike has no such legitimacy. Both sides are lush with money, both are senselessly obdurate, and neither seems concerned about the reaction of the fans who make the games possible. It seems to me little more than a sullen "me-first" slugfest. In terms of talent, most of today's players are already overpaid. Some clubs are bilking the public by fielding entire teams masquerading as major-leaguers. As far as I can tell most fans feel betrayed; their sense of fair play and fair pay has been violated.

On a deeper level one is angry at the overpayment for pleasure when so many good causes are crumbling. School systems are sheared of employees, aid to the sick, poor, and disadvantaged is diminished, but the players and owners want even more. Soon, as the game grows increasingly expensive, it will be played by the rich for the rich, while the rest of us watch it on a small screen.

Baseball is a great game. Even a grouch like H. L. Mencken and a

satirist like Shaw enjoyed and praised it. It is a highly skilled game —
only some six-hundred men in our nation enter the major leagues.
Gifted writers like Ring Lardner and Damon Runyan have celebrated
it. All sorts of people enjoy it, from lushes to poets and philosophers.
Even the Reverend Mr. Jerry Falwell occasionally flees to New York
to see the Yankees — courtesy of the private plane of a devotee. As a
boy I thought it infinitely more important than translating Caesar. A
trip to the old Yankee Stadium in the Bronx — the bleacher seat in the
sunshine overlooking green grass in the infield and outfield, hearing
the hard crack of wood on the ball as Ruth powered it over the right-
field fence, pushed his barrel-like torso around the bases, touched
home plate, took off his cap as he walked to the dugout — was a
highlight of summer. I saved baseball cards. I had all the great players
of the twenties and the decade before. While I was at college, my
mother gave all those cards to Tony Pasquali, our neighbor's son. If
Tony still has them, I envy his good fortune. I still enjoy ball games,
especially at the park in the sunshine. I would like to go again to
Wrigley Field, home of the Cubs, where I went from time to time
when I studied at Northwestern. It is the most beautiful park I have
seen, and now they want to invade it with artificial light.

Today the bleachers are empty, the fans disillusioned, and the players and owners competing in greed. It is not inconceivable that after
the strike the bleachers will be harder to fill.

Alice and the Deacon

The Reformed Journal (September, 1972)

For three years now we have lived next door to
Alice, her five children, two prospective husbands, and a succession
of police cars, as David, a friend, was regularly ordered out and his
belongings hurled on the driveway. The turbulent drama, now in a
quiet and hopefully permanent phase, has given us opportunities for
understanding, Christian service, and friendship.

What does it mean to live next door to Alice? It is an experience of
the mystery in human nature and of two different worlds separated

by a fence. The sense of time is different; there is more room for lounging and laughter. There is less planning because there is so little to plan with. Churches are unentered buildings. There is often little food, and Woody at the door at first refuses a snack because he has been taught to, but after he relents, he sneaks off to the garage to hide part of his food for future use. Things wear out, but repairmen don't work for charity. If my garage roof leaks, I hurry for shingles, but Gene, her husband, observing the holes in his roof says, "Don't worry about it. I never seen the rain come down straight. It always comes down on a slant." Ordinary conversations reach a volume one normally attains only in trying to sing "The Star-Spangled Banner." When Kaylise Faylene, the illegitimate child of David, was about due, I found myself hurtling down Eastern Avenue before dawn and being told by the policeman at the parking lot at Butterworth Hospital to hurry on although the lot was empty. When the children came over for breakfast, Anne Marie said, "My mama was crying this morning because none of our people would get out of bed and help." Later, Anne Marie, ten years old, came to borrow soap so that she could do the laundry, mop the floor and basement stairs, and have it "all nice and clean when my mother comes home." For my wife it has meant mending, making dresses, ministering at midnight to a forehead bloodied by a hurled glass in a family dialog. Alice, in turn, out of innate generosity and despite poverty, has brought over, among other things, a box of good cigars, a ham, and an unnecessary hot-water bottle. The little children have brought pleasure and sunshine.

Alice is black and poor, an A.D.C. mother, and might have been considered, to use Lamb's phrases, "a rebuke to your rising," "a haunting conscience," "the one thing not needful." Yet she and her family have been a blessing to ours.

We have learned that one needs experience to understand. Much of what happens at Alice's home is the result of fragile subsistence and unchosen predicament. She once said to us, "I was never brought up." An A.D.C. allowance allows meager living. Even used shoes and clothing for five and simple food cost money. Appliances break and furniture wears out. Alice needs a baby-sitter when she goes out to work, and the baby-sitter may steal as well as watch the children. She needs a car to get to work, as well as to rush an asthmatic child to the hospital on occasion. Unpaid bills pile up and repossession commences. The cycle grinds endlessly on.

Secondly, mutual confidence is nourished by staying put. When the family across the street moved in, the fourteen-year-old son said to me, "I suppose you'll be moving out now." It was a sad remark. Age and infirmity may make such a move necessary but one gets trust by remaining.

Those who live in areas like ours need support from the larger Christian community. A few months ago a deacon-at-large was appointed by the Christian Reformed churches in Grand Rapids. His office serves to bring the needs of the poor of any race to diaconates and individual Christians who are able and willing to aid. Recently, Alice faced a need, a need beyond the capacity of neighbors to alleviate. I referred this urgent matter of need to the deacon-at-large, who responded immediately and enthusiastically. He brought the problem to the diaconate of the nearest church, which investigated the request carefully and promptly. Within a week Alice was given funds which will enable her to work her way out of her difficulties. When she came over later to thank us for our help, she said, "I'd like to do something for the church. Are there any old people who need their floors washed? Or their house cleaned? I could do that." I believe this pattern has splendid possibilities in similar communities. Here is a highly responsible way in which generous Christians can help deserving and unfortunate people whose needs they can never be personally aware of.

Finally, the fourth response would be that neighborhoods like ours, if they are to grow or even survive in a pattern of amicable and fruitful integration, need young married couples. We need their enthusiasm, idealism, energy, and above all their children who adjust best of all and will receive as much as they give. A physician once told me that he had gone to a cheap tenement house to give free medical aid. At one apartment, he found an immaculately groomed young lady sitting on a chair, pad and pencil in hand, writing down suggestions for the ailing woman, her slovenly house, and disheveled children. He said to the social worker, "You ought to get off your chair and wash the floor." We need help like that. A good way to bring the love of Jesus is to show a little of it while you tell the story to the hurt and discouraged. Emerson said many dubious things, but he also said:

> Nor knowest thou what argument
> Thy life unto thy neighbor's creed has lent.

Whatever Happened to Alice?

The Reformed Journal (March, 1976)

Long ago, in *King Lear*, Edmund says that "when we are sick in fortune — often the surfeit of our own behavior," we behave as if we "were villians by necessity, fools by heavenly compulsion." If many comfortable people lay their troubles "to the charge of a star," heredity, environment, the bad break, the wheel of fortune, how much more appealing such refuge is to a person greatly locked in the whirlpool of heredity, environment, and personal weakness?

When misfortune strikes, Alice says, "That's the way the cookie crumbles." The strategy of coping is not a matter of inner reformation, but a shift of scene, a new boyfriend, new tactics in escape or acquisition. As one watches Alice and her family flounder in a whirlpool her own efforts cannot escape, one needs a lifeline stronger than a neighbor is able or society willing to furnish. A neighbor's lifeline draws her from the deep water temporarily, but the massive social lifeline necessary to give her security is not available, and the depressing fact is that if it were, her personal weakness would probably destroy her grasp — just another bad break. Let me try to make all this concrete.

Some four years ago, a little after D. B., Jr., the father of her last child, was ejected with appropriate rhetoric and all his belongings hurled on the snowy driveway, Alice, always interested in and interesting to men, welcomed Gene into the family. Since he had a job and was kind to the children, we urged them to marry. For their honeymoon they went to a Holiday Inn, after packing the children off to Grandma. At four in the morning Alice came home and my wife said, "The honeymoon is over already," but Alice had only returned to put a turkey in the oven. She went back to relish to the full the splendors of the motel. Characteristically, they had spent far too much on wedding rings, and for months we got calls from Fox's Jewelry, asking us to remind them of their debt. Gene, who has a talent for working in wood, could have supported the family; he also has a great talent for inertia. Neither one worked; it was somewhat like children playing at being a family.

Trouble was soon at every door, and instead of meeting it through responsible work, they decided to move to the West side of Chicago. As I looked at the U-Haul loaded with the furniture, the children, and the poodle setting out on this dubious odyssey, I could foresee only bleak disaster. It came within six weeks. Alice phoned me, begging for money to return to Grand Rapids. Her mother-in-law had tried to sell her furniture, hit her in the face with a hammer, and threatened to kill her. Fortunately, at the last moment they had left the children with Grandma.

Alice came home to a house without heat, light, or water. The furniture was still in Chicago, and the children had to sleep on the floor. It was late October and even the poodle was cold. Since she had left town, there was no welfare check available. Fortunately, the diaconate and the pastor of a nearby church came to her aid; the utilities were restored and food contributed. Gradually the furniture returned, some of it partially hacked to pieces by her mother-in-law. Welfare checks were restored. We thought that Gene would now seek a job, but, except for delivering telephone books for a few weeks in January, nobody worked at much of anything. It was a marvel to us that six people, a poodle, and an automobile could exist in such an effortless way.

Idleness, however, has its own perils and tensions and tempers mounted, reaching a bizarre climax. Gene had a cousin over from Chicago. According to Alice they spent the afternoon popping pills and smoking pot. When Gene and his friend went out for wine, Alice bolted the door. When Gene came home, we were jolted out of sleep by the crash of glass and the splintering of wood. Alice tried to bar him after he kicked down the door, but he beat her about the head. Woody, the little boy, frantically pounded on our door, shouting, "Call the police! Call the police!" We did and they arrived in three cruisers. Gene and his friend went galloping down the street, each with a long-barreled gun, one of which had a telescopic sight. Gene was caught but the cousin merged into the small crowd and the police first hand-cuffed the wrong man.

The police eventually confiscated the guns, but let the men go. That was a big mistake, as I tried to point out to them, since I knew Gene would return. He did — about 1 a.m., when we were again awakened by a pitiful screaming. Gene was then beating his wife with an immense iron pole used by the city to turn the water off and on at the curb, and previously stolen by him to turn it on when the city turned it off. Back to the telephone. More cruisers. Alice in our living room with a bloody towel over her head; three of the petrified children on the floor; the poodle howling in the night. During the last hours a man high on drugs, carrying a formidable lethal weapon, smashing a door, hammering his wife, and keeping the street in an uproar was still free, and so he remained. Irritated beyond measure, I went to the cruiser in pajamas and barefeet and asked the officers, "Would you please tell me what a misdemeanor is?" Later I was told police officers hesitate to arrest black men because their women seldom carry out a complaint. At about two o'clock, Alice and her children went to Grandma's, that huge, kind lady, only forty-three years old, who once said to me of my wife, "She done get her reward."

By means of the unfathomable adaptation that goes on next door, Gene was back in a few days with his pleasant grin, gaudy clothes, and cheerful "Howja doin?" Alice had taken him back on the condition that he go to work. He obtained work at a first-rate furniture factory and made good money which he spent largely on himself. Life seemed returning to normalcy, but not for long.

After a night of slamming doors and stormy talk, early in the morning Alice streaked away with the children. At seven in the morning, a neighbor's child said Alice wanted to see me. When I came to the door she was in complete daze and had blood on her clothes. The dining room table had a layer of blood on it. I went home and told Grandma to call the police. When my wife went over with a cup of coffee, she noticed an overwhelming smell of gas. All the jets were on. When Alice had asked me for a cigarette, I told her I had only had cigars. I gave her some. Fortunately, she had not lit one of them. When Grandma arrived, dressed like African royalty, she cleaned the table and the house.

The gruesome cause of Alice's attempted suicide need not be clinically described. She had come upon her husband molesting her little daughter. The effect on her was overwhelming: she could not face the horror and disillusion. This time she pressed charges and honored them, and Gene was put in jail and later divorced.

Alice works, but the wages she makes cancel her welfare check and are inadequate to meet the mounting minor crises: the ailing car, needed for work, but expensive to repair, the turned-off water and the mobilization of resources to get it turned on; the ceiling that fell down and was finally repaired; the robbery of several hundred dollars with no insurance; the deterioration of a property she cannot maintain, with its swinging storm doors, four splintered windows in the front door, the mounting back payments on the house, the torn jackets, dresses, and slacks my wife repairs, the layaways she pays on but always fails to buy because of waning funds. Furthermore, there is the merciless exploitation of finance companies. Once she was charged fifty dollars for the proper signature. Then there is the tiresome dependence upon neighbor's telephones. Once a relative from Chicago called at 3 a.m. to fetch Alice to the phone. When we refused, she said, "I'll never call you again." Even though she is trying hard, there is always too much to carry. All we as neighbors can apply is patchwork and veneer.

Six years ago Alice moved next door, and her way of life has been a revelation to us, almost always on the edge of disaster and sometimes in it. Six years later and the life of the family as insecure and ramshackle as ever. Four children and the mother locked in by environment, heredity, personal weaknesses, exploitation, social conditions, and the "mystery of iniquity" in a fallen world. At the center is Alice, sometimes aggressive and flamboyant in a flaming red coat, puffing a True cigarette, sometimes tender and generous, believing in God, quoting texts such as "Vengeance is mine, saith the Lord," and adorning her dining room with a large picture of Jesus. We have never succeeded in getting her or her children to church; yet she appreciates what the church has done for her. She says, "My people just talk and pray but the Christian Reformed help me out." Finally, one is filled with frustration as one confronts the labyrinth of problems that press upon her. One cannot change her character or the society that shaped her, and one cannot transfer faith by inoculation.

How pleasant it would be to end with a Dickensian picture of Alice shepherding her children to church regularly, never leaving them alone at night, spending the little money she has on their needs instead of her own pleasure. We have achieved little — a witness and five friends. After our exchange of Christmas presents, all four children wrote us letters with a lot of heart and bad English, one of which said, "I love Mrs. Timmerman, I even love Brandy [our dog] and Mr. Timmerman."

It's not what we hoped for but it is something.

2

"Fixing our Eyes on Jesus"

SUNDAYS AND SERMONS

*P*rofessor Timmerman is the son of a Christian Reformed minister, the Reverend John Timmerman, and grew up in what he calls "the golden age" of the denomination. It was an age of unified hearts and minds, but also an age which made tremendous demands upon the talent and versatility of its ministers. After one year of teaching at the Presbyterian Seminary in Dubuque, Iowa, Reverend Timmerman spent thirty-eight years as a minister in the Christian Reformed church, including four years of teaching at the short-lived Grundy College whose noble but checkered history is recalled elsewhere in this book. Reverend Timmerman served Christian Reformed churches in Cincinnati; Wellsburg, Iowa (a bilingual, German-Dutch congregation); Pella, Iowa; Grandville Avenue in Grand Rapids; Orange City, Iowa; and Paterson Four in New Jersey. He retired in 1934 and moved to Grand Rapids where he served as an assistant pastor at Alpine Christian Reformed Church for many years before his death in 1946.

Growing up in a minister's home, in a growing and lively denomination, left an indelible imprint on Professor Timmerman. A profound respect for the church, a deep love for worship, a thoroughly informed theology; these mingle with his abiding realism which is also willing to admit human frailty and occasional foolishness. The following essays are of two kinds; reflections on the church which are tempered by autobiographical reminiscence, and assessment of theological questions in the modern church.

Old Year's 1926

The Reformed Journal (December, 1977)

I have attended Old Year's worship services almost uninterruptedly since I was a year old, a fact that has made quite an impression on me. At first I didn't know why I was there; now I wonder why others are not.

During all these years I moved from unconscious to reluctant and then to appreciative attendance. There is always the reading of Psalm 90 to anticipate, a Psalm whose magnificent rhythms and austere yet tender wisdom vibrates with universal resonance. I always enjoyed singing "O God Our Help in Ages Past" as composed by the Reverend Mr. Herbert, a melody now out of favor with the musical *cognoscenti*. The sermon, usually based on a verse from Psalm 90, accentuated the transience and uncertainty of human existence, a somber message about our frailty. The solemn accent on man's mortality and the precious pledge of a dwelling place beyond the fever of history moved both heart and mind.

The first Old Year's services I remember were conducted in the Dutch language in Paterson, New Jersey. The occasion involved a slight sacrifice. My father had to omit hearing the calm, reassuring voice of Lowell Thomas, who took the sharp cut out of the news for him as long as I can remember. I had to give up the Happiness Boys, Willie Jones and Ernie Hare from WOR, Newark.

After the members had come walking down the hill, or arrived in T. or A. model Fords, or even on occasion by horse and buggy, Mother, Grandmother, and I entered the church from the front — always an embarrassment to me but an apparently inescapable ministerial fringe benefit. With the strange visual clarity that seems to enhance memory as one grows older, I can still see most plainly the neighboring families in their pews with all their children. When services were about to begin, my father and the six elders and six deacons filed in through the same door to special seats on the right and left at the front of the church where they were not only prominently displayed but were in a splendid position to keep an eye on the congregation. They stood

Fourth Christian Reformed Church, Paterson, New Jersey

during every prayer and during the "long" prayer some of them slightly swayed.

After this prayer the deacons came with their purple velvet bags attached to long poles, a mechanism which made certain that only your right hand knew what your left was doing. The sermon followed with its usual clarity, insight, and deliberate pace. Ministers then had to do without the enormously labor-saving device of a loudspeaker. In a sizable church, such an omission meant hard work to be heard. Some ministers developed a "*preektoon*," a shrill booming voice with basso and crescendo which seemed to get where it wanted. My father did it with clear enunciation and a slow pace which allowed the sound to find its target. When the service ended the members went home to whatever meager festivities they could afford. We had none; my father had to preach the next day and the house was still.

The street and the city, however, were far from still; and the shrill contrast between the two deepened the effect of the service. Shortly after the church service ended, the young Italians in the neighborhood congregated under the dim light at the corner. These Italians had their own quartets, the Nineteenth Street quartet, the Fourth Avenue quartet, and so on; and their untutored voices were singularly attractive. (I once worked next to an Italian in a silk mill for almost a year who sang endless operatic melodies in a tenor I thought remarkable.) They harmonized for a long time ending with "Auld Lang Syne." Nondi Damato, a few doors down, was delivering illegal beer in a hearse.

Across the street, even through closed windows I could hear Tony Dioro's little orchestra belting out waltzes. Pasqualis, next door, were being comforted by the wine he had pressed with bare feet the autumn before.

At midnight the city quivered with the sound of church bells and factory whistles. For once the piercing whistle of Weidman's Piece and Dye Works summoned men to good cheer instead of ten hours' toil in acrid smells and musty air. If the weather were good there was hugging and kissing in the streets. Sporadically, during the night some stumbling singer burst into maudlin song or angry talk. Although we did not hear it, Times Square was slowly subsiding from the hysteria celebrating the beginning of 1927. 1927 — how long ago it is since Calvin Coolidge sat in the White House, a lean and laconic Puritan, presiding with thin-lipped inertia over Babylon as the twenties rolled on. Coolidge was against sin and for business and did next to nothing about either, which was a typically American attitude in 1927.

Old Years' services and New Years' services face us with a paradox. According to Psalm 90, man's lot is brief, encumbered with grief and full of sin. Iniquities and secret sins will be increasingly grave. Jesus tells us that the direction of worldly culture will deepen in godlessness, so that time will have to be shortened for the elect's sake. The world will become a moral wasteland. On the other hand, it is equally clear that Christians should never cease to serve as salt and light, to struggle to make it a better world, to make a happy new year for all men. The Christian's own dwelling place is secure, but he must work to improve a world that is destined to become worse; he may not cultivate only his own garden — whether spiritually or physically understood.

Over a century ago Alfred Tennyson, depressed by the loss of a dear friend in a universe apparently a vast machine weaving a dark meaningless web about all things, wrote a poem of hope, rising out of his experience "That there is not a flower on the down that owes as much to the sun as I do to Christ." Despite the apparent purposelessness deep down in things, he wishes the New Year's bells to ring out all grief, injustice, "faithless coldness," false pride, and the "lust of gold" and to ring in justice, "love of truth," a nobler life and the spirit of brotherhood through the power of Christ.

Whether or not one shares the thought of the subtle and original melodies of Tennyson's poem, I believe a Christian should ring out the meaning of Christ for both sinners and their culture and work hard to realize it in our common life. We are involved in and contribute to a dimension of earthly existence that will triumphantly survive the dissolution of the old order. Work in God's kingdom, in which a thousand years equals a moment of memory, will last. Though the world will grow sodden with sin, Christian witness is mandatory and eternally fruitful.

The Reluctant Angel

The Reformed Journal (December, 1979)

Emily Dickinson and I have had one thing in common. We both had fathers who, in her words, "frowned on Santa Claus and such prowling gentlemen." My father also had two objections to the Christmas tree: it was a pagan custom, and the tree itself belonged in the snow where God put it. In our home nobody hung gaudy stockings about. Christmas Eve was a silent night. My father was meditating on his Christmas sermon, and I was somberly meditating on my participation in the Sunday School Christmas program. Maybe for once I would have a real headache rather than malingering one, which was soon unmasked by the rapidity with which I ate the big orange and the box of candy my parents sympathetically brought home. Christmas morning with its presents was a happy time, but at the edges of frolic lurked images of the program in which I invariably, inevitably and ineluctably had to participate. I had either to recite singly or in unison, or to sing, for obvious reasons, always in unison. Intimidated by shyness I dreaded the Christmas program and participated in it with tingling nerves.

Non-participation was unthinkable because I lived in the manse, and the teachers were unflagging in assuring me that compromising the family honor was inconceivable. At four in Orange City, Iowa, I began my inglorious career as a speaker by reciting a little Dutch poem. When halfway through it, I noticed all the faces and beat it for my mother's pew. In those days, the minister's family always had a special pew, the fourth row from the front arranged between the side-pews where the elders swayed upright during the long prayer. There was no retreat during the next seven years and I edified audiences in the Dutch, German, and English languages. Singing in chorus was not so difficult because it was slightly anonymous and one could rely strongly upon proper facial movements. At twelve Sunday school was over.

Over the years most of us have enjoyed Christmas programs. Our children have carried a fair share of staves, shepherd's crooks and stars. None seemed to suffer and to one of them it was like wine — the longer the piece and the louder the song the better. Yet I always see some little fellow squirming on the platform, awkward and bumbling, eyes riveted on ceiling or floor, feet shifting uneasily, or immobilized by unease. I respect these little people immensely. I think their courage, sense of duty or just plain grace under parental pressure among the most affecting features on the program.

This may all appear sentimental to the bouncy extrovert who can't wait to march in as a King of the Orient or as Mary dressed in blue. Yet there is nothing sentimental in appreciating the freeze of shyness. The carapace that experience shields us with should not allow us to forget the vulnerability of the timid child. He does have to screw his courage to a sticking point. In this Christmas season I want to salute every little boy and girl who hates to get on that platform but does it.

Safe in the Eye of the Storm

The Reformed Journal (April, 1978)

Tolstoi begins the novel *Anna Karenina* with a striking sentence, "All happy families are alike; all unhappy families are unhappy in different ways." One may wish to dispute that statement, but I think most of us would agree that the amount of happiness or unhappiness in a family greatly determines the future happiness of its members — as long as they live.

Life and literature provide countless examples of this. Ernest Hemingway detested his mother who detested his father, and Hemingway's novels are generally peopled with disagreeable women. Eugene O'Neill had a lonely and embittered childhood, which festered in him his entire life and burst into violent and depressing expression in a play of his old age entitled *A Long Day's Journey into Night*. Anthony Trollope, the English novelist, tells us in his autobiography that he had always "a desire to be loved, to be popular. No child, no boy, no lad, no young man has ever been less so." He was not physically abused, just completely neglected. When his parents spent a year in America, he was left alone in a decrepit farmhouse; when they died in Belgium, he was not even notified. When he became a famous writer, his mother and brother showed only amazement. He was forced to fashion a new personality to face the world, but the raw wounds of his family home were never obliterated. The stories are legion; I would like to write a short account about a happy childhood in a happy home and what made both possible.

Our home was happy, partly because of the character of my parents, but largely because of their pervasive and profoundly real belief in the providence of God. My father was a solid theologian but also something of a mystic. The Holy Spirit was a living reality in his daily life, not Someone he preached about on Lord's Day XX. For him the providence of God directs all of life to the minutest operations of natural law. If he lost something, he not only searched his memory, which was extraordinary, but also sought the guidance of the Spirit. All events, even the devastating losses in the great depression, were for our good, a cause indeed for sorrow but not repining. Both of my parents were singularly unworldly, not in the sense of a naive ignorance of evil and sin in the world or in themselves, but in the sense of disassociation from secular prizes. Though we lived in a comfortable manse, we had few luxuries — no car, no vacations, no expensive furniture and the like. They had no interest in clubs, cottages, or caviar. My father lived through the depression; in fact, he anticipated it in our family by lending money to Christian institutions and persons with a talent for bankruptcy; he added to it by turning back part of his salary. My mother had an irrepressible urge to empty her pocketbook on everybody but herself; she was always emptying herself for others and thereby being strangely fulfilled. Tender and impressionable, she had the gift of intuitive sympathy. My father, on the other hand, had a kind of unbendable, billiard-ball set of convictions centering on salvation in Christ and the providence of God. Concretely, these characteristics fused into creating a happy home rooted in an unswerving conviction of God's loving care.

One of Frost's characters says,

> Home is the place where, when you have to go there
> They have to take you in.

What a cold, loveless picture of home that is. Some homes fall short even of this soulless necessity; they are places to flee from. No one who has ever had a home can escape its ineradicable impression. The days one spends there can never be dropped into a forgettable, meaningless void. The children of irresponsible or fragmented homes often need, like Trollope, to fashion a new personality to compensate for and cover their scars. Children are often emptied and distorted so one or the other of the parents is fulfilled. On the other hand, a Christian home develops a sense of identity, meaning, and belonging, since its members belong not only to each other but all belong to the family of God from which nothing can dislodge them. Seldom does a child from a Christian home need to undergo Trollope's ordeal, or like a girl from Anderson's *Winesburg, Ohio,* need to begin "trying to force herself to face bravely the fact that many people must live and die alone, even in Winesburg." If there is one splendid truth a Christian home etches in the heart, it is that Christians never live or die alone. They are members of the most permanent home in the universe, the home of God's kingdom of which our homes are but faulty reflections.

In the world, however, the Christian has to deal with the mystery of iniquity. Job said long ago, "Man is born to trouble as the sparks fly upward." No human memory of any years' duration exists without its images of horror, personally experienced or read about. I saw a little girl, running across the road in summer sunshine to a playground, smashed to death. I have stood at the graves of highly gifted friends torn from the world in the middle of brilliant careers. Years ago I saw the huge, black clouds of dust darkening the rich land and piling in drifts the height of a man. Last summer the incomparable beauty of the Big Sur forests was reduced to rubble amid the incineration of wild life.

The moral evil in the world shouts from every newspaper. The raw violence of street crimes, the current depraved obsession with sex, the ramshackle poor who barely survive in crumbling shacks, the inordinate waste on luxury, the piling up of the means of unimaginable destruction while whole populations starve — what uncontrolled sin and evil in the world. Looking at it all, James Joyce has pictured God as paring his fingernails in serene indifference to the universe. If there be a God at all he is either powerless, indifferent, or outside his world. Every thoughtful Christian struggles with these problems, but through grace and faith he sees this warped world in the light of our redemption in Christ and the ultimate renovation of the fallen world. He knows that in the world he will be hurt; he also knows the counterweight of grace to bear an ultimate healing. Some day, he believes the mystery of iniquity will be dissolved in the blazing glory of Christ's return.

Our home, like every home, had its pains and sorrows. My father
spent seven weeks in a hospital. I will never forget the faith, resig-
nation, and gratitude for healing. The experience gave eloquence to
his faith and tenderness to his life. My mother spent eleven weeks in
the same hospital, but left it with permanent lameness. I never heard
her bemoan her crippled condition, grandstand for sympathy, or weary
people with complaint. She regarded her affliction with a sweetness
and submission revealing not only a noble, heroic character, but the
presence of grace. Emily Dickinson wrote a stanza that described my
mother over a period of twelve years:

> To fight aloud is very brave,
> But gallanter, I know
> Who charge within the bosom,
> The cavalry of woe.

God cared for her so that she was a source of strength in manifest
weakness.

When a Christian reflects on his life, its twistings and turnings,
surprises, appointments and disappointments, he sees, to use a phrase
of Henry James, the figure in the carpet, the design and craftsmanship
in the Maker's purposes. These purposes, in the end, have little to do
with secular success, but much to do with faithfulness to God's will.
We learn the folly of banking on the false providence of personal
health and friends. Some of these will certainly fail in life; all are
pointless at its end. The Christian also learns that although God may
not answer our prayers according to our wishes, he always gives us
something better according to his.

Whatever Happened to Sunday?

The Reformed Journal (February, 1981)

The Reverend Mr. R. T. Kuiper, travelling from
Willervonk, the Netherlands to Graafschaap, Michigan in 1879 with
seven motherless children, waited in Passaic, New Jersey, to catch the
train on Monday, since "the trains do not run on Sunday in America."

He adds that he was glad "to rest on the Lord's Day according to the commandment." One hundred years later in America few passenger trains are running in America, but almost every thing else is. Two blocks from our home the C&O freight trains rattle by day and by night. More than a hundred thousand cars hurtle down Twenty-eighth Street in between. Anyone looking at its malls, shops and eating places would be hard put to distinguish Sunday from Thursday. Kuiper's Sunday exists only in albums.

Willa Cather speaks of the "incommunicable past." One can communicate facts of Sunday in my boyhood in a little Iowa town: the air full of bells three times that day, the well-filled churches and horse-barns under August sun and January chill, the nature of the church services, the pietistic regimen that controlled all activities. What is difficult to convey is the ubiquitous sense of Sunday that pervaded the day from dawn to dusk, from the first cock crow to the last wan chirp of the cricket, the stillness of the town. I never experienced such Sunday stillness again.

Sunday was church in Orange City, Iowa, in the first decades of the century. I suspect that it is so even now in the little pockets of piety that dot Northwest Iowa, though it can't be as still in the town or in the homes as it was in my youth. There were three services which I attended with simulated docility. The preacher delivered three sermons before his often critical sheep, dressed in a sombre Prince Albert, sweating it out in August afternoons without air-conditioning before a whir of variegated hand-propelled fans. He spoke in these churches, some large, without the aid of electronic devices; and a voice of good timbre could be heard on the street through the open windows. There were always competitive babies in the crowd, quieted not by artful jouncing but by breast feeding. As the sermon pounded on, squirming little boys were pinched. Sometimes fractious older boys in the back seats were policed by elders. Dutch psalms were fervently sung while a lathering janitor pumped the bellows of the organ in 110 degrees. There was no choir — an irrelevant impertinence. The sermon was the centerpiece of the service; upon that the evaluation of the preacher and the determination of his ecclesiastical fortunes depended.

The heart of the service was the sermon; then, as it was well into the sixties, as rhetorically fixed as the terza rima. Apparently all texts were best analyzed and interpreted in terms of three points. I remember a preacher saying, "One more point and then we go home." Whether the content were brilliant or mediocre, it was formulated in terms of an introduction, three divisions, and application. The three points were often chosen with care and memorably phrased. These pegs to remembrance enabled certain people to remember sermons for years. A lady of eighty-eight wrote me recently saying about some sermons she had heard, "I know the introduction and application he made and often talk about them." She also gave the three points of several sermons she had remembered for fifty years. Such fixed rhetoric may seem wooden, but its mnemonic helpfulness was striking. As a boy, of course, I had no interest in these sermons; I spent my time counting the pipes in the organ, the panes in the colored glass windows, watching the consistory up front and day dreaming. I am glad that later I learned to appreciate the meticulous preparation, craftsmanship, and meditation that went into their making. Some of these older ministers operated on volubility, but others on a lot of mind and heart; not a few had style and some had class.

The rhetoric of these sermons is now old-fashioned and has been replaced by more free-wheeling forms, many times abetting a freshness of phrase and imaginative presentation, and at times a fog swirling about directionlessly. When the older prosody of rime and metre gave way to free verse, there was both gain and loss. Free verse allowed freedom, experimentation, and variety, but it is often diffuse and always difficult to memorize. A conversational style and meandering approach is easy to listen to but hard to remember. What one remembers is not the sermon as a unified whole but imaginative perceptions and moving effects. I am talking, of course, about members who try to retain what was said as a strengthening spiritual experience for the week ahead, who seek the stimulus of nourishment rather than the pleasure of an amusing flick.

These older ministers, whose spiritual authority was enormous and sometimes tyrannical, had fixed minds. Their influence is sometimes hard to understand when every Tom, Dick, and Sadie with a strong *D* average in high school has the right to expressed opinion. Then, when preachers said, "Thus saith the Lord," they were inclined to believe it. Some of them had a center of Zion complex, abrasively attacking other Christian communions, microscopically scrutinizing their fellow preachers for theological slippage, and a general sense of thorough comprehension of the full council of God. One admires certain qualities in such people, their intelligence, spiritual concern, uncommon diligence and zeal for the church, but one grows weary of their omniscience. One gets tired of people who are always right, whether they be professors, preachers, or editors of church papers. In all the years I have observed ecclesiastical controversies, I do not remember a protagonist who admitted being wrong about anything that really mattered. It frequently proved easier to start a new denomination.

After the preachers had had their say on Sunday in Orange City, Iowa, in 1912, there wasn't much of the day left, and there wasn't much choice as to how to spend it. There were no radios, television sets, Sunday newspapers. There was, of course, the church paper, impeccably sound. Carefully chosen secular books might be read. In some homes there were sets of Kuiper and Bavinck, generally unread. Outdoor amusements were frowned on. A family who hitched up a team or cranked up a Model T to tour the corn fields risked censure as well as appearing somewhat ridiculous. Three services, three trips to church, three meals as the choices pretty well consumed the day. What time there was remaining was to be used in a way compatible with the spiritual tone of the day. To many this all sounds like "a hard, hard religion," as well as somewhat of a bore. Indeed, it took something out of one but it put something real into one also. The church was a sanctuary, a renewal of hope, a confirmation of faith. These people did not have easy, pleasure-filled lives. They had a profound sense of the mystery and misery of human life. There were no protective barriers. Death even among little children had often to be endured. I remember my mother crying over deaths of little children. They were sometimes marred by small pox, weakened by scarlet fever, dead of diptheria. Diseases, now almost routinely cured, carried off parents, leaving fatherless and motherless children. Fearful accidents occurred on the farm. Hail, storm, and drought brought destruction to their crops. But the death of the saints was precious in the sight of the Lord and in the eye of the storm was the providence of God. How often they prayed for a rainbow, how often they found a spiritual rainbow in the church where God spoke to them through his servants, and promised cure for all misery.

At that time and even into the sixties, there was a remarkable consensus as to the meaning and practices of Sunday. Although the Bible did not specify the number of services to be held on Sunday, congregations attended with notable faithfulness and did not appear to grow weary of that kind of well-doing. Even though the services in the earlier decades of the century were a surcease from loneliness on the empty prairie, a stay against loss of identity in a strange land, and the warm concourse of friends, these reasons did not bring them to church. What did bring them to church was a felt spiritual need and a sense of duty. They believed God wanted them to come as often as they could and that it was good for them to be there. That kind of consensus has been eroding for years, whether out of spiritual amplitude, secular diversions, boredom, or alienation. So also has the drawing power of popular preachers. It has been decades since I have seen churches packed to hear a particular preacher. I can name half a dozen preachers during the thirties and forties who packed the evening service wherever they went. The sense of duty in going to church and the pleasure anticipated through the sermon have both waned, so that today churches with excellent ministers rope off many pews for evening services during the summer, while some of the saints go marching off.

The consensus as to how church services should be conducted has also been eroded. I can imagine how astounded a church would have been in 1912 if a minister had greeted them with "Good-Morning!" No congregation would have bellowed it back. The minister conducted everything that happened on the platform. Liturgy was fixed and sparse. Some today feel the need both of modification and amplification. Forms for Communion and Baptism, laboriously prepared by Synodically appointed committees were punctiliously adhered to. Now they are revised, abridged, or supplemented. In some churches women pass the plate; others would fight to the last woman to prevent it. Some judge that children, under certain conditions, should be invited to the Lord's Supper; others think that no one in his right Reformed mind should approve it. Echoes of academic controversies about the nature and authority of Scripture receive a divided reception. Some of these matters are relatively trivial, but the controversies on the nature of Scripture are of the utmost importance to all but Laodiceans. The trustworthiness of the Bible is crucial; there are no acceptable lesions. It may be conceivable to live a relatively happy life on false assumptions, but not if one is aware of them. No thinking person would bet his life on illusion or agree with Swift that "happiness is a state of being well-deceived." I can sympathize with the indignation of those who think such trustworthiness is threatened. When it is, the heart of Sunday is disinherited.

The consensus on Sunday behavior is also waning. Whereas in the early decades of the century, attendance at church three times was common, today attendance twice is lessening. The blue laws have almost vanished. If a member of my old church in Iowa had spun his Buick over to the Blackstone Cafe at Sioux City for a Sunday dinner of Prime Rib and Cocktails, he would have been in danger of losing his membership; if one does that in Grand Rapids today he is only in danger of losing his shirt. The old blue laws were based on the idea that the Sabbath is a "day of sacred assembly" and that "wherever you live, it is a Sabbath to the Lord." They thought God made the Sabbath for man to insure rest and spiritual growth, not to do what he wanted. The older generations were uptight and possibly self-righteous about Sunday. The present generation is relaxed and self-righteous about it.

Several of my friends have written vividly memorable accounts of Sunday in the Iowa area from which we all came. Their memories have more acid than mine, a bit of a sardonic tone. I could say that my memories antedate theirs by several decades and that the high tide of Sunday had already crested. I hereby say so. That homogeneous culture was severely affected by World War I. Under the governorship of 120 percent, flag-waving patriot, Americanization was stridently forced, and the movement and turmoil of the war crashed through social and religious barriers. Neither the church nor the nation was ever the same. I would grant, then, that their portraits of foibles are true. The fundamental outline of Sunday, its mood, church services, and dominant activities were not enormously changed by the thirties and forties. What is certain is that none of us has escaped the indelible impressions of that Sunday. To me the Sunday of my boyhood in Iowa and my youth in New Jersey meant two things supremely. Sunday was to be markedly different from Thursday in church attendance and in other activities which should be spiritually centered, positively contributory to the distinctiveness of the day. The second, in that honorific and stilted phrase, was the preaching of the word. The latter is still, however brilliant or bumbling it may be, the heart of Sunday services. I am thankful for the spiritual insight and inspiration I have received over the years from many sermons. To have attended half of them would have impoverished me; to have fragmented the spirit of the day with antithetical secular diversions would have made it almost indistinguishable from Thursday.

The Sermon in Disrepute

The Reformed Journal (April, 1972)

I grew up as a minister's son in what may now be called the golden age of the ministry in the Christian Reformed Church. My father enjoyed respect, confidence, authority, and affection. He was a dignified man when the ministry enjoyed great dignity. He meticulously prepared his sermons, which possessed both art and insight. They were listened to by intelligent audiences, even though many had little formal education. He felt it his duty to proclaim what he considered the full counsel of God as far as his abilities permitted. The minister and audience constituted an harmonious unit. None felt the urge to muscle in, share rare wisdom and searing hang-ups or personal encounters with the Lord. The audience felt instructed, inspired, and cleansed. Audience participation would have been regarded as intrusive, unmannerly, and unprofitable as we would regard it in a good play, where no one but a fool would rise to reinterpret *Macbeth*. That day, to my deep regret, seems to be about finished.

Many people seem to relish the new day coming, the day of audience participation, the day when the worm will turn and ultimately devour the lark. Some want not only attenuation of the minister's role, but are ready to scrap every custom about worship. This, I suppose, includes the role of the clergyman, who will become some sort of moderator or facilitator.

He will be engaged in arranging the movable seats so we can see each other better; he will be busy hustling about with hymnbooks and contemporary ballads, patiently tolerating seven rambling opinions on neighborhood projects, ordering the holding of hands and the letting go of hands, seeing to it that everyone is listening actively while preparing the next spontaneous remark, plugging people into new programs, guiding the mass analysis of texts, and summing up the consequences. Having done all this:

> At last he rose, and twitched
> his mantle blue.
> "Tomorrow to fresh fields and
> pastures new."

Audience participation is the sparkling word today, but I don't like audience participation in the exposition of texts in Sunday services. Some say the single voice in front is a bore and a drone, but are seventeen bores any better? The participators are as likely to be neurotic exhibitionists as mature and gifted saints. If a group wishes to discuss the sermon afterward, and the minister wishes to participate, that is another and probably a profitable matter, but to invite instant opinion on the meaning of texts seems absurd to me. A well-prepared and substantial sermon to which I actively listen means infinitely more to me than comments even by gifted people, who can't be masters of everything.

The Sunday sermons are the most significant and often most plea-surable parts of the Sunday services to me. The poetic caliber of many hymns is slight; the responsive readings in uneven pace and frequent dissonance are not always an inspiration. Many are so intent on read-ing words that words is all they hear. I greatly prefer a trained and articulate reader. If the sermon disappears, a fine and rewarding ex-perience will vanish, and I shall be poorer for it. Discussion of Scrip-ture on Sunday by many voices holds no attraction for me. There are suitable societies for such activity, where many of the severest critics of sermonic exposition never appear. Finally, I fear that if the sermon goes, the audience will diminish too, but maybe that is what some members want — no organized church services but little cells where congenial spirits meet to talk to each other about the religious life.

Modern Communication and the Sermon

The Outlook (September, 1975)

Communication has changed enormously in the last fifty years. Anyone who grew up as I did under the formative influences of Victorian poetry, fiction, and criticism realizes how the forms of fiction and poetry have been ruptured and then reconstructed into novel and even bizarre patterns. The permissible content has been so extravagantly enlarged that chagrin, repulsion, and even boredom have often characterized the humane, non-religious reader. The irra-tional and the absurd have sometimes replaced the sane and the nor-mal. Literary criticism has introduced many new standards for excellence. Radio enlarged the boundaries of communication. Then came television, a medium spectacularly influential and possessing extraordinarily sophisticated instruments largely devoted to junk. God must be angry at what man has done with this marvelous medium. Instead of great plays, we have "Kojak" and "The Edge of Night"; instead of great music, we have "Tony Orlando and Dawn." There are some fascinating interviews, but most of them are exercises in animated backslapping. Some religious programs embody the means of television to provide spectacular settings and florid showmanship. One clergyman accompanies a disjointed series of comments with meandering piano playing. Shouldn't that Victorian relic, the traditional sermon be pepped up? Doesn't it need some aid?

The Editorial Board of *The Outlook* has asked me to comment on this question, not, I am sure, because I am any kind of expert on the sermon, but probably because they know that I have an abiding and high respect for the traditional sermon. I do not believe it to be an archaic relic to be entrusted to a museum with other valuable objects that have outlived their usefulness.

All the sermon really needs today is a competent clergyman and the English language. A thousand years of rich human experience, intelligence, and the work of many geniuses have made that language an incomparable instrument for expressing human thought and feeling. To supplement it in a sermon with flannel graphs, cartoons, drawings of flora and fauna, illustrative objects like toothpaste, sound effects, audience participation and hysteria demonstrates the intellectual poverty of all involved. No one would deny the religious value of art, but I don't enjoy mixing the arts, accompanying the sermon or prayer with good music. A good sermon is an oratorical unit and should not be invaded. It is primarily a matter of words and gestures to which personality and sincerity are the only important aids. I believe this is all the sermon needs; but it is not all the contemporary audience needs, as I shall point out later.

Communication through a sermon is not easy. No worthwhile speaking or writing is, and there are no effortless solutions. Words are slippery; they are often many-layered in meaning; they alter in meaning through the generations. The strong words of one age become weak or unusable in another. When someone was called silly in Chaucer's time, he was denominated saintly; today he is ridiculed as a fool. One of the rich words years ago was *gay*, a word now so debased one scarcely dares use it. Doctrinal terms, since they are not part of daily life, have to be incessantly taught because substitutions are hard to invent. To fix the right meaning in the right words is an everlasting task for the minister. If he accomplishes it well, he should not need aids, at least not in our churches.

Dissatisfaction with the traditional sermon is, in my judgment, not so much caused by the inadequacy of the sermon itself as it is caused by a cultural context increasingly hostile to it. Let me illustrate. The Reverend Mr. R. B. Kuiper, whom many of us remember with affection and gratitude was an outstandingly able preacher in matter, manner, and expression. In my youth he attracted overflowing audiences. Probably many of us walked a long way to hear him. I doubt whether it would happen today if he were among us. Various influences have shouldered the sermon out its former centrality in the life of our members. In some of our churches, possibly many, the worshipers at evening service are becoming an endangered species. The evening sermon competes with the beach, "Kojak," visiting, indifference, and inertia. The authority of and the taste for the sermon have diminished. I do not think the fault lies in the sermon. I hear many fine sermons today. The basic fault lies in a new sensibility on the part of the church members. How to modify that is the real problem. I do not believe it will be modified by refashioning the sermon in drastic ways. In the words of Pogo, "We have met the enemy, and they is us."

Ministers and writers in our circles who wish to stimulate wide response face hard times not because they cannot communicate but partly because a portion of the potential audience resents intellectual effort, and partly because another portion has been attracted to and alienated by influences in our culture which have decentralized the Word and the word. Ministers and writers are urged to be brief. Transparent, obvious, and captivating — one page articles immediately digestible and fifteen minute sermons. If this pattern prevails it is the prelude to disaster as far as the Reformed tradition is concerned, an intellectually tough tradition that can never be kept alive by hasty reading of bits of devotional and theological prose. The magazines that try to keep this tradition alive have a disappointingly meager subscription list. Solid reading is rare. The *Banner* has its problems especially with the age group in the twenties and thirties, a group that should be the foundation for future development. In all these cases, I do not believe the real problem lies in inept communication; it lies largely in indifference to what is communicated. How to change this attitude in an age that disparages authority, exalts individualism and is geared to the idea of instant wisdom baffles me. Anyone who has taught college students during the sixties knows how overwhelmingly powerful the spirit of the age can be. Professor Jowett, the famous Oxford don, once told a student who professed to be an atheist, "You believe in God by 10 a.m. tomorrow or you will be expelled." He wouldn't have done it in 1968.

The past was not perfect; many sermons were not masterpieces, and the services were not ideal at all times. Keeping awake on a sunny August afternoon was sometimes beyond the power of some of the elders up front. I remember a man snoring. Babies were yammering until they received natural nourishment. The minister faced a tempest of waving fans, and the elders at times had to police naughty boys in the back row. But the congregation was there, and the majority came to listen and to learn. I was there — three times a Sunday. The minister was expected to exegete the Word, and he did not have to be a spell-binder. The minister was like Philip who said to the eunuch, "Under-standest thou what thou readest?" In answer to the eunuch's reply, Philip opened his mouth and explained the Scriptures. When the mul-titude was assembled at the mountain side, our Lord opened his mouth and taught them. The only way I know to master a passage in litera-ture is to read it word after word, and, if I am baffled, further ex-planatory comments. This strikes me as neither old-fashioned in a derogatory sense nor sterile. Formerly the audience was willing to do its part. If the sermon fails today, I would fault the audience more than the minister. Mr. Blythe makes a comment applied to another matter, but it has relevance here: "The old people have gone and have taken a lot of the truth out of the world with them." In this case a lot of the truth about preaching.

In Praise of the Sermon

An address delivered at the annual meeting of the Reformed Fellowship, Inc., October 6, 1972.

When I was a boy in rural Iowa, the church and the sermon in the church were close to the center of experience. Here for a few hours each week, the harsh toil and long loneliness of farm life were forgotten. In the fellowship of believers, the singing of long familiar psalms, and above all in the sermon the members of the church found security, spiritual nurture and new strength. Though it was a long, long day for a little boy as the sermons seemed to stretch endlessly on under the hot summer sun, yet even then the church and the sermon provided a kind of stability and fixed point to life which endured with me.

Can the sermon survive?

Willa Cather prefaces one of her finest novels with the Latin words, "Optima dies . . . prima fugit," (the finest days fly first). Whether the early decades of our century were the best years of our church may be debatable; that they were good years and that they are gone is not. The pastoral context is largely gone, the minister's preferred position and authority has lessened. The roar and sweep of our industrialized and standardized culture has muted our distinctiveness.

American thought and especially American psychology have changed the ways we think. Our obsessive "presentism" has hit the young hardest, and they often abandon the past not with a sigh but a shudder. There is a feeling abroad that regard for tradition is an absurd loyalty. Everywhere there is a revolt against authority: decency in literature and the arts, standards in language, doctrine in religion, instruction in education, and reason in experience.

The question we face is whether the sermon, as the central element in the church service, can survive in a world in which whirl seems to be king, the termites are always at the pillars of the temple, and good things die everyday. I hope to show that it should.

Sermon as oratory and rhetoric

The sermon is a major example of the arts of oratory and rhetoric. The type of sermon we are accustomed to hear has risen out of a long literary tradition. Our church has very rarely ordained a minister without long education, which has always included homiletics.

This literary tradition goes back to the middle ages in which there were elaborate theories on effective preaching and critical sheep in the audience to test them. In the seventeenth century sermons were the greatest form of prose literature. In Puritan New England books of sermons were best sellers, and Samuel Sewall gave them to the woman he was courting. This concern with the artistic dimension of the sermon continues to this day.

Furthermore, the sermon has been a very flexible form, amenable to freshness and variety without loss in dignity or identity. It has ranged from the homespun clarity of John Bunyan to the silks and satins of John Donne, from the "close, naked, natural way" of the Puritans to the urbane and sophisticated prose of Cardinal Newman, from the austere dignity of the "Pardoner's Tale" in Chaucer's *Can-*

terbury Tales to the colloquial style of Moody. It has room for the preacher's personality, the nature of the messages, and the temper of the time. It can serve a devout, spiritual purpose with all the resources of art. It is, in fact, often the most organized and sustained speech its audience hears all week.

Sermon as a medium

The sermon is still an highly effective medium. I know that effectiveness is hard to measure. I remember working hard to teach a class the definition of an *heroic couplet*, two rhyming lines of regular verse. When the tests came, one of the students defined it as follows, "A heroic couplet is when two young people marry and have a tough time of it but stick together." Perfect communication is seldom possible. The speaker may be somewhat cloudy, the hearer not alert. Words too are hard to handle. Eliot has said that words:

> Crack and sometimes break, under the burden,
> Under the tension, slip, slide, perish,
> Decay with imprecision, will not stay in place,
> Will not stay still.

But to say that sermons have been bouncing off the heads of audiences for generations as if they were masses of imperceptive clods is the other extreme. There are those who neither listen nor learn; dull in faculty or enveloped in a miasmic mist of egoism. But there are many who know what was said and can discuss it.

The responses I received to my little piece on the sermon help prove this. There were, to me, surprisingly many — oral and written. They came from unlettered laymen, from physicians and lawyers, from many of my colleagues at the college, and from a good many ministers ranging in age from 27 to 82. Among these ministers were a good many whom most of us would consider the ablest in our church. The sermon still works and to a good sermon can still be applied the words of Emily Dickinson:

> Some say a word is dead
> When it is said,
> I say it just begins to live
> That day.

Sermon in the apostolic church

Many critics of the traditional sermon, ignoring other passages in the Pauline letters, ground their convictions on the alleged general practices of the apostolic church in which one taught, another sang a psalm, a third spoke in a tongue and a fourth interpreted this. The specific Scriptural passage referred to in *Called to Serve* is I Corinthians 14:26-33. But in a minor masterpiece of suppressing the evidence, they fail to continue with verses 34-35, where Paul says "It is a shocking thing that a woman should address the congregation." Now, one can't have it both ways. Either verses 26-35 are all normative today or the verses describe an expression temporary in character.

I believe this was a legitimate form of worship at the time, but superseded by the long tradition of the sermon as we know it. One of our ministers who had just taken graduate work in the life and literature of the first and second century apostolic church wrote me that his studies made it abundantly clear that such dialog services were held only until competent preachers arose and that when they did the sermon became central in the worship services.

Authoritative voice
versus democratic colloquium

I believe, furthermore, that the minister fills a God-ordained office in preaching, that he literally represents, in spite of human frailty, the voice of God to His people. There are excellent commentaries on the Bible, and many helpful spiritual books, but only in preaching does a living, human voice confront us directly as God's messenger to us. The minister cannot share this office. In a dialog service this is lost; instead of an authoritative voice we have a democratic colloquium. The minister has been lengthily and expensively trained to perform this office, and it is not the business of unprepared people to offer instant wisdom on knotty Scriptural passages. The minister has the special training, the gifts, experience, and time to explain Scripture in a way that most of us are too preoccupied with our daily tasks to do.

The sermon seems to me irreplaceable in worship. No other way of conducting services embodies the values I have emphasized. I do not think any intelligent critic would deny the esthetic dimension of the sermon. If one is dubious, let him read sermons by Donne, Newman, and R. B. Kuiper; then, if he is still dubious, one can safely dismiss him as a blockhead. The opinion of the sermon as invariably dull and soporific strikes me as adolescent in origin and weightless in argument. Not all sermons are brilliant, but I have never heard a carefully prepared sermon by an intelligent man that did not have something worth listening to. In no other service does the minister speak with the authority inherent in the sermon.

If these convictions are sound, interwoven dialog is both erroneous and ineffective. Where the sermon is held in high esteem "passive listeners" will be limited to the daydreamers, self-appointed geniuses, sleepers, and hostile witnesses; eloquence will not be confused with contrivance; and libelous language which describes our traditional preaching as replete with "ponderous phrase and esoteric language, intellectual conceits and theological smokescreen" will not be madly spoken. Good sermons will continue to nurture our faith, stimulate our love for God and neighbor, inspire compassion, work repentance and faith, give light for darkness and hope for the morrow.

Monuments and Myths in Temple Square

The Reformed Journal (October, 1976)

Last summer I read Vardis Fisher's long novel *The Children of God*, a remarkable saga about the Mormons from their origin in the alleged visions of Joseph Smith to their permanent settlement in northern Utah. It is an impressive novel that rises to greatness in the magnificent account of the Trail, the long journey of the believers on foot, by oxcart and wagon, as they inched their way over the lonely prairies of Nebraska, the treeless aridity of Wyoming and between the spectacular Wasatch mountains of Utah, where they found water in green valleys and birds in the air. Winter awaited them in a desolate region bordering a great salt lake. They weathered the hard winter through almost super-human courage and endurance. They built a city and created a strong society. Had the gold rush not occurred and had the Civil War been lost by the North, they might have created an independent empire.

The book teems with struggle and drama. There are many unforgettable characters but dominating them all is canny, imaginative and iron-willed Brigham Young, an acutely realistic man, who accepted the doctrine of the plurality of wives with initial misgiving but practiced it later with heroic diligence. Young was a remarkably ingenious man, who managed a kingdom, but couldn't cope with his thirty odd wives and had a tough job remembering all his children. The spirited account of the Trail, the undaunted nerve and conviction of the immigrants and the building of greatness in the face of terrible odds makes this a book to remember.

The massive impressiveness of the novel prompted me to check its authenticity. *The Gathering of Zion*, by Wallace Stegner, a scholarly and imaginative account of the Trail, as well as shorter authoritative articles support the basic factuality of the work both as to major events and specific doctrines. The Latter-day Saints paid for their convictions with bloody persecution and inhuman cruelty wherever they went. They were saints according to the Book of Mormon but not according to St. Paul. Furthermore, since I had the opportunity, I determined to visit Temple Square in Salt Lake City, where the shining monuments to Mormonism are.

We approached Salt Lake City from the southwest, driving for many miles through an eerie wasteland. On either side of the highway lay the heavy salt, like snow in summer. As we came closer to the city, forbidding, sharp-edged mountains loomed on one side of the road, and the endless salt on the desolate earth on the other side made a fit place for bombing practice by the Air Force. Gradually, the patches of salt grew wetter and became pools and then little lakes of salty water, until suddenly we saw a strange, gleaming body of salty water, hard to look at in the brilliant sunlight. The same dazzling whiteness blazed from the buildings in Temple Square, lush in varied flowers and dark green grass spacing the brilliant architecture, spruce and immaculate.

As one enters the sacred area, one is struck by the fact that unlike most notable attractions, everything is free, and that, unlike others, everything has proselytic intentions. There are guides for every place and their lines have been carefully learned. Suffusing the whole place is an air of having arrived, a smug aura of certainty, a disturbing arrogance that faintly mars even the strikingly beautiful murals and reaches its peak in the row of prophets from Abraham to Joseph Smith and our Lord. The trim lecturers speak with curt dogmatism. Even the spectacular acoustics of the tabernacle, in which even at the back one can hear a pin drop and a whisper reverberate from the platform, enhance a feeling of self-satisfied perfection. There is an ornate solidity about the square, opposite which is the massive bulk of the Bank of Utah, housing some of the financial clout of the Latter-day Saints. The bedraggled refugees from Nauvoo and Missouri have made their mark, and with the terrible images of the Trail in mind, one is filled with admiration and amazement.

The amazement deepens as one reflects on the spurious visions of Joseph Smith, the nonexistent golden plates from which the dreary, unreadable details of the Book of Mormon were allegedly transcribed, the later visions in which Smith was divinely ordered to a plurality of wives and unabated production, which together would determine a saint's place in glory. Though the latter doctrine is temporarily in abeyance, its deliverance has not been repudiated. Two by two the missionaries in sleek and natty dark suits evangelize the world, deliver if possible the dull book and meet with astonishing success as the Church of the Latter-day Saints flourishes and the true church diminishes. Why? That is, of course, for the theologian and scholar to explain, but as a curious observer I thought I detected some of the appeal of this church.

In the first place, the Mormons demand a great deal of their members. Every Mormon devotes part of his life to the church and a sizable part of his income. There are many people who respond to rigorous demands, who achieve a new meaning in their lives through expectations and genuine effort, a sense of wholesome identity with a supposedly great cause.

In the second place, there is the palpable material success of the Mormons, apparent not only in the magnificent buildings and the independent Mormon society, which gives welfare instead of taking it, but also in their thriving, often ruthless, private and corporate business enterprises. Brigham Young's own home, "The Beehive," is an appropriate symbol of this fact both in name and physical reality. Begun while the valley was still desolate and fearsome so that it needed a stout wall for protection against animals and Indians, it was largely completed in the early years of the settlement. Built by cunning craftsmen, elegantly but chastely furnished, rising four stories high, the Beehive House was a triumph of beauty and utility, worthy of the President who occupied it. It is enviably impressive today; it must have been a visible evidence of material success in the semi-wilderness. Today Temple Square is a monument to both faith and prosperity.

The most telling appeal, to me at least, was dramatically revealed in the official film presented to hundreds of thousands of visitors annually. The film pictures a young man struggling to find a meaning in life — and the film purports to give it. The climax of the picture, the ecstatic moment of glory, the meaning of life lies in the permanence of human affections and the presence of those with whom we share them, particularly the family circle. After a scene of mourning at a snow-covered grave, the film moves from the corruptible to the incorruptible, from dust to heaven. The grandfather who was mourned is seen entering a green meadow and being greeted by old friends and relatives in shimmering robes. The family survives intact in glory. Those who have been singing "Tell Mother I'll be there" are. Yeats once said:

> Think where man's glory begins and ends
> And say my glory was I had such friends.

In this Mormon heaven, there is no more than a grand family reunion. The Lamb and his light are absent and the shimmering robes give no hint of having been washed in His blood. Powerful as the scene was to many in the audience, it left us cold. The meaning of life is not based on human hopes and values, but this film is.

However magnetic to man such a notion of the meaning of heaven may be, it is pure humanism and dishonors God. It is of a piece with the humanism in the novel, in which the dominant motifs are human myths, motivations, and rewards. Christ had no preeminence in the life portrayed in the novel or in *The Gathering of Zion*; He had no place in the film. The Christian yearns for the fulfillment of Christ's promise, "Today thou shalt be with me in Paradise." Although, through God's grace, he may enjoy the peripheral happiness of meeting those he loved in life, his real happiness lies in enjoying the infinite perfections of God The Christian should not forget that Jesus said: "He that loveth father or mother more than me is not worthy of me: and he that loveth son or daughter more than me is not worthy of me."

3

"Let Joy Break with the Storm"

ON CALVIN COLLEGE

A college is founded on principles. It has goals and objectives to which its staff and its constituency devote deliberate effort and many dollars. A college constructs a curriculum to achieve a purpose, and devotes countless hours of committee meetings, countless pages of documents, countless informal discussions to explain and defend that purpose.

Finally, however, a college is primarily about people, for people act on purposes, principles, beliefs. Some people greatly affect the entire course of a college. Many people, far more than the students and staff, may benefit from the college.

The college, then, may best be seen as a living being, continually shaped and transformed by its living parts.

This is true of Calvin College. Thousands of private histories contribute to the history of the college. Thousands of private futures link with her future.

This section recalls some of those private histories which have formed the tradition from which Calvin College will find her future. Because they contribute to the college's history, these are also our stories.

In Debt to Alma Mater?

The Calvin Spark (February, 1980)

The first "Calvin Alumni Letter" appeared in October, 1935. In 1953 it became *The Calvin Spark* and reaches all discoverable alumni from Purewater, South Dakota to Yemen. Once one spends a semester at a college, he becomes one of the unforgotten. Friends may forget or ignore you, but Alma Mater sends mail until informed of your demise. She lets you in on all the news and how to pay for it. That semester you spent in college, even if you flunked half your courses, insures a lifetime of regular mail. Brimming with affection in one eye and expectation in the other, Alma Mater reminds you periodically of red cheeks, sound teeth, hair, lost youth, and the benefits you received and others should.

What precisely does an alumnus owe? Something, obviously, because not one of us ever paid the cost of our education. When I went to Calvin the Christian Reformed church and private donors paid the difference. Since 1945 the proportion paid by private donors and governmental bodies increased dramatically. Since I am no longer on the staff, I can add that some of the cost is assumed by teachers who could command larger salaries elsewhere.

The intangible debt is more difficult to determine. I will describe mine, aware that the impact of Calvin was probably greater upon me than upon high school graduates today because of greatly changed circumstances, but I hope the essentials are similar.

In 1920 the Christian high school I attended opened its doors on the third floor of a second-hand public school, with over-waxed floors, chipped and legended desks, and the pungent smell old schools used to have. I entered the school in 1922. Its principal was a rigid disciplinarian with linguistic delusions, who believed *food* should be pronounced like *good* and did so in a well-known prayer. The young teachers, most teaching non-major subjects, were building a school on top of a grammar school. One taught English, German, Mathematics, and leftovers. Our gymnasium was the floor between pillars sustaining the building. We exercised under the supervision of a charming and beautiful young lady. I liked that class. In 1924 we moved to a remodeled house with an adjacent barn which we dismantled on successive Saturdays. The library was a little room without books in the basement. The teacher of Reformed Doctrine was an elderly minister, who stared out of the window, lecturing in a rigid whine on another track. Because of the scarcity of electives I took a semester in Spelling. I don't now remember what we did there. I also took, for no good reason, Commercial Law, which I enjoyed. Our teachers tried hard against blasting odds. We had one superlative teacher whom we idolized, a "natural" like Shoeless Joe Jackson or Babe Ruth in baseball. He made a lot of philistines appreciate learning.

At Calvin I entered a school where everybody seemed to know what he was doing and why. For the first time I encountered teachers who used words whose spelling I guessed at and had to look up when I got to my room. In my first week I had to wrestle with a scarlet-covered book, over four hundred pages long, entitled *Principles of Psychology*; this text by Wm. McDougall, was brimful of ideas I had never heard of and crammed with words I had to look up. I spent hours on a Greek grammar. I chose to write a term paper on *Paradise Lost*, without any real idea of what I was getting into. For some poor reason I found myself with a group of juniors taking Reformed Doctrine. The contrast with my previous education was dramatic, jolting, and beneficent.

Many years ago a student nearing the end of a course at Calvin asked a former colleague what his name was. He then shook hands. Bizarre? Some may think it bizarre that I remember the names and personalities of all the forty-five teachers I had, from Miss Graham, a real cracker, to Professor Thorpe, an authority on Keats, who said to us once, "If you don't believe me, read my book." What strikes me now in the tranquil objectivity of retirement is that four of the seven genuinely outstanding teachers I had taught in Christian schools. The other three taught at Michigan and Northwestern. Too frequently graduate scholarship makes for brilliant dullness, memorable aridity, something like a piece in the P.M.L.A. going on hour after hour. A friend of mine was in a one o'clock seminar at the University. After a time, dulled by his own voice, the professor dozed off. What graduate student in 1932 would have dared to waken him. Some teachers at Calvin may have put students to sleep, but none has provided visual aid. When I remember that most of the professors I had at Calvin occupied a suite instead of a chair, I note gratefully that only two of the teachers I had could have been magnanimously called mediocre. Three of them were as good as anybody going.

Calvin taught me the significance and resources of a library. In

1927 Calvin had 16,000 volumes; now it has over 250,000. Then public libraries barred patrons from the stacks. In March 1928, the attractive and beautifully appointed Hekman Memorial Library was dedicated, and shortly thereafter the stacks were open by special permission. The joy and sense of discovery, as well as a flattening sense of ignorance as I browsed among these books I have never forgotten. The college then as now made sure we knew how to use the library. One of Calvin's splendid achievements is the quality of its present library and holdings.

Up to 1946, when seven-hundred veterans suddenly doubled the enrollment, Calvin's size permitted an intimacy and friendliness rare today. One could take many courses with a superb teacher, although one might also have to endure them with an ineffectual one. Several features of college life then enhanced this intimacy. The more than twenty clubs on campus, in almost every field, permitted unusual opportunities for companionship and intellectual growth. The men's dormitory of eighty students was an energizing powerhouse of discussion, intrigue, pranks, and politics. What I owe to these friends, discussions, and dormitory life is as inestimable as what I owe to the teachers and library.

How does one evaluate such debt? When a teacher makes a man's life, four hundred years gone, as vivid as yesterday and stimulates an interest in biography, which never lets you down, what do you owe? When another introduces you to a Greek philosopher and a way of critical thinking that adds a new and permanent dimension to your life, what do you owe? When another shows a series of paintings with infinite zest and impresses you indelibly with the paintings, his personality, and the value of great paintings, what do you owe? When a man with startling eccentricities reads and interprets poetry so that it touches you to the bone, what do you owe? When they and others light up the infinite mass and maze of learning with the grace of the Spirit and the love of Jesus, what do you owe?

Return from the Rhine

"Centennial Reflections," *The Banner* (February 20, 1976)

During most of its history, Calvin College was changed from the inside by insiders. In two cases, however, Calvin was profoundly altered by events from the outside, events which Calvin in no sense originated nor controlled. World War I had relatively little impact on the college, but World War II and Vietnam affected the college crucially. The members of the Armed Services who served from the jungles of Guadalcanal to the storied and bloody Rhine, in the skies of many lands, and under perilous waters returned not only to swell Calvin's enrollment but to affect its basic perspectives and deepest ideals. When they returned, both students and teachers, in the late forties, they were a distinct and powerful element in the life of the college, and as a group exercised an unparalleled influence on its history.

The veterans were among the finest groups Calvin teachers ever taught. Schooled in hard discipline, far-ranging in experience, mature and independent in attitude yet unfailingly courteous, and eager to redeem the time, they introduced a dynamic atmosphere of intellectual and spiritual concern. Many brought to the college a strong faith, toughened by extraordinary stress and peril. Some were willing to share it in papers and conversation. I distinctly remember a student who had been in more than ordinary danger. He told me how often he had murmured to himself Bryant's lines.

> He, who, from zone to zone,
> Guides through the boundless sky thy certain flight
> In the long way that I must trace alone,
> Will lead my steps aright.

God's presence was real to him and all his work showed it.

The stress and peril sometimes lingered long. One of my students had been a prisoner of war in Germany. He survived on a diet of bits of moldy black bread and reeking potato soup. Day after day he had to march on this diet. He got water from ditches and patches of snow in the open fields. When he went too slowly he was nipped by German police dogs. Finally, totally exhausted, he was dumped in a ditch for dead. He was later rescued by British prisoners of war but remained unconscious for fourteen hours. He recovered slowly at home and among friends, but he was ill at ease and often bewildered.

Most of the veterans outgrew their memories, but I knew one student whose tensions expressed themselves in erratic behavior and finally required hospitalization. If a professor looked wan, he would come up after class and say "You look as if you have stomach trouble; now, I take these pills." One day he wanted to make a chapel speech and went to President Schultze's office and said "I want to talk about battling for the Lord," and then whipped a sword out of a sheath at his side. There was never a way out of the war for him. Happily, I never heard of another veteran at the college who shared his tragedy.

The impact of the returning veterans was unique in the history of the college. Their large number made them distinctly noticeable, their experiences made them interesting, and their talents and discernment made them valuable. Their contributions to the spiritual and intellectual life of the college were essential. I have learned to distrust all generalizations about one generation of students being smarter than another, but I can plainly tell whether one generation works harder than another. This group had plenty of talent and they knew how to work. I have never taught any group with less loafers. In later years American society has owed them a lot, and Calvin College had drawn from this group many distinguished members in both administration and faculty.

The Faith and the Funds

"Centennial Reflections," *The Banner* (January 30, 1976)

Some wit has said, "Idealism is best supported on an income." During Calvin's century idealism or faith has been steadily present and also, often in a remarkable way, the income, or funds. The budgetary contributions of our church families over the years have been the envy of many colleges and still constitute an indispensable source of Calvin's income. From a minute fifty cents per family in 1900, they have today risen almost ten thousand percent in many of our churches. These funds have been enormously augmented by various financial and developmental secretaries, a host of Calvin supporters, a benevolent government, and munificent private donations.

The Reverend Mr. J. Noordewier's enthusiastic support of Calvin's first major building project boxed him in as our first officially appointed collector of funds. Such service required sacrifice. He had to abandon his ministry at an attractive congregation in Fremont, Michigan, a place of idyllic charm. He traveled to some ninety congregations, often by slow trains and in even slower buggies. He did this in the lean years of the early nineties when even pennies were scarce. His achievement was notable, sacrificial, and prophetic.

In the history of Calvin, the support of what Abraham Kuyper called the *"kleine luiden"* (the small man) has always been indispensable. Generous and nameless to us, yet we know there would have been no college without them. There are also many who are known and remembered. The Reverend Mr. J. J. Hiemenga, Calvin's first president, effectively illustrates the fusion of faith and the acquisition of funds and serves well as a model.

When the Reverend Mr. Hiemenga enrolled as a student in the Theological School, as it was then known, he was a model of faith and a lack of funds. He spent seven years in deepening the former and in managing to acquire enough of the latter to subsist. A haberdasher in Zeeland supplied him with free clothes for seven years; a shopkeeper there supplied him with free shoes. He worked in a barber shop on Saturday afternoons and on the other week-day evenings for seven warm meals a week. For a time he enjoyed bread, molasses, lard and cold water for breadfast. Finally, he discovered a place where he could get seven warm meals a week for a dollar. His room cost him seventy-five cents a week. One must have deep respect for a faith that for seven years can survive on such funds.

The Reverend Mr. Hiemenga assumed the presidency of Calvin in 1919. Synod had previously rejected the idea of a president because it feared "he might have too much influence on events." Some of the faculty shared this feeling, and "stonewalling" was not unknown. The new president had a well-defined, courageous, and imaginative vision for the college. He urged the development of a strong Christian school system under Calvin's leadership; he stressed the importance of academic excellence so that Calvin would be "able to compete with any institution of its kind." He stressed physical expansion and set about to acquire a million dollar endowment fund. His leadership was, however, sharply criticized by certain elements in the church; consequently, only $100,000 was raised. He did succeed in acquiring a boy's dormitory, and that is an interesting story.

He raised $80,000 for the new dormitory, $40,000 of which was contributed by Mr. William Van Agthoven of Cincinnati. When he informed the Board that he wished to make a trip to Cincinnati to ask Van Agthoven for a gift, the Board said, "You don't have to go there. He'll give you ten dollars and it'll cost you more than ten dollars to go there and come back again." Hiemenga arranged to preach there; he paid his own fare. Van Agthoven met him at the station with horse and buggy and treated him to a grand tour of Cincinnati. Later he gave him $10,000 and promised another $10,000 if Hiemenga would raise a similar amount elsewhere. Hiemenga went back to Grand Rapids with ten negotiable $1,000 bonds in a brief case. He made the trip three more times, each time with a small fortune in his briefcase and no Saturday Special in his pocket. He raised $80,000 in all. The dormitory was built, containing a gymnasium where the equipment in the words of Dean Rooks "comprises all the apparatus necessary to the latest and most approved physical exercise."

President Hiemenga resigned in 1925. He had done much for Calvin, but as he himself said, "When I was President of Calvin College I missed my congregation."

Vision in a College Classroom

"Centennial Reflections," *The Banner* (February 13, 1976)

A teacher who meets a former student is sometimes confounded by what the student relates as his outstanding memory of a course. Not infrequently it turns out to be a trivial aside or a brash, impromptu comment blown up into a principle.

Professor Johannes Broene, with his gift for phrase, elaboration, and low-key dramatic remarks said many things in class which I have not forgotten. One day in the late twenties, he was commenting on the serene beauty and valuable holdings of some older American colleges. He then said something like, "Some day these will come to Calvin too." There was so little on or off the campus to generate such a vision that its apparent preposterousness drilled it into my mind. There were three buildings: a rectangular, serviceable, and pedestrian dormitory, an adequate administration and classroom building, and a new and attractive library. There were slightly over three hundred students, about half of whom paid the entire tuition of one hundred dollars a year. The church numbered 22,500 families, who paid $3.50 a year per family to the support of both college and seminary. There were few rich families in the church, and five of them had already done more than their share. Omens of the great depression were flickering on the horizon. Was the statement a romantic dream or sensible prophecy?

President Broene was a cautious and realistic man, chary of excess in any form. He never made a plea for many students; as a matter-of-fact he encouraged students without brains, means, and industrious habits to stay home. He was reluctant to diversify or expand the curriculum. He had no aptitude for magnetizing money. Furthermore, he was fully aware of the deliberate pace at which the college had grown. The number of non-theological students had grown very slowly from twenty-nine in 1895 to sixty-one in 1915. It took another decade for the number to reach three hundred. There seemed small reason for great hope; yet after another half century Calvin College, born fifty years earlier of a noble vision, and brought to maturity through unremitting sacrifice, intelligence, hard work, and the grace of God had become widely known for its academic success, administrative and faculty excellence, and a large and beautiful campus, designed and executed with brilliance. At this writing, student enrollment stands at the peak in the history of the college.

President Broene's prophecy will never become completely true, but it is still amazing to me that so much of it has. When I think of Calvin's meagre resources in 1928 when I heard that statement and compare them to the present I am deeply grateful to God for all that He has permitted Calvin to become and to accomplish.

What President Broene knew when he made that memorable prophecy was the temper, generosity, and the gifts God had entrusted to our people. He knew what faith, intelligence, and hard work can do. He also knew from study and experience what was formerly often expressed in our circles by the presently archaic word *Ebenezer* (Hitherto hath God helped us). In a quiet but compelling way, the history of Calvin College makes that plain.

Two Who Won

The Banner (November 14, 1975)

Mr. George Kamp spent almost fifty years working at an old-fashioned upright desk for Standard Oil at Cleveland, Ohio. "If I hadn't done that," he says, "I'd probably be even shorter than I am now." As one gets to know his unfailing grace and poise, one soon realizes that he stands tall in about everything except his shoes. Surrendering but slowly to the frailty of the years at eighty-two, he never seems weary of well-doing, whether greeting members at the East door of Calvin church twice a Sunday or serving Calvin College as a statistician. His petite and winning wife, Anne, supports these activities with selfless zeal.

When Anne's family moved from Amersvoort in the Netherlands to Edom, Saskatchewan, they disembarked at a lonely railhead on the western frontier and were then transported thirty-eight miles to isolated farm country and primitive housing. The family consisted of a widowed father and eight children. Since there was no school, Anne had to interrupt her endless household duties to teach her younger brothers all she knew. There were two bachelors in the neighborhood, an eccentric Englishman, whom her brothers found reading in a bed surrounded by classics, while the rain dripped upon an umbrella poised over his head, and an ardent Welshman, about whom Anne says, "But I was reserved for a Dutchman." She found her Dutchman in Cleveland, where she went after working as a dressmaker in Minneapolis. When she first saw Mr. Kamp, he struck her as a staid, married man, a dignified deacon, passing the plate with calm expectancy. The deacon, however, now in his late twenties, and rising steadily in his occupation, had been waiting for someone special. Fifty-three years of the happiness to be found in marriage proved him a wise man.

Born in Almelo, Overijssel in 1892, George Kamp emigrated to Cleveland with his family in 1904. He had almost completed his education in a Dutch grammar school, but had to enroll in the first grade in Clevelend and memorize stirring sentences like "Let us chase the squirrel up the hickory tree." A month later he was in the fifth grade and ended grammar school as the valedictorian of his class.

The Reverend Mr. J. R. Brink urged George's father to educate the boy for the ministry, but family circumstances made this impossible. Instead, he and a boy named Kemp applied for a position in Standard Oil, for which Kamp beat out Kemp. He worked for this firm almost fifty years, most of them as manager of cost and sales in the Barreling and Marketing Department. Kamp had among other duties to scrutinize the cost of fodder for the horses, many of whom he got to know by name (\$.50 — oats for Nellie). In his last years with the firm he was a sort of trouble shooter. When he retired at sixty-three, the earnest solicitations of Calvin officials led him to serve the college as a statistician in the business office where he has been employed ever since. His work, like that of Mr. Joe Orlebeke who occupies an office with him, has been much appreciated.

If one is looking for a man to whom hospitality is an inborn grace, diligence a lifelong habit, cool intelligence a daily exercise, unruffled poise second nature, and a profound commitment to the Lord devotedly sought and exercised, he will find them in Mr. Kamp. Few members of our church have a more avid interest in it: its history, clergy, classes, synods, and statistics. He knows over five hundred ministers personally; the *Yearbook* is one of his hobbies, and he manages the arrangements for synod with the tact of a master.

His wife has some fine stories about his unruffled poise. "George," she says, "never loses his cool." One evening as Anne heard sirens wailing in the neighborhood, she rushed to the window and then began to wonder about her own house. As she hurried downstairs she went through the smoke-filled rooms to find flames in the basement. Rushing back to George imperturbably resting in bed, she screamed, "George, the house is on fire!" "Don't get excited," said George, "the walls are still cool. Wait till I get my pants on." Only then did he go to the phone to inform the fire department in the low-keyed voice of a statistician reporting another detail, "We have a fire." On another occasion, the house began to shake, and a sound like a crashing locomotive filled the air; objects began to drop from the walls.

"What's that?" asked Anne.

"That's an earthquake."

"What will we do?"

"Do? Nothing. Stay in bed."

On still another occasion Kamp had to read the sermon to the congregation since they were without a minister. He announced the final psalm, but his father, the organist, was sound asleep. So George unceremoniously left the pulpit and played the organ to accompany the audience's singing. Later his father laughed and said, "You put me to sleep."

During World War II when Mrs. Kamp was enrolled in a first-aid course, one of her assignments was a simulated resuscitation of George at home. Feigning unconsciousness, he was really resuscitated. He ached all over. The next day he looked so weak and wan at work that he was sent to the dispensary, where the nurse discovered that the frail Mrs. Kamp had broken his rib. The Kamps tell the story as if a broken rib were a mere detail when one is zealous in well-doing.

George Kamp is not only unusually knowledgeable about our church and deeply interested in Reformed thought, but he is also a self-made scholar. He has over the years translated between fifty and sixty articles that first appeared in solid Dutch journals. Such writing is usually not strikingly smooth, but his translations, of which I have read many, are marked by grace as well as accuracy. He has also translated pieces from Afrikaans, including an Inaugural Address by the President of Potchefstroom University, South Africa, entitled "Function of Native Chiefs in the Government of South Africa." He has translated addresses on Mathematics and Sociology. For those interested in their family past, he has translated genealogies. He has selected and read many sermons for his church in Cleveland. During all these years he has had a keen ear for sermons and is especially appreciative of doctrinal and exegetical preaching. He has served in the consistory for over thirty years. His mind and heart have been devoted to the cause of Christ as it is served in our denomination, and in all these tasks his wife has shared his concerns.

Mr. Kamp and his wife, as well as many others in our denomination, have made essential contributions to the life of our church out of love for the Lord, and without pay. Such men and women, whether in obscure mission stations or prominent churches, serve selflessly year in and year out. Many a minister can say about them, as Paul did about Timothy, "He has been at my side in the service of the gospel." The Kamps have been such servants for over fifty years. Age has not withered their love nor their zeal.

When I was a student at Northwestern University, I attended a Lutheran church. Every Sunday the church bulletin had a picture of the Lord Jesus with His sheltering arms tenderly extended over the old. His arms have sheltered the Kamps for over eighty years and they never weary. Through the grace of God, the Kamps are winners in the truest sense. Nobility without heraldry has stamped their lives. All who know them are grateful for them and their victorious service in the kingdom of God.*

---

*Mr. George Kamp was one of many whose selfless labor and love enriched the kingdom of God in this world. In August, 1981, Mr. Kamp died and joined God's eternal kingdom.

4

"The Muse in Harness"

MEMORIES OF CALVIN COLLEGE
DEPARTMENT OF ENGLISH

The following history of Calvin College's Department of English focuses particularly on the years from 1927, when Professor Timmerman enrolled at Calvin College, to 1975 when he retired from active teaching. A span of nearly fifty years is bound to have uneven, turbulent stretches, and these are faithfully recorded. Not only do the personalities of the professors in the department come to life, but also their handling of important trends in literature and literary criticism. We find portraits of students, from the earnest small groups of the twenties and thirties, to the hard-eyed, tough-minded veterans after World War II, to the bare-foot wanderers of the sixties.

The Department of English has always had an important role at Calvin College. All students take required courses in Rhetoric and Literature, always according to demanding standards. The Department has produced well-recognized scholars in its own ranks, and internationally known authors from among its majors. As such, this history is more than that of one department, but touches upon the heart of Calvin College and its alumni.

The Muse in Harness
Memories of Calvin College Department of English

Grandfather Tifflin in Steinbeck's *The Red Pony* lost his heart to the past. When he visits his son, he bores the family with his reminiscences of the great westward movement: the dust and the heat, the stupendous buffalo herds, the justifiably hostile Indians, the daily endurance and courage needed to keep the wagon wheels rolling through the endless, empty spaces. As he is talking, he says, "I guess I must have told you that story"; whereupon his son says, "Lots of times. Course I'd like to hear it again." This deflates Grandpa, who says, "Maybe it should be forgotten." He, however, cannot forget and he should not. What he remembers is not only the physical strain of westering, but westering as an attitude and a dream, a push toward new horizons. Of course, the early years of pioneering in the English Department of Calvin College were pallid pioneering compared to Tifflin's but there were real struggles: the occasional harsh opposition to what was taught and how it was taught, the logjam of students after World War II, the crises occasioned by certain publications which the department sponsors, the swirl of the sixties. Now that the department is organized like a phalanx before which the philistines have vanished, now that it is composed of gifted men and women, teaching with widespread appreciation and producing fine poems, stories, learned articles and books, it may be neither meaningless nor inappropriate to recall some elements of the long journey to where it is now.

In 1894, when there were thirty-three students in the Literary Department of the Theological School, Professor J. G. Vanden Bosch was there. In 1907, when the John Calvin Junior College was established, Professor J. G. Vanden Bosch was there. He was there in 1920 when it became Calvin College, and he designed the first English Major. Professor Vanden Bosch taught at Calvin College for fifty years. Professor J. Broene said he had ". . . a personality all his own. There is not another Vanden Bosch on the faculty. I do not know whether it would be desirable to have one, but this Vanden Bosch I should not

want to lose." Calvin kept him until he was seventy-five. That he was
genuinely eccentric, generally effervescent and quite often frightfully
opinionated did not make him less interesting or impede his endeavor
"to let my Christianity speak in the classroom." This very able man
did that with clarity and fervor in an astonishing variety of courses
for fifty years.

When I enrolled at Calvin in 1927, the English Department consisted of Professor Vanden Bosch and two assistants who taught other
subjects as well. For almost forty years he was the English Department as Professor Jellema was the Philosophy Department and Professor A. E. Broene was the French and German Departments. He
had, indeed, transient assistants, often gifted, but they taught only
Freshman English. I took ten of his courses from Shakespeare to
Contemporary English Drama, as well as Principles of Literature and
Advanced Rhetoric. Considering the enrollment of some 315 students
in the late twenties, his classes were well-filled. I don't think I was in
a course under fifteen students. He never ran dry and not to have
done so involved an enormous amount of preparation.

He was an ebullient crusader with passionate loyalties and ani-
madversions. For him truth, beauty, and goodness were one in God
and ought be one for man. His esthetic principles were grounded in
Reformed and Puritan thought. He was allergic to idealistic philosophy and caught its scent in many places. For him idealistic humanists
like More, Foerster, and Sherman, the reigning literary critics of the
day, were stimulating but often in error. Critics like H. L. Mencken and
Van Wyk Brooks were a species of literary vermin. He detested the
naturalism of Hemingway and Dreiser, whom he regarded as termites
gnawing at the pillars of the temple. Against both tribes he employed
all the best Reformed insecticides he could muster. He believed a
literary artist should follow the gleam, the light that never was on
land or sea; he should use his talent to instruct and delight. Such
ideals alienated some students who found compelling truths in Dreiser
and Hemingway and felt that he was too concerned with providing
"moral pap for the young." This caused friction between him and the
realistic practices of the creative writers at Calvin at the time. The
great majority of his students, however, appreciated his learning,
thoroughness, Christian convictions and real, though sometimes
oblique, affection.

During the years of his chairmanship, Professor Vanden Bosch established four traditions, at that time by no means always found in
English departments of comparable size or character. The first was
his affirmation of the value of the study of American literature, which,

during his career to the present, has provided Calvin students with perennially popular courses. The second was the effort to serve students with sound guidance in literary criticism, an effort sustained for years and now spurred on by the intensive and fruitful efforts of Clarence Walhout. The third was to give time and course credit to students interested in advanced, creative, or original writing, whichever term sounds least immodest. This difficult course has been taught frequently, and in recent years has enjoyed the gifted leadership of Stanley Wiersma and John H. Timmerman. Finally, even if somewhat shrilly and dogmatically, Professor Vanden Bosch brought his Christian convictions to bear on all he taught, and that is a feature of Calvin's educational effort at its very best and most important.

Professor Vanden Bosch, like all the English teachers succeeding him, had, apart from the fact that the great majority of them were Dutch and Christian Reformed when that still meant something in terms of language and awareness of ecclesiastical roots and doctrines, a perennially similar variety of students. There were those indifferent to composition, immune to literature, and eager to be done with both; there were the average students with a mild competence in both; there was the very sizable group who wrote competently and appreciated literature. There were those excellent in language and literature who became first-rate scholars or could have been if they had wanted to. Finally, there were the writers, and they were of two kinds. On the one hand, there were the genuine or self-appointed representatives of the artistic temperament:

> A most intense young man
> A soulful-eyed young man
> An ultra-poetical, super-esthetical
> Out of the way young man.

The poem doesn't say, but there were such women too. They were writers who arranged and aroused notice:

> Fire in each eye, and papers in each hand
> They rave, recite and madden round the land.

These students were weary of the received tradition, often iconoclastic, eager to beat their own rhythm out. Some of them achieved national recognition. But over the years there have been other gifted writers, some of them on the present staff, who absorbed, mediated and built upon tradition, and assiduously honed their craft, enriching the college

without embarrassing it. Their poems and stories inform new config-
urations with old wisdom.

Gifted writers, from the stunning fivesome of the DeJong brothers,
DeVries, Manfred, and Smitter in the space of a long decade to the
present, have been both to the department and Calvin a source of
pride, mixed feelings, and apology in two senses. They have often
received in terms of departmental time and energy in service as men-
tors, judges, and defenders of literary controls a great deal of expensive effort. I have wondered whether this miniscule fraction of our
majors who pay no more tuition than others were overly attended to.
I say that with full awareness of their brilliance and skill, the sharp
edge they gave to teaching as well as their occasional abrasiveness
and ingratitude. How do they fit into the aims of the department? Was
it right that I sometimes spent more time in a semester on the "creative
work" and its results of one student than I did on all the term papers
in a class? Should "creative work" be channeled into classes on writing? It is a difficult question when one admires a student's work,
wishes to be helpful and has a desk piled with papers and some of
one's own one wishes to work on. I have struggled to answer it in the
light of what I consider the aims of the department as I see them.

The English Department, it seems to me, exists to serve six major
concerns. It should teach the elements of composition and their successful employment. In the second place, since many students share
an attitude expressed in the following jingle, it should work hard to
change it.

> As I was laying on the green
> A small English book I seen.
> Carlyle's "Essay on Burns" was the edition.
> I left it laying in the same position.

In the third place, the department should stimulate its able students
to greater appreciation and critical sensitivity, and in some cases to
enter upon graduate work. In the fourth place the department has a
strong obligation to participate in the training of future teachers of
English. The department should also encourage real writers without
shortchanging the others. Finally, in a college like Calvin, it should
make clear and appealing the importance of Christian experience and
value in relation to literary judgment. Scholarly publication which
grows out of or contributes to these aims is greatly to be praised, but
not necessary to their realization.

In trying to achieve these aims one has the perennial pleasure of surprise. To balance the oafs that sometimes wander into a college classroom, are the students compact with charms; to balance the freshman who wants to write a term paper on the seeing eye dog are those who write, as one did, a forty page paper on the atom, or, as another did, on the diaries of Virginia Woolf. To balance the final examination that shows a genius for unawareness, is the final examination I received in which the answers were convincingly proved by abundant and precise quotations. I received a critical paper on one of Chaucer's Tales written in commendable heroic couplets. I received one final examination paper in which the writer complained that I taught Chaucer in Middle English, and then went on to recommend some modern translations. In the late sixties some students complained about their low grades; I have had thousands of students, but no one has ever complained about his grade being too high.

As might be expected, however, the marvels appeared in unsolicited manuscripts. The problems, of course, did not surface in the promising and exciting efforts. The real problems came in evaluating doggerel, verbal fluff, and baloney. I had to comment on a poem in which the author was being stifled by city air and "Acking for clean air" in the country. After many lines of lament, I was almost moved to tell him that what he needed was artificial respiration. I received a poem composed of several pages of adverbs. It was ingenious but pointless, like a large horse standing on his hind legs on a small block of wood. So what? The "creative mind" is often obsessed by self. Once at 3 a.m., a student, seeing a light in our living room where my wife was feeding the baby, rang the bell and asked if he could talk to me. He had been caught in poetic parturition and wanted help. Another student, who failed to win a coveted literary prize, holed up on the cold shores of Lake Michigan for a few nights to cool off. How many times members of the English Department have had to mobilize to regret or defend a literary product. I wish to compliment the members of the department who have with ingenuity and patience taught the course in "Creative Writing," in many ways the hardest course to teach in the department. It is fitting also to congratulate and thank the Wm. B. Eerdmans Publishing Company whose interest and generous literary prizes over many years helped make the problems possible.

When I was a student at Calvin only two faculty members had offices, infrequently used, and just large enough to hold two filing cabinets, not there, a desk and a chair. Today's English Department has quite a few offices, some of them attractive, and all heavily used. One of them is so packed with books, scholarly publications, student papers, and other detritus, and the inhabitant is so consummately industrious, that I was always tempted to post a sign on the door "Do not disturb. Scholar working." Professor Vanden Bosch had no office and he was not a counseling man. If you wanted more than comments on a paper, you had to ask for it. He left his elegant study at 856 Bates Street with the departmental agenda in his head, the day's scholarship in his briefcase, and no post-class interruption to fear. However, in other cases, I think students may miss being invited to a teacher's study in his home to discuss his problems over coffee and pie. In the college of that time academic counseling occurred only upon student request; today it occurs on schedule twice a year and often in between. Nobody counseled us at registration; it was assumed that a college student could figure that out with the aid of the catalog. If one ran into a severe problem, you consulted Registrar Dekker who had the answers or made them happen. In the twenties one had to force oneself on the professor; today the professor is forced on the student.

The end of World War II transformed the college. It doubled the enrollment over night and began the "Golden Age" of education at Calvin as well as in the rest of the country with grants, gifts, and soaring enrollments in most colleges. For decades to come, the faculty was steadily enlarged, and for many years adequate staff was hard to achieve. The English Department was understaffed and overworked for years. Freshman English classes ranged from thirty-five to forty-five. Teachers with graduate training were hard to find, and many sections of Freshman English were taught by experts in history, education, theology, and languages. Dr. John Bratt switched his calm and penetrating eye from Amos and Ezekiel to sentence structure and "Why I came to Calvin College"; Dr. John Daling during one year, moved effectively, if not always enthusiastically, from syllogisms and philosophers to the seven ways of developing a topic sentence; Dr. Earl Strikwerda deflected his gift of language from the teaching of American History, to polishing term papers on the Orient Express. Some wonderful souls taught five sections of Freshman English. Knee-deep in papers, red in eye and fingers, they gave a full measure of devotion. Fifteen hours, six days a week, and one hundred and fifty students was not uncommon in the department. I heard groaning but little grousing; the future was in the air and the lights were all green.

In 1950, the leadership of the department changed. Professor Vanden Bosch had retired completely if reluctantly at seventy-five. Old professors do not fade away; they are retired. After he had retired we were talking about Browning's "Rabbi Ben Ezra" and the famous lines:

> Grow old along with me
> The best is yet to be,
> The last for which the first was made.

He then remarked with typical unexpectedness, "You know, John, that is a lot of baloney." Dr. Henry Zylstra was appointed Departmental Chairman in 1950.

Dr. Zylstra received his M.A. in German from the University of Iowa and his Ph.D from Harvard in Comparative Literature. He taught at Calvin on various occasions during the Thirties and was appointed Instructor in English and German in 1941. In 1943 he was appointed Associate Professor of English. After serving in the United States Army, he returned to Calvin in 1946 and became chairman of the department in 1950. He brought to that task a brilliant mind, wide-ranging scholarship, uncommon pedagogical skill, ready wit, and unstinted idealism. He led by attraction and example. He, like Vanden Bosch, ran the department out of his vest pocket. Although he had to call a few quasi-departmental meetings, they resembled a scholarly coffee-kletz and did not become a habit. Dr. Zylstra, like Vanden Bosch had a deep appreciation for continental thought; he never disavowed literature's function to transform, humanize, and ennoble; he and the rest of the department now put as much emphasis on *delight* as *instruct*. Literature was a pattern of beauty as well as morality, and beauty itself had a moralizing influence. The department became contemporary in attitude and subject matter. Vanden Bosch's influence was not derailed but enriched. Henry Zylstra died in 1956 in The Netherlands while on a Fulbright Guest Lectureship, to the deep shock of all of us.

Immediately after World War II, our problem of staff was, as I have mentioned, extremely difficult. It was difficult for twenty years. Right after the war it was hard to find adequately trained teachers; after the fifties it was difficult to get them to come to Calvin. The sixties were the promised land for Ph.D's. Some of them came to their interviews with the Educational Policy Committee with several appointments in their pockets. One prospective candidate informed me on the way from airport to college that he had ten appointments. It must have been a grand feeling. During the disconsolate depths of the Depression I walked miles to East Grand Rapids, to Wyoming, and to other places to apply for non-existent positions. Finally, I taught one course at Calvin for a year, and oddly enough I still have twenty-two dollars coming. This candidate, a very able one at that, did not accept our appointment. For me in 1945 Calvin had been the promised land; this

CALVIN COLLEGE
ENGLISH DEPARTMENT

1965: L to R, Mary Ann Walters,
  Arie Staal, Kenneth Kuiper.
  Seated, Winifred Holkeboer.

1955: L to R, Gertrude Slingerland, Henry Zylstra,
Peter Oppewall, Steve Van Der Weele, Richard
Tiemersma, John J. Timmerman, Betty Duimstra.

965: L to R, seated, George G. Harper,
enrietta Ten Harmsel, John J. Timmerman.
tanding, Stanley Wiersma, Richard Tiemersma,
teve Van Der Weele.

1965: L to R, Gertrude
Slingerland, Bernie Van't
Hul, Peter Oppewall.

1977: L to R front row: Steve Van Der Weele, George Harper, Henrietta
Ten Harmsel, Richard Tiemersma, Charlotte Otten, Henry Baron, Clarence
Walhout, Irvin Kroese. Back row: Mary Hietbrink, Stanley Wiersma,
Kenneth W. Kuiper, Linda Spoelman, Mary A. Walters, Robert Meyer, John
H. Timmerman, Edward E. Ericson, Peter Oppewall.

chap was just traveling through. During the sixties we began recruiting candidates before they ever left Calvin. Sometimes, it paid handsome returns, as in the case of Harmon Hook, a most-gifted young man who died at thirty-two to our lasting sorrow. Two others also came and later left to our intense regret. The English Department is unique in its tragic losses through death and departure. During the early part of this period, the first woman was appointed to the English staff to spend all her time in the department. Miss Gertrude Slingerland served the department for many years as a gracious, gifted, and popular teacher. We were later strengthened by the appointments of fine teachers such as Mrs. Winifred Holkeboer, Dr. Charlotte Otten, Dr. Henrietta Ten Harmsel, Dr. Mary Walters, and Mrs. Mildred Zylstra, each of whom contributed to the variety and competence of the department.

During the fifties and early sixties there were two notable influences on the department and one expression of student and staff association now defunct. The first was the thought and poetry of T. S. Eliot. The influence of T. S. Eliot during these years was momentous and unforgettable. In 1956, Eliot lectured at the University of Minnesota to a crowd of thirteen thousand that had to gather in the football stadium. For that lecture he received an honorarium of $2000, the largest sum ever paid up to that time for a literary lecture. Eliot was not a sparkling lecturer; his rather prosaic delivery and subtle humor, tightly-packed thought, and dogmatic style never made him the glittering event that Dylan Thomas, another favorite of that day, always was. Yet he was in great demand. At Calvin his thought and poetry attracted much attention and loyalty among many students. Eliot's critical thought especially on the relation between Christianity and literature was helpful to us all. His poetry was irresistibly attractive to teach. Eliot's poetry gave a professor who had studied Matthiessen and Williamson an enormous advantage. One could appear erudite and masterful, opening new doors. When one taught Robert Frost, there was only the poetry, which looked so simple but wasn't. The fun there was to prove it. Eliot's influence was pervasive until the middle sixties when non-literary passions moved English majors more than old masterpieces.

The second important influence was the temporary hegemony of the "new critics," Brooks and Warren, Tate and Eliot. It is not easy today to imagine the revolutionary impact of these critics and the textbooks the first two provided on the teaching of English on the college level. They infiltrated the graduate school much more slowly and never as completely. Their work resulted in a shift from talk about poems, paraphrase, and summary to a close analysis of the poems, from preoccupation with literary history to a study of literature, from a major concern with ideas to a consideration of art, from a thoughtful study of the relation of life to letters to, in extreme cases, the total isolation of art from the life that begot it. I have seen, examined, and dumped a text composed solely of poems, without even identifying their authors, as if an acknowledgment of their existence were irrelevant and somewhat shady.

The new critics did perform a valuable and overdue service. There had been too much literary history in many English courses and not enough examination of how the author put his art together. The new critics developed a series of code words like irony, myth, archetype, symbolism and, above all, ambiguity. They often became tricky and authoritarian, and their methods failed in cases where the code words were inoperative. Even Eliot denigrated their "lemon-squeezer technique." Furthermore, eighteenth-century poetry, tight and rigidly organized as it is, cannot be well understood without a knowledge of biography and literary history sensibly applied. This, however, does not eliminate their great services.

In 1954, there were eighteen student clubs on campus, each one sponsored by a faculty member and devoted to various modes of extracurricular study in a particular discipline. The two English clubs, one for men and the other for women (and nobody thought anything of that), studied contemporary drama and Dante and Thomas Mann respectively. In a few years there were four. The first English club, organized in the twenties and called the Pierian Club, numbered over thirty men and women and devoted itself not only to imbibing at the immortal spring, but adding a trickle to it. Frederick Feikema (Manfred) was a member of that club, and I can see him in imagination, all six-feet-nine of him, swaying gently as he read his prairie poems. As I took a few minutes to look at the pictures of the young men and women in the literary clubs of the fifties, I was impressed again by their stellar talents and the distinction most of them achieved in their careers. The works we studied, the papers, prodded into excellence by the presence of peers, the sharp and sometimes flamboyant dialog that followed are a treasured part of my memories of the English Department. I think Professors Harper, Oppewall, Tiemersma and Van Der Weele, who served as sponsors also, would corroborate that judgment. These clubs floundered in the hubbub of the sixties, and attempts at revival failed.

After Dr. Zylstra's death I served as chairman of the department for a decade. Though it was no longer possible to run the department out of a vest pocket, I tried. I did it for almost ten years without an office; we are, I suppose, such creatures of habit that when I was finally assigned an office I couldn't stand to sit in it. I would rather talk to students with problems in my study at home. I was assisted by a wonderful private secretary, my wife, who typed countless letters with impeccable accuracy and unheralded goodness. In a bit of skillful strategy, I appointed Dr. Richard Tiemersma, the rhetorical conscience of the department, as Director of Freshman English. He performed a most valuable service in organizing, directing, and patrolling the Freshman English program. His distinguished gifts as a teacher enhanced his value as director. Later on Dr. Steve Van Der Weele, that stellar combination of talent and indefatigibility, made valuable contributions to this course, as he has done in many other places. Most recently Dr. Henry Baron employs his gifts in a similar function. Miss Slingerland relieved me immensely by agreeing to teach the course "Principles of Teaching English," a course in which I had exhausted my store of pedagogical wisdom by six weeks and which I kept going through the study of literary criticism and composition. Dr. Kenneth Kuiper later taught this course with ingenuity, wisdom and great practical pay-off for its students. Dr. Stanley Wiersma, a somewhat shy and extremely polite student in my earlier classes at Calvin, now widely known for his enchanting poems, sometimes mordant but always vivid, of the products of Reformed piety in Iowa, employed his talents of critical acumen and sympathy in the course for original writing. These years were also enriched by the linguistic talents of Dr. Louis Rus, and the incomparable verve, originality, spice, and solid scholarship of Dr. Bernard Van't Hul, both of whom left us. What I am trying to say in this rather rambling paragraph is that whatever success the department enjoyed during my tenure was the result of loyal and skillful service by devoted colleagues. It was, in fact, an era of good feeling until departmental discussions on the 4-1-4 took place in 1966.

In 1965 the faculty began its discussion of the proposed new curriculum — the 4-1-4, with four courses available to the student each semester and an interim of curiosities, novelties, limited in-depth probes, and other assorted goodies in between. After a sustained and illuminating discussion on the aims and practices of education, the faculty adopted the new proposals. The Educational Policy Committee, of which I was a member, sat through sixty-six meetings in which it considered the adjustments of every department in consonance with the program. Prior to these discussions the departments had met lengthily to make such adjustments. Since in our department the literary orchard had not only to be rearranged, pruned, and in parts uprooted, the dialog was not uniformly saccharine. There were ruffled feelings and some severe disappointments. Many of the final decisions depended upon one vote. The major clash arose over the reduction of Freshman English from two semesters to one. To some that appeared to be an undesirable truncation. Furthermore, limiting students to four courses a semester instead of five, six, and sometimes even seven, would appear certain to diminish the participation of non-majors in our advanced courses. They diminished. Two well-filled sections of Chaucer dropped to twenty-five students; two sections of Eighteenth Century Literature dropped to one, so sparsely attended that it had to be offered in alternate years. Proponents of the 4-1-4 say they didn't do it. They did.

It became the task of Dr. George Harper, the new chairman, to iron out the wrinkles in the new program, to face the hard choices in assigning courses to departmental members since many of the plums were gone, and to guide the department through the stormy late sixties. He did this with remarkable coolness, patience, wisdom, and selflessness. His adroit handling of departmental meetings, concern for his staff, time-consuming interest in his students, ready wit, and devotion to the highest ideals of the department marked his entire career as chairman.

The late sixties was no paradise for pedagogues. Our students though mildly affected by the turmoil of the times were affected in ways that made some of us uncomfortable. The notions that the past was a "bucket of ashes," that wisdom peaked before thirty, that everything had to be, in that abominably abused word *relevant*, with the connotation of immediately meaningful, were disconcerting. Class discussion, often without emphasizing its quality, became the earmark of good teaching. There was grumbling about grades, thereby giving an edge to student evaluations. There was a loss in dignity and manners. Some of my friends think I was born with a tie on — a gaudy one at that, but I never thought sloppiness enhanced appearance. When some students shuffled in with hair like a haystack and beards that reminded me of the pictures of the elders hanging on the walls in my father's consistory room in Orange City in 1912, I was irritated. Some years before I had a boy who came to class with bare feet. I told him, "Listen, Robinson Crusoe, you have your man Friday shoe you before you come back." I told the Dean that I liked neither the sound nor the smell of bare feet. He replied, "It will soon turn cold." One boy with an ample sweater and long, groomed hair confused me and I called him Miss — till I received the mid-semester bluebook and

saw that he was Andrew. However, he never resented it, returned the
next semester and we became good friends.

My main concern for over forty years has been students — thousands of them. I have often been asked two questions about teaching
them. When I began teaching at Calvin I was asked how high school
teaching compared with college teaching. The second question I was
asked most frequently during the late sixties: "Aren't students more
gifted today than ever?" No. First, of all, because in general I see no
progress in the sequence of Pericles to Warren Gamaliel Harding or
in that of George Washington to Ulysses S. Grant. The very idea is a
blow to evolution. Secondly, I found no evidence of it in my experience.
Students of one age may know more than those of another, may be
peculiarly stimulated by the excitement of a particular culture, but I
don't see them getting smarter. The bright students of the sixties
seemed to me no brighter than those of the fifties, and, of course not,
of the late twenties. The gifted students of the sixties were electrified
by their passionate commitments and the fortifying environment of
outspoken assertion.

There are outstanding teachers in high school and in college, but
excellence in one place is not always transferable to the other. If a
good college teacher should move to high school, he would immediately encounter a fact of life which would fill him with nostalgia for
the oasis he had left — the maintenance of discipline. College teachers
may be disturbed by occasional whispering, a bellicose disputant, a
harmless dozer, or a knitter of afghans, but that is about all. A college
teacher may be as soporific as Sominex, his presentation like smoothed
cement, but he is unlikely to be fired, especially if he teaches a required
course which only he can teach, or publishes erudite pieces which
only he, the editor, and a few savants have read. His tenure is like a
piece of the rock. It is radically different in high school; the lava is
usually moving below the surface and unless the teacher has imagination, a sense of drama, manifest interest in and affection for his
students, and a forceful personality, it will erupt. I remember a colleague in high school, a sunny, sweet person, a pushover. One day as
the principal and I were talking in the hall we heard the rumors of
disorder in his room. The principal asked me, "What's he teaching?"
I said, "The Tempest," and he replied, "It sounds like it." He lasted
just a year. High school students are often more outspokenly loyal
than college students, but you have to win them from the beginning
of the first class. With good discipline high school teaching is a great
pleasure; without it Room 205 is a chamber of horrors.

On the other hand, a first-rate high school teacher never has to publish a line or make a speech outside of chapel, if there. Even if he does, the authorities are unlikely to notice either, and if they do, are unlikely to comment on it. The writings are nothing more than unrewarded serendipity. In many colleges, however, even if mistakenly, publication is extremely important; it can be tabulated; it is recognized outside the college; it indicates industry. Yet some of the best college teachers I know have published little; some of the least impressive have published every other Thursday; a very few have excelled in both teaching and publication. I have always felt that a teacher who channels his reading, research and thought into fine teaching, fulfills his obligations to the college. I suspect, however, that even the most brilliant of college teachers who do not publish have a minor sense of frustration.

The English Department, which never had more than three full-time faculty members until 1946, has now seventeen full-time members and ten assistants. Its chairperson is now Dr. Henrietta Ten Harmsel, an excellent student in one of my first classes at Calvin and some years later an admired colleague. Her marked skill as teacher, scholar, and superb translator are well known. The achievement and quality of the present English staff speaks for itself.

The department has expanded in striking ways. It is humming with courses we would never have thought of introducing or dared to introduce in the forties. A course in Black American Literature has been successfully pioneered by Dr. Peter Oppewall, who has fruitfully served the department for so many years. Dr. Irvin Kroese, whose sprightly critiques of movies in *The Banner*, would have triggered an ecclesiastical eruption in 1945, has offered a course, Introduction to Cinema. I also noted an Interim course by Dr. Harper, The Films of Alfred Hitchcock, whose course description says, "Ken, this is only a movie. Let's not go too deeply into these things." In 1928, no one would have dared go into it at all. Even the course, The Bible in Literary Perspective, might have roused the warriors on the walls at that time. Solzhenitzyn, C. S. Lewis, Canadian Literature, Vision and Fantasy have been offered, even an interim in Minstrel Shows. The department is, indeed, humming with a freedom, openness, variety, and self-confidence unknown years ago. Since professors now occupy a chair instead of a living room suite, and since they have become specialists instead of generalists, they have time to offer graduate courses and to produce both commendable scholarship and poems and stories. If founding father J. G. Vanden Bosch could return for a look, I think he would be astonished and pleased.

5

"A Cloud of Witnesses Surrounding Us"

ON CALVIN COLLEGE ALUMNI AUTHORS

*I*n his centennial history of Calvin College, Prom-
ises to Keep, *Professor Timmerman devotes a chapter entitled "Little
Foxes in the Vineyard" to those students in Calvin's history who
have waged varying degrees of warfare with their* alma mater. *He
observes:*

> Calvin is committed to giving Christ preeminence in all things: work
> that imperils that ideal cannot be tolerated. I think it is worthwhile to
> remember a comment of the poet and critic Allen Tate: "Poetry does
> not dispense with tradition: it probes the deficiencies of a tradition.
> But it must have a tradition to probe." However incorrect one may view
> their probing, I think Calvin College has given its rebels a tough tra-
> dition to rebel against. They weren't slugging it out with Styrofoam.

*Most of those rebels expressed themselves quite noticeably in col-
lege publications. Some continued to do so through other vehicles
for some time after their graduation. Sometimes it was little more
than preening of feathers and verbal strutting. But sometimes they
were authors of rare and gifted brilliance who have now themselves
become a part of that "Calvin tradition." In the selections that follow,
Professor Timmerman reflects on Calvin's authors. The section concludes with Professor Timmerman's reflections upon the possibilities
of the Christian novelist, a topic further explored in the section on
literature.*

As I Knew Them

Dialogue (April, 1975)

*D*ialogue has asked me to share some of the information accumulated in writing a centennial history of Calvin College. Since excerpts or fragments from it may prove obscure, and since whatever interest the book may have will come from reading it as a whole, I shall share some memories of the Calvin writers students have often asked me about. All four of these writers attended Calvin while I was a student there from 1927-1931, though never all at the same time. A kind of myth to which some of them contributed has developed. Here they are as I remember them, part of a student body of 315: Peter DeVries, all four years from 1927-1931; David DeJong, for two years; Meindert DeJong and Frederick Manfred for one, although in the case of Manfred conversation and correspondence have often occurred since friendship has been sustained.

Calvin College at the ebb of the twenties was but a tenth of its present size. There were but three buildings on the campus; no coffee shop, and a tiny gymnasium. Chapel was held every day, and there were regularly held classes at 7:10 in the morning to which some students came by streetcar for a nickel from the south and west sides of Grand Rapids. There was then so much history to learn that every student had to take two courses in it, so much English that every student had to take four, and so much Bible that every student had to take five courses in the subject. Clubs abounded, oratory and debate were major school activities, basketball scores of 31-28 were common, the A Capella choir was not yet organized, although the men's quartets were popular. There were two Broenes on the faculty but no Broene Center. If you had a problem, you had a problem.

I said rather hyperbolically that I knew the DeJong brothers. Dave was rather unknowable, Meindert inscrutable. They moved in silent splendor through the halls of Calvin, impenetrably aloof. They were distant and unobtrusive. Anyone, however, interested in writing was soon aware of the imagistic and often enigmatic poems of David, which, together with occasional short stories, appeared regularly in

111

the *Chimes* and *Prism.* Dave had a reputation already in prep school, then in its last year as part of Calvin. Formerly the pictures of graduates in the *Prism* were accompanied with epithets, often revelatory. The epithet beside Dave's picture in 1925 was:

> The iconoclast. He excels in four things:
> Cynicism, haughtiness, wit and poetry.

In the same *Prism*, he and a friend, Johannes Stuart, a self-appointed genius with abundant and flaming red hair and gaudy, clashing clothes, wrote as follows:

> After years of patient clamor for recognition we have finally obtained the meritorious degree from Professor Vanden Bosch (English), of being dubbed the most obstinate, unruly and pachydermatous class in school.

Johannes did the clamoring, Dave delivered the goods, but what he delivered in the school papers revealed little of his deepest tensions. When he was graduated from Calvin in 1929, the epithet beside his picture was:

> My blood is cymbol-clashed and
> The anklets of the dancers tinkle there
>
> Harp and psaltery, harp and
> psaltery make drunk my spirit.

I'll let you figure that out.

Though I was in several classes with him and accepted his rather disdainful attitude toward ordinary mortals like myself as a mark of his talent, I had no idea at all of the gnawing resentment he bore toward "the self-righteous Christian Reformed Grand Rapids Dutch" or the contempt he harbored toward Professor Vanden Bosch, who recommended him enthusiastically for a fellowship he later received at Duke University and whom he ultimately repaid with slander in *With a Dutch Accent.* After he was at Duke I asked him for poems to publish in *Chimes,* where they later appeared. His first novel, *Belly Fulla Straw,* and his autobiographical *With a Dutch Accent,* which missed being a Book-of-the-Month Club choice through the adverse vote of Clifton Fadiman, reveal a deep persecution complex compounded by emotional elephantiasis. Such incredible touchiness as these books reveal strikes me as unconvincing. I never heard anyone at Calvin speak disparagingly of him. All he got publicly was incense, but never enough. His book *Old Haven*, a novel about Friesland had, however, plenty of incense coming. Professor Howard Mumford Jones of Harvard hailed it as a work of genius. It is a superb book and the local manifestations of Frisian Power can legitimately rejoice in it.

Dave's brother Meindert moved through Calvin on little cat feet. He was at that time amazingly shy and uncommunicative. After graduation, he filled a position as instructor in English at Grundy Junior College in Grundy Center, Iowa, hardly an American Athens. After teaching for a week or two, he slipped away during the night by bus. He supported himself for years by manual labor until his rarely excellent children's books made him internationally famous.

Peter De Vries was an entirely different person. He was about as inconspicious as a flamingo. Suave and sophisticated in looks, chic and natty in dress, with a walk full of bounce and a vocabulary fully adequate to all occasions, he burst upon the campus like a meteor. He never did much for class, and I once saw him ordered out of one. He was sharing his wit too loudly. He was an extremely gifted orator whether competing in a state oratorical contest massively attended and cheered by the students or mounting the counter of the De Luxe Cafe and giving a spontaneous oration on Buffalo Bill. He was an amiable and likeable person. For one semester he served as an innovative editor of *Chimes*, writing brilliant, breezy editorials and introducing the newspaper format. He retired after the first semester, presumably from nervous exhaustion. This may well have been true because beneath the vigorous manner, the troubles that later hospitalized him with tuberculosis may have been beginning. I once visited his apartment on Wealthy Street next to the old Wealthy Theater. In the course of the conversation he engaged in a heated diatribe against a print he had hanging on the wall. He then opened the refrigerator, took out an egg, and hurled it on the middle of the print. We all watched the egg dribble to the floor. Later it struck me as a prophetically symbolic act. After graduation I once spent a delightful evening with him at the home of a mutual friend in Evanston. He was then an editor of *Poetry* magazine. When his first book *Who Wakes the Bugler?* was published, he asked me to review it for *The Calvin Forum*. In addition to a good deal of praise, there were a few suggestions. I have written reviews of some of his books since, but not because I was asked by him. If someone had asked me in our senior year at Calvin, "Is Peter De Vries going to be somebody?" I would have said, "Most certainly." If he had asked me "What?", I would have said, "Mayor of Chicago."

In an article in *The Banner* some ten years ago, I said that "Peter De Vries is the most prominent writer to come out of our group." Soon afterward I received an angry letter, which, together with other hostile details, said of De Vries, "His career and work have nothing to say to Christians." But he *is* the most prominent writer to come out of our group, and some of his best short stories, and especially *The Blood of the Lamb* have a great deal to say to us. Furthermore, his scintillating satires on suburbia are a cleverly executed attack from the inside on the vapidity of its life.

Manfred came to Calvin when I was a senior; at six-feet-nine his visibility was obvious and his tremendously gregarious nature accentuated it. He came from a corner of northwestern Iowa, which has in former years sent a host of able students to Calvin. The town was Doon, where a friend of his years later erected a sign "Doon, the home of Frederick Manfred." It was removed. In his book *The Primitive* he recounts in minutely realistic detail the long journey by tin-lizzie to Grand Rapids. The four bedraggled boys were glad to reach the "rooster-coop," as he calls the dormitory. The book is rich in accurate topographical detail, many clearly identifiable characters, and some that are composite. Its chief character, Thurs, he claims to have invented. What he does not include is also significant. He does not include, for instance, a mild form of hazing which he and his friend De Bie experienced after having listened to Billy Sunday strike out sinners. When they returned a large group of students were milling about the dormitory; a minor group detached itself and, all calling each other Al, approached De Bie and Feikema. They ordered Feikema to strip to the waist and painted a huge red *F* on his back, after which they covered the letter with newspaper and made him don his shirt. The group then escorted the boys to the new Seminary building then under construction, made them go up into the pitch dark attic, and then removed the ladder. As they left, a student tossed up a book of matches. Manfred's magnetically impressive size invited various forms of attention.

Manfred was drafted into playing basketball. He had not played the game in high school, but in the relatively slow-moving college basketball of his day, his height permitted easy tip-ins, and he proved invaluable to the team. He also endured a great deal of physical punishment: undetected jabbing of elbows, jarring shoves, and painful stomping on highly available feet. He was also a fine baseball player, a sport not then sponsored at the college, but sporadically engaged in on campus until the shattered glass in school buildings and neighboring houses abruptly ended the sport. I remember pleading with

President R. B. Kuiper to at least allow us to play catch on campus, but the furious protestations of janitor Norden made him implacable. We then made up a team and played a few games at Garfield Park in which George Stob, later a professor at the seminary, made one of the finest circus catches I have ever seen.

Manfred was always a real writer; everything else was secondary. He was a genuine self-starter. Manuscripts were constantly accumulating, and they were frequently revised. The early poems and stories he showed me were already marked by impressively accurate detail. Rural Iowa, in which he had such deep roots, was evoked with pictorial vividness: the man-sized grasses, the whirling and singing of birds above them, the rustle of non-human life at their base, the hot summer sun and the bleak, deep snow of winter. His talent for observation and accurate recording was apparent in his poems and stories, which he published in the school papers. He was always bent on improving his craft: sometimes "the old lizard," as he calls his inspiration, manipulated his work, but that he strove for form as he understood it was evident from the beginning. He had to work his way through college, mopping floors, cleaning windows, sweeping the gymnasium, but he never scanted his writing and reading. Even in the summer after a hard day's work, long after everyone else had turned off their lights, he read the classics. He had a gift, but he spared no effort to enrich it. In *The Primitive* and elsewhere, he seems to imply a certain amount of persecution. I never met a student or faculty member who did not admire and like him, though not all were in agreement with his esthetic or philosophic convictions.

Manfred over the years has produced a shelf of books, some of mammoth size. He has accomplished a great deal: a multi-level saga of the evolution of an area of our country from the pre-white era to the present, the creation of a great variety of characters drawn from all walks of life, an original and fruitful experimentation in language and technique, at least three novels which deserve a place on a small shelf of first-rate Western fiction. He has done this in the face of poverty, neglect, obscurity, a long bed-ridden siege of tuberculosis, and even hostility. He has never engaged in pointless recrimination or senseless revolt, but has lived steadily by a vision of his craft and the place of man on this earth which one need not share to respect.

Siouxland and Suburbia

The Reformed Journal (October, 1959)

Five of Calvin College's alumni have received national literary distinction. Their books have been published by reputable firms, reviewed in quality magazines, and in the case of each author at least one of his novels has been well up in the best-seller lists. Writing reviews about the books of two of these authors raises nobody's eyebrows. Writing about the books of the other three in our publications is a challenge to literary nuclear warfare. The reviewer thrusts himself into a no man's land awaiting simultaneous hostile fire from the puritan and the avantgardist. If he escapes wounds, it is because he is unread—a pleasant dilemma.

Anyone who knew Peter De Vries or Frederick [Feikema] Manfred at Calvin College sensed that when they would be graduated their literary future would not be past, but the most perceptive critic could hardly have predicted their rather amazing products of 1959. *Conquering Horse* by Manfred goes back to primitive Indian society for its inspiration, to a pagan world dense with myth and symbolism, a world of fetish, trance and medicine man, a world without a white man. *The Tents of Wickedness* by De Vries is as contemporary as the last *New Yorker*, a striking pastiche of Marquand, Faulkner, Proust, Hemingway and others, as well as authentic De Vries. It is an acrid portrait of an indecent society living in Decency, Connecticut, a cerebral dance of wit, pun, and parody proceeding from the lips and pens of some of the zaniest characters in fiction. Drama merges into melodrama and melodrama clanks into farce. Here is suburbia, slick, sophisticated, and suppurating.

The two books, though strikingly different, reveal important similarities. Both are imaginative creations. *Conquering Horse* is an imaginative form of historical fiction. Terrain, characterization, and plot, though doubtless authentic, are illuminated by poetic feeling and poetic insight. This recreation of an alien culture is no pedestrian, factual, historical novel. *The Tents of Wickedness* is surely a social fantasy, if not a social nightmare; if there is really such a social structure, Alice lives in Wonderland and you can write her a letter. Both are remarkable in their nomenclature. Manfred's book abounds in the picturesque symbolism of such names as Circling Hawk, Owl Above, Moon Dreamer, and Redbird. De Vries specializes in such fantastic handles as Chick Swallow, Beth Appleyard, Pete Cheshire, Colonel Bickerstaffe, a "Waccy" woman, and the Groteguts. Neither shows appreciable indebtedness to the Christian tradition, though there is a certain magnanimity and moral grandeur in some of the characters in *Conquering Horse* that seems rooted in the Christian sense of the dignity of man. Dignity is lost in Decency, except in the case of Mrs. Swallow, who in this book of psychiatric case histories resembles the normal taxpayer.

The most striking difference between the two books lies in the contrasting cultures portrayed and in the contrasting visions underlying and informing their depiction. *Conquering Horse* is a simple and moving story of a young man in search of a significant name. No Name, as he is called at the beginning of the story, must attain a meaningful name through a god-given vision and a series of brave deeds. The book is the search for the name and the ensuing heroism once the vision is given. Running parallel to the search for tribal status through the acquisition of a proper name is a tender love story, pagan and frank at times, but never salacious. The action, and the life of the Sioux, are governed by religious feeling, vision, and prophetic interpretation by Moon-Dreamer, the tribal priest. The gods speak to man in visions, dreams, and natural phenomena. The word of the gods is real to the people and in the highest vision, the life of the spirit is eternal, for as Redbird says before his miraculous translation to the spiritual world, "My Son, it does not matter where the body lies, for it is grass. But where the spirit is, there it will be a good place to be." The world of Conquering Horse is religiously orientated, though the religion strikes the reader as a maze of gross superstition.

The Tents of Wickedness is the story of Charles Swallow, columnist for the *Picayune Blade*, popularly known as "The Lamplighter" for his advice to the lovelorn and maladjusted. Swallow is a writer and amateur psychiatrist, drawing his inspiration from literary and psychological sources, both of which prove chimerical rush lights to him in his search for answers. He ruins more people than he helps. Beth Appleyard, a giddy whirl of ideas and feelings trying to be born, is a gifted but psychologically dislocated poet, walking the thin edge of normalcy from childhood. "Sweetie" Appleyard is Swallow's main project in moral rearmament. Following his regimen for maturation, she swirls through Greenwich Village with abandon and ends her pilgrimage to the good life with Swallow as the putative father of an unborn child. Swallow also tries to rehabilitate his brother-in-law, Nickie, and ends by splitting Nickie's personality. The minor characters, like the major ones, are witty, cerebral, and bohemian. Further documentation is needless. They move in a world of moral fog, luridly illuminated by glittering wisecracks. Swallow finally comes to feel himself a sort of fool, and says that "the conformity we often glibly equate with mediocrity isn't something free spirits transcend as much as something they are not quite up to." Yet there is no remorse in the book, only relief at escaping consequences. Convention is pragmatically safer than revolt, but the conviction has no religious orientation. To that *The Tents of Wickedness* have their flaps shut.

There are other notable differences. Manfred's novel is a good example of artistic impersonality. There is no ubiquitous authorial *I* in the story. The Yankton Sioux are authentic Indians, living in a prewhite world from which the contemporary has been amazingly refined. The novel is a surrender to objective subject matter in characterization, description, scene, and point of view. It is a remarkable advance for Manfred because his earlier novels suffered from personalistic intrusions. De Vries, however, is ever with us. His gaudy aquarium of queer fish speaks with the fantastic rhetoric of De Vries himself. Swallow, Crystal, Nickie, Mme. Piquepuss, even the minor characters, revel in the well-turned phrase. Swallow, of course, is sometimes little more than a series of phrases. The fantastic story, the switches in narrative technique, the purple emsembles of styles — all are De Vries keeping his puppets hopping. Manfred's characters enjoy an objective life in an heroic, almost epical, dimension; De Vries's characters are almost literary clothes-horses to model his verbal dexterity. Finally, the styles, though notably effective, are sharply different. De Vries, when not engaged in parody, or conscious imitation of some contemporary stylist, writes with metallic brilliance, a taut, polished prose which reaches its peak of deft excellence in the superbly realized party scene at Flickendens', where the bower of Decency blows with tropical rot. Manfred's prose has thrown off many of the excessive onomatopoetic neologisms of his earlier work and is a carefully wrought concrete medium, simple yet rich in its minute accuracy of detail, its sensitivity to natural beauty, its frequent rhythmical grace. In the best passages, as in the visions of No Name and his pursuit of the great white stallion, who has some of the dimensions of Moby Dick, it reaches an evocative magic of distinction. The battle scene between Black One and Dancing Sun, the two great stallions, throbs with onomatopoetic power. The staccato beat of the prose perfectly echoes the masculine savagery of the battle.

The Tents of Wickedness, which has received wide publicity, is now a best seller and a Book of the Month. The Seaboard papers and journals have praised it vigorously, using phrases like "best comic novelist" and "irresistible." The sheer literary tour de force is undeniable; the dazzling variety of successful stylistic imitations from Marquand to Joyce, the play of wit, and the dexterous if fantastic handling of situation are delightfully clever. The puns are sometimes good: in talking to a dealer in evergreens, Swallow says, "I phoned your office but deciduous out." They are, sometimes, "corny": "His present concern was to favor his feet, which he had more than once described as on their last legs." The figures of speech are often strikingly original: "an island of coagulated stockings known as a hook rug." The epigrams are pungent: "The English ate as they talked, the Americans merely talked as they ate." The literary comments are shrewd: "the miles of relentlessly combed Jamesian syntactical fleece." The light verse parodies are brilliant. But there is a plethora of wit; this battering assault of bon-mots wears one down. There is too much verbal polish and not enough enriching vision. The plot is absurdly, if hilariously, contrived; the characters are generally unconvincing. The satire lacks the moral indignation of Swift, the outraged sense of decency in Twain. Lamplighter Swallow, trifler Nickie, giddy Sweetie Appleyard arouse no deep human concern. They are literary conceits on a moral holiday. Passages are frankly prurient. Judged by Christian perspectives, Decency is a world of hollow men, which, to use De Vries's own pun, does not end with a wimple. Russel Lynes says that De Vries is a moralist but never a prig: The moral never rises higher than pragmatism, and even to think of De Vries as a prig requires a massive imaginative exertion.

Conquering Horse has had scanty and ungenerous recognition. Yet, it is in many ways an enriching novel. The authentic Sioux culture, the high seriousness, the heroic dimensions of some of the characters, the simple and compelling story are all solid values. There is frankness in the treatment of Leaf and No Name but no pruriency. The book is at bottom a spiritual odyssey. Manfred's treatment of Sioux mythology is amazingly objective. There is never a note to suggest that what can only be read as incredible legend is anything but history. Since the material is so utterly legendary, it seems to me the point of a reminiscing narrator might have been more convincing than that of an omniscient historian. Then the events, fabulous as they are, would have seemed misty and distant, and would have put less strain upon a "willing suspension of unbelief." However that may be, one can recommend the book enthusiastically to the adult and discriminating reader.

"In our unpleasant century, we are all mostly displaced persons,"

says Basil Willey, and twentieth-century literature has been much concerned about finding some kind of home again. Obviously, Manfred
and De Vries are displaced persons as far as their common spiritual
and cultural heritage is concerned. Rootless, disenchanted writers
have groped for a meaningful center. Some have found it in dogmatic
Catholicism, some like Hemingway have tried to root a stoical code
in nothingness as a center, some like the Beatniks seek security in
shameless histrionics, some like Steinbeck in a vague pantheistic mysticism. De Vries and Manfred in their literary products show no devotion to the Christian faith. Manfred seems to be seeking roots in a
primitive past, in a sort of mystical appreciation of the continuity and
consanguinity of man and nature. De Vries sees "the worm in the
Marquandian apple" all right, but he tries to accommodate "the worm,"
the dissonance in existence by persiflage, and satire. Man is to be
corrected by pragmatic common sense.

Novelists create their own world, that is their moral right and their
moral responsibility. One does not dictate a writer's vision, but the
reader has the right to judge it according to his basic convictions. A
Christian writer cannot be a divided critic, compartmentalizing the
aesthetic, moral, and religious judgments. Pure aestheticism is impossible because literature always deals with life experienced by a
human being who is inextricably involved in moral action. Hence the
Christian reader completes the purely aesthetic and moral judgments
with religious insight. Judged by these convictions both books lack
the Christian dimension, and whatever one's regard for author or
book, one is troubled and regretful that two of the most prominent
Calvin graduates write books untouched by the Christian vision.

Book Reviews of Alumni Authors

Old Haven, David Cornel DeJong

The Calvin Forum (January, 1939)

One of the ironies of a culture is that it, even
against express intention, provides an environment and an intellectual
equipment which enables a later product most handsomely to discover
its flaws. *Old Haven* is a book that could have been written only by

an initially gifted intelligence operating upon a background familiar to us all either by primary experience or tradition. The same could not have been true, for instance, of "The Gold Bug." As far as "The Gold Bug" is concerned, Poe might have lived in Babylon or Sioux City. Such appropriation of a culture for literary purposes should be judged, it seems to me, by two criteria: the veracity of the report and the quality of the execution.

Old Haven is the drowsy village of Witsum on the North Sea. Over its eternal somnolence broods, however, the perpetual threat of the sea; over the lives of the sea-folk in Herring Court hovers the weird of the endless wave which may spill huge waters into simple homes at any time, snatching life and property without ruth or stint. At any time storms may rise and the anxious wives begin pacing the dike with eyes gazing for returning craft. Below the calm social life is the acid jealousy of fisherfolk and landfolk. On a hill, dominant and austere, bestriding the town physically and mentally, stands the village church. Into it on Sabbath morning pour the villagers, the bold rude sea folk sitting in the rear, the solid farmers farther to the front, and in the foremost pews the petty aristocracy in small town eclat.

A landscape of vivid green fields upon which drowsy fat sheep and colored kine graze the long day, covered by a great blue sky and crisscrossed by canals, constitutes the physical setting of this memorable story.

In my mind the genius of the story is scenic. The impressive imagery of sea and land and air lingers on; the multiple activities of man and beast upon this canvas remain etched in the mind. The sea, quiet or furious, and always latently hostile; man's tiny fidgetings upon this vast shore; the village life, unhurried and simple, with an undertone of savage social jealousy; the slow march of the bearer of sad news as she makes her way through the village while hearts are frantic till they see her pass; the pomp of the burial of a local aristocrat while the heavy bell tolls; the dike and its precarious security "brewed from decades of agony"; the intrusion of human vanity into the little church-service as the golden-helmeted wives march to the foremost place; the magnificently executed skating scenes when whole villages hold holiday on the ice in a vigorous air — such are the images that fasten on the memory.

Tjerk Mellema is the central character of the novel and in him we have a focus of various conflicts. He is a sensitive boy, impressionable and poetic, yet indecisive and more or less adolescent to the end. He dreams too much, and thinks too much, and fidgets his way out of one problem into another by procrastination. He has an itch to paint, and an unusual sensitivity to beauty. He has aspirations. Had life given him freedom to mature, he might have been an artist. But life has an atrocious way of paving a boy's way with conflicts. Social, religious, and moral dilemmas are thrust upon him and he solves them by postponement leading to final frustration. His father is one of the haughty landfolk, his mother of the crude fisherfolk, and they and their class struggle for his social allegiance. Great Beppe is an aristocrat and has her dream for Tjerk; while his mother loves her humble folk. Pake Hannia has an austere version of religion, while little Beppe is mild and loving — and they complicate Tjerk's conception of God. Gosse, his father, tender, sensitive, and great in loving-kindness supports Great Beppe in desiring Tjerk to be an architect, while Tjerk hates trade and building. Tjerk postpones his ultimate decisions by entering the army, and finally precipitates a show-down by bringing a tempestuous girl into the sleepy village, a girl who scandalizes the town and flames gossip into hate and finally causes Tjerk to solve the problem as usual — by retreat.

The house of Mellema is an interesting creation; it has breadth, vision, and resistance. Much of Witsum is the fruit of its hands. The genius of the house, however, is Great Beppe; and Great Beppe is a character. Her presence is firm and unbending at eighty-five; she has quality and she doesn't need a gold helmet to show it. She is ruthless, independent, shrewd, implacable, and yet withal there are soft spots in her heart. In the decline of her days, she still exhibits great force of character. Her cynicism is tempered by humor, and her grim aims by common sense. She meets disaster just as a Roman senator should meet a boastful Gaul; as the twilight of her dynasty settles over her at eighty-five, there is a grandeur in her words to Gosse, "We'll have to keep our heads up, son. From now on it's going to be harder." Elinor Wylie's words come to my mind —

> In masks outrageous and austere
> The years go by in single file;
> But none has merited my fear,
> And none has quite escaped my smile.

Pake Hannia, Tjerk's grandfather on his mother's side, moves through the book like a forbidding cloud. His presence is grim, and his soul is sere and unforgiving. He is harsh, unsympathetic, and downright ugly. The only redeeming thing about him is his faith — and that is unbalanced. If the author meant him as an isolated product one could accept him; but I feel that he is rather meant to be a typical

Calvinist. There may be such dour and detestable people among our faith, but it would be libelous to make him typical. In pointed contrast we have Little Beppe, as lovable a woman as one can imagine. An interesting feature is that the grim Pake has faith and no love; while the gentle little Beppe has much loving-kindness and weak faith. One wonders whether DeJong feels that this, too, is typical — that strong faith flourishes best in a harsh, single-tracked, and relentless mind. If so, I think that, too, is untrue. There is, it seems to me, no psychological necessity for such a union. Paul was a man of preeminent faith, and he surely had great loving-kindness.

The report *Old Haven* gives is intensely interesting, rich, and substantial in content, penetrating and convincing. A whole way of life arises in this novel, varied in detail and memorable in incident and activity. The novel has body; there is nothing thin about it. The characters *as individuals* are, in my mind, without exception clearly and convincingly drawn. The theme is significant and it is developed with great skill. From a material point of view, it is a rich and significant book.

There are, as could be expected, elements which grieve a Christian consciousness. There is some wholly unnecessary exploitation of loose living in the book. I see no reason structurally for Klaas's intrigue with Antionette. The final conflict could have been precipitated without it. There are more such exploitations which mar the story. The strong Christians in the book are hateful, whereas the weak Christians and the non-Christians are lovable. There is bias here; and it is unpleasant. An author, of course, has the right to produce whatever sort of a book he wishes; but it is no impertinence either to point out elements distasteful, I think, to many sensitive readers.

The ease and simplicity of style is a constant source of delight. The language is so skillfully and quietly varied, so subdued and unobtrusive that one forgets the artist — and that is great art. There is great clarity of description and vivid dialog. There is a fine portrayal of the various moods of a people. The story moves slowly, almost too slowly; and what we have is a succession of fascinating scenes accompanying the psychological development of Tjerk which is the real story.

This book, if read with detachment, is a great book. True, it leaves one with a sense of frustration and disillusion. Ideals lie in tatters on the last page. One has a sense of the waste of life. But life is wasteful and great art so presents it. What a waste of life there is in *King Lear*! How much more wasteful if there are no abiding horizons. If one cannot read this book with admiration for a great artistry, it seems to me to argue an adolescent inability to discriminate.

There lingers in my mind that matchless death scene of little Beppe to whom "Heaven was an endless green slope like the dike on which the sun would always shine." Little Beppe's faith is as feeble as a candle in high wind, but she meets her going with quiet heroism. She slips from the solid shores and approaches the great sea of forever. She sees a far gate and it is open. The gate is very near, and as she dies we feel that she is

> striding up through morning land
> with a cloud on either hand.

Conversations with Frederick Manfred, Frederick Manfred with John R. Milton

The Reformed Journal (October, 1974)

This is a fascinating book whether the reader knows Frederick Manfred and his work or not; if he does it is even more so. Through the skillful and perceptive questioning of Dr. Milton, who knows the right questions and who also knows how to redirect the torrential Manfred, the book succeeeds in painting a lifesize portrait of Manfred.

There is in addition a lively and arresting estimate by Wallace Stegner in the Foreword. Stegner sees Manfred primarily as a myth-maker, for whom reality is too small and language "too arthritic." He sees him as a gifted, largely self-educated primitive who "trusts his old Lizard more than I would trust Mine." I would be inclined to agree. Manfred knows his country and he can tell a story. It is a sparkling introduction to a sparkling book.

Through the conversations one sees Manfred plain: his winning personality, rare narrative gift, meticulous planning of his books, ar-duous effort to beat out his own rhythm, varied and assimilated read-ing, love of earth and landscape, historical gift as well as a profound sense of myth, sense of humor and occasional leg-pulling, lifelong and impressive devotion to his craft, and an unwavering confidence in himself despite early neglect and never adequate recognition. When I read of his animated plans for ever greater books, even as old age approaches for him, I think he must like Keats be haunted by:

> fears that I may cease to be
> Before my pen has glean'd my teeming
> brain,

> Before high-piled books, in charactry,
> Hold like rich garners the full-ripened
>   grain.

Manfred prizes storytelling, especially if the story has extra dimensions; and his best novels exemplify his gift for it. In this book a large part of the interest lies in the numerous and greatly varied anecdotes and stories. There are stories about quirky people he met, strange incidents observed, adventures while hitchhiking or squirreling material for books, visits with celebrities, college experiences, and farm life. He explodes little dramas at us in a few words. There was for instance the man in rural Iowa, living in a shack, who "got stewed one night and burned up in his little shack." He claims somewhere in the book that early in life, with many children in the family, he was taught to "observe the other guy as well as himself." The variety of characters he portrays confirms this; they speak with many voices and reveal distinct personalities. Whether Manfred operates in cameos or epics, he has a great gift for telling a tale. Manfred has a good deal to say about the craft of fiction and his practice of it. He feels that the academic atmosphere of the classroom impedes creativity. Since he observes closely and remembers tenaciously, he says he is "a very fine recorder of what people say and do." Ultimately his inspiration wells from deep inside him, from what he calls "the Old Lizard," something deeper than the unconscious. He says, "I've dreamed about all the characters in everyone of my books." But he works over his materials from whatever source with great care. He is almost Poeesque in his insistence on preconceived design. He likens his finished book to a bird in flight, "but I know before it flies where every bone and every gut and every drop of blood and bile [are]." Always interested mainly in "what happened and what is," he never wants to disavow fact or their uncomfortable nature. The story may have mythical dimensions but must be essentially true. Even after soaking himself in historical data, he seeks his own rhythm of treatment. In order to achieve such ends he revises a great deal. He wrote *The Golden Bowl* seven times and junked nine hundred pages of another novel and rewrote the whole work. He refashioned his lengthy trilogy. For him the novel is the greatest of arts and in the scheme of values "that the human being gets involved in the creative arts are top." To him the artist is a true child of God and must follow his vision.

Although I respect this kind of devotion and the immense effort it engenders, it would seem to me that the artistic vision is subordinate to a vision of God that seeks to keep all his commandments, of which the supreme commandment is to love him and our neighbors, a commandment which may at times involve a repression of the "Old Lizard."

Manfred was born and reared in a Christian Reformed community and educated in Christian schools. He says he read the Bible *through* seven times before he went to college. He was a student at Calvin from 1931-1934, a freshman while I was a senior. He knew Peter De Vries, who graduated from Calvin in 1932 as I did. He did not know the DeJong brothers whom I knew (as far as a merely mortal and contemporary student could know them.) Manfred says they were all "outcasts on the campus." I would consider an outcast to be somebody thrown out by his community. If anything seems true to me it is that the DeJong brothers threw themselves out. They were aloof and impenetrable, especially Meindert. But Dave's work was regularly published in *Chimes*; Prof. Vanden Bosch wrote a strong recommendation in support of his application for a fellowship in English at Duke, which he received. Manfred was a very popular student, an athletic hero; his poems and other pieces were occasionally published.

In the conversation, Manfred makes some judgments about the college and the community which supported it which seem to me unjust, whether because of inaccurate memory or prejudice. He berates his freshman English teacher for trying to make him shape up according to her prim, metronomic standards of diction, style, and logical expression. This teacher had a fine reputation at the time for a tough but reasonable insistence on formal standards. I can understand the tension, but I suspect that the "Old Lizard" was a little riled. He says, "I had a fine philosophy teacher in college, the only good teacher really I had there." No graduate of Calvin who had this teacher would disagree with the first half of this statement, but the second part strikes me as unjust and naive. There were other excellent teachers there, and if every college faculty to be considered good had to be staffed only by teachers of the outstanding teaching caliber of William Harry Jellema, there would not be a good college faculty in the country. Equally harsh is his comment on teachers. "I saw what happened to them. Particularly in the closed circuit of the Christian Reformed Church." I like what Manfred says about "What Happened and What Is." In these matters, and some others like them, I do not doubt his honesty but his veracity.

Manfred received a tumultuous welcome on his return to Calvin in 1959. He made himself available with unsparing hospitality of both person and ideas during his visit then and also some years later. As his work has come into better perspective and the quality of his best fiction apparent, he has become widely respected at the college for his artistic integrity and achievement although there are substantial disagreements with the soundness of his vision and use of materials.

Alien Fruit

The Reformed Journal (April, 1963)

Calvin College's graduates have written many articles and books. They have written about others, about each other, and against each other. In so doing they have often split dogmas, churches, and hairs. One can hardly pick up one of our periodicals in which somebody is not pummeling somebody else. We bicker. Somebody is always taking on everybody.

Whether we owe this literary cantankerousness to Protestantism, heredity, boredom, conviction, or sheer spleen, it is a fact that the literary temper of our group has a large element of contention in it. Hence, it is hardly surprising that our most gifted literary graduates should be characterized by active or passive revolt. Mutual appreciation is hardly our literary forte. Though there has always been a great deal to appreciate in our group, human nature being what it is and writers being what they are, it is hardly news that none of our professional novelists have treated their culture with the loving realism of Willa Cather or even the humorous acceptance with which Hardy treated the rustics of Wessex. Except for Bastian Kruithof's very promising and sadly neglected *Instead of a Thorn*, our writers have reflected their heritage with distaste.

There are, of course, other influences which have helped to produce this alien. I should like to suggest some reasons for the past and to express some hope for the future.

One must seek to understand the literary milieu in which these novelists matured, the dizzy whirl of twentieth-century culture. The nineteenth-century novel matured in a culture, eroded indeed by doubt and despair, but maintaining throughout an ethical center in which man was important and values real. Shocking as Hardy's novels were in the late nineteenth century, even they affirm human dignity and human values. The fiction of that century had propriety, restraint, and ideals. The novels still had structure or plot. The twentieth-century novelists jettisoned the old faith, challenged traditional values, and produced novels of startling impropriety, cynical undertones, and violent experiments in language and techniques. *The Sound and the Fury* replaced *Adam Bede.* Furthermore, the twentieth century was an age of extreme critical diversity in which the humane tradition was at bay and the noisy voices of the impressionists, humanists, incipient new critics, and psychologically oriented critics filled the air. Ezra Pound called *Paradise Lost* a "conventional melodrama" written by a "coarse-minded, asinine, disgusting, and beastly man." Yvor Winters describes Henry Adams as "the radical disintegration of a mind." and Brooks calls Joyce "a sick Irish Jesuit." Nowhere was there a commanding center of critical authority or guidance.

Young writers are naturally imitative. Having read widely in the secular literature of our time, without the counteracting critical authority of Eliot's later essays, they imbibed a spirit and a form which reflects the chaotic age in which they were maturing. Furthermore, an author wants to be sold. He is not interested in empty pews. Debunking was in full sway in the 1920s. Biographers concentrated on faults; novelists dredged queer fish out of skid row, and sex became obsessive. Moreover, frankness in diction, novelty in imagery, and experimentation in technique were found everywhere, from the staccato beat of Dos Passos to the swirling, polysyllabic "non-stop" sentences of Faulkner. New metres, new symbols, new myths were introduced. All of these factors contributed to the shocking effect of the books of our novelists among our group.

One must take into account the nature of the artistic temperament, which is seldom placid or receptive, but generally arrogant, self-willed, and iconoclastic. Since the artist is hypersensitive, since he does see and feel more deeply than most of us do, since he is usually egoistic and often neurotic, he is commonly intent upon realizing subjective rather than objective patterns. He is likely to want to beat his own metres out. Flushed with his gifts, he tends to extremes in technique and the shocking in subject matter. Appointing himself a genius, he regards the received tradition with a fishy eye, morals as mere mores, deep-seated convictions as ancestral shibboleths, and everybody who doesn't agree with him as a square or hypocrite. Writing out of such a mood and conviction, he pours out prose and verse that goes far beyond responsible Christian realism. When the product evokes understandable hostility, he often retreats into a grudge and persecution complex. The rift has been made and steadily deepens. Neither the public nor the poet is without blame, but the alienation is real and usually progressive.

Our writers have been nurtured by a religious community which professes exceedingly high moral and religious ideals. We claim the finest system of theology; we aim at God-centered living. It is a profession that demands heroic effort, prayer, and grace. And, in all fairness, much is achieved. Despite all kinds of cynical comments, the sacrifice, the nobility, and achievement of our group have been notable. My major grudge against our professional novelists is their imperceptive and jaundiced account of their cultural and religious origins. I was there, too, and that was *not* the way it was. They have tended to emphasize our spiritual fragility, our inadequacy. When one professes a really high ideal, failure is inevitable, but the striving should be remarked. Surely, we are sometimes guilty of hypocrisy; we often act like pragmatists; we are sometimes smug, self-righteous, and impatient of legitimate dissidence. We are, like everyone, fair game for satire, but the satire should be responsible and reasonably fair. One too often feels that the satire is powered by dislike and hate rather than proper moral indignation.

The writers under discussion in this issue shared an atmosphere in which there was much verbal contention; they matured in a world of cultural fragmentation and literary confusion and experimentation; they were influenced, I believe, by current public interest; they shared the artistic temperament with its tendency to revolt and nervous instability, its unwillingness to abide by group formalism and convention; they reacted with violence to certain rigidities and assumed or real hypocrisies in creed and life. If one adds what a careful biographer might convincingly adduce — familial and educational antagonisms which exacerbated these alienating influences, one has what seems to me some reasonable suggestions for their products. Furthermore, their early work was generally received with stony indifference and public scorn.

There is one more problem to discuss, and it concerns the judgment that Calvinism and Calvinists cannot because of the very nature of their deepest beliefs produce full-orbed and convincing fiction. Calvinists, it is asserted, make men puppets; Calvinism is an iron creed that shrinks human nature in a procrustean bed so that a complex and realistic picture of man is impossible. In its crudest form the idea is that a Calvinist can neither write nor appreciate a true image of life. Both ideas seem to me false.

Let us begin our answer in a negative way. Whether or not Calvinism can produce Calvinistic novelists, Calvinistic communities have shown an uncanny ability to produce illustrious literary rebels. Writers like Stevenson, Carlyle, Burns, Twain, Dickinson, Glasgow, to mention but a few, arose out of Calvinistic cultures. They were rebels, indeed, but Calvinism gave them something important, solid, and real to rebel against. The Calvinistic emphasis upon the transcendent majesty of God, the immortal implications of the drama of life, the obvious reality of human sin and guilt, the necessity of personal responsibility in choosing for or against Christ, and the inescapable pressure to view life in the great Taskmaster's eye made them agonize, reflect, and react. They were forced into tension and out of that tension came literature. The bland gospel of the Unitarians couldn't do it. Even if Calvinism did not produce Calvinistic writers, it produced writers.

I realize that this is but a pallid answer to the main problem: Can Calvinists produce a novel that is a genuine illusion of life? The problem is deepened by inability to adduce outstanding novelists that have done so. But I believe there is nothing in the beliefs of Calvinists to impede such writing. Calvinism is often misrepresented by critics who have not read Calvin and who mistake its excesses for its genius. Calvin knew the classics and appreciated pagan writers. His literary standards were of course limited by the perspectives of his age, but his insistence upon honest observation, objective creation, sane evaluation, and perspicuity of style would permit the kind of fiction Willa Cather produced. Furthermore, later Calvinists, enriched by the literature of three hundred years, could greatly widen both the range of subject matter and the employment of techniques without violating the spirit of Calvinism. Calvinists have never been afraid of reality. I doubt whether any group of people had a greater awareness of the sin-drenched nature of man than the New England Puritans. What Calvinists have resented is not a true novel about real men, but the mistaken perspectives behind what passes for a true novel about real men. What the Calvinist resents is sin without moral judgment, implicit or explicit, life pictured as meaningless, man as an accidental freak in pointless circumstance. In other words, the quarrel is not with honest portrayal but erroneous spirit and vision; it is basically a quarrel about theology. Graham Greene gives as relentless a portrayal of depravity in *The Heart of the Matter* as any modern writer, but the Calvinist accepts it with appreciation because the perspective is Christian. Although I have a great problem about what a distinctively Calvinistic novel would be like, I have no doubt that a Calvinist could produce a novel with an underlying Christian vision. Nor do I have a doubt that properly trained and responsible elements in the

Calvinistic community would receive such a book with profound gratitude.

In the maturation of a novelist both the artist and the public have responsibilities. Both take advice sourly, but since this is an honest and unpaid article, I hope you will permit me to perpetrate some. Our public, I believe, should be patient and understanding with young and old writers. We should all do our best to develop the Christian mind in the artist, the self that loves God. We should not immediately hack, hew, and expel. We should allow room for experimentation and original response and show gratitude for it. We should expand our notion of the artist's challenge. He may treat not only the beauty of the universe, its wonder and mystery, "the splendid silent sun, with all his beams full dazzling," but also "the tarantula rattling at the lily's foot." He may treat not only King Arthur "wearing the white flower of the blameless life," but also the shattering of commandments. He may deal not only with "the light that never was on land or sea," but also "the debris, the debris, the debris of the slain soldiers of war." In short, the writer may deal with human life in its glory and degradation. The artist, on the other hand, should not dismiss the public as having brains of oatmeal and critics as annoying gnats. He must be truthful and only a true artist knows how hard that is. Truthfulness must not be confused with verbal efflorescence. He must represent life, and the representation must add up to something. Unless a novel in some way enlarges one's vision, deepens one's sensibilities, and bestows vision, it is only printing or rare diction. If the novelist reflects our heritage, he should reflect its nobility as well as its pettiness. If he wishes to write a novel we can thank God for, he should illuminate the contained experience with a Christian vision, a world in which the providence and grace of God are concretely operative. These themes have had trivial treatment enough; it is time for grandeur. To deny the possibility of fusing the superb creative gifts of a Christian with his deepest commitment seems to me to deny the validity of the novel as an art form.

6

Memories of Grundy College

A HISTORY

*T*he short-lived Grundy College provides a fascinating insight into midwestern culture in the early part of our century. Started by visionary and energetic persons, crippled by economic and political pressures, the institution remains, nonetheless, an interesting if minor footnote in American and church history. The following essay, through reminiscence and research, provides a portrait of that place and that time.

Memories of Grundy College

Grundy Seminary, College and Academy was located in Grundy Center, Iowa. The town was not named after Mrs. Grundy, a captious, puritanical lady in an English play, although some of her descendants seemed to have moved there.

Grundy Center is 9 miles from Reinbeck, 14 miles from Dike, 240 miles from Dordt, and 457 miles from Calvin. According to its first catalog, Grundy Center had paved streets, only partly true, since the streets along the college were black dirt; it had free mail delivery, true; a "fine library," a pardonable hyperbole, although the library had generous holdings in Irwin Cobb, Clarence Buddington Kelland and *The Literary Digest.* The catalog goes on to say that this town of fifteen hundred inhabitants had "the conveniences of a large city, but is free from its temptations." You had to invent your own. It had only a public school, where I sat as a boy of eight next to Eels, Willoughby, and Dalglish instead of Bontekoe, Krombeen, and Oole in Orange City, Iowa. My teacher was no longer the pretty Miss Zoerink, but Miss Graham, a gaunt, lanky lady out of *The House of Seven Gables*, slightly horse-faced and a real cracker. We had dancing lessons, and in the spring were trained to skip about a Maypole holding ribbons in our hands. I got out of both as a conscientious objector. There were five Protestant churches and one Catholic church. The Grundy College church, where I attended to sermons in Dutch and German was the soundest.

Grundy Center in 1916 was bounded by the Rock Island Railroad, the Fair Grounds, the cemetery, and the open cornfields. In the center of the town was the courthouse square and in the center of that was the courthouse. On fair days the band played Sousa and the choir sang Stephen Foster. Opposite the courthouse to the east was the fine library, to the west lived the snobs, to the north lived the slobs; in the east was the college near which lived Peter Bonk. Moving slowly down Main Street to see the sights, one observed Holden's Drug Store, the Ritz Variety Store, Groves' Haberdashery, Canfield's Shoes, Moore's Cafe, law offices, and the medical center containing Drs. Lucas and Carpenter. Milk, coal, and groceries were still hauled by horse-drawn vehicles. The railroad rather than the highway tied the town to the outer world. Near the railroad lived Slosky, the rag picker and his pretty daughter; and in its coal-heated station the town loafers puffed their corncobs. The town baked under the summer sun and shivered in the winter snow. Its pride in itself and the state was strong and to demonstrate it we had to memorize the names of ninety-nine counties from Adair to Wright.

On May 4, 1916, at a meeting in Lincoln Center, Iowa, Classis Oostfriesland, comprising thirteen congregations with five hundred families, voted to establish a theological school, two years of preparatory college, and an academy. The whole works at once like Minerva from the head of Zeus. The headaches were to come later. The thirteen churches were largely German and were served by German pastors and *Der Reformierte Bote*, a German *Banner.* German-speaking pastors were hard to acquire since World War I had stopped imports. Hence the need of a seminary. After deciding to establish the school, the twenty-six delegates went to Grundy Center to inspect the old McKinley high school, an attractive brick building with seven classrooms, a chapel, and an office. They liked what they saw and the Reverend Mr. Hoefker put a dollar down to cement the purchase: $7500, a sum toward which the merchants in Grundy Center contributed generously. The institution would be supported by gifts, tuition of $37.50 a year ($17.25 for ministers' children), $2000 a year in Synodical rebates and self-sacrifice on the part of the staff. Whatever else Grundy achieved, it was a training in professional economy. My father, for instance, took a stiff cut in salary, gave up the use of an elegant manse and other ministerial perquisites. Throughout the eighteen years of its existence, the staff was soundly underpaid; even the lemons were squeezed.

The initial staff consisted of six men and two women. They served fifty students in the fall of 1916. Grundy never had more than one hundred students, and always by necessity rather than by intention, a student teacher ratio of ten-to-one or less, the only respect in which it equaled Harvard. It was unique in the fact that instruction was offered in three languages: Dutch, English, and German. I think this student-teacher ratio helps explain the phenomenal loyalty of Grundy alumni who still meet annually in Grand Rapids after the school has been dead for fifty years. The students became intimate acquaintances of the staff. I taught there from 1932-1934; I think I could still write adequate recommendations of most of my students without consulting a record book. I still see Wilson Cheney, chunky, short, redhaired and freckled, sweating out the pronunciation of German umlauts. German

is a difficult language. An American belongs to the United Mine Work-
ers Union; the German may belong to the Handwerkerwitwensunter-
stuetzungsverein. I still hear William Main, a local loudmouth who
mistook wisecracks for intelligence. There were Alyce Boxum, a bit
of sunshine from Kansas; Mr. X from Texas, who maintained his unwavering mediocrity by dedicated effort; and Chester Brockway, a
local Baptist who combined unusual intelligence with profound Christian experience. Small colleges always want to get bigger and as they
do their announced appeal to individual attention diminishes. The
larger the student body, the less unified the impact of the staff.

Dr. William Bode, Grundy's first president, was a gifted man from
a distinguished family that dominated Classis Oostfriesland from
1890-1950. His father the Reverend Mr. C. Bode traversed the prairies
by ox-cart, horse and buggy, coach and freight cars, establishing
churches, tiny struggling churches almost dwarfed by the tall prairie
grasses. His brother was a minister as well as his two sons, William
and Henry. The Reverend Mr. Henry Bode, like his brother, was a
stalwart tall man, a Saxon in energy and steadiness, who served Wellsburg I for twenty years. I heard him preach from time to time. His
sermons had a fascinating dullness and were always closed with a
rafter shaking "Amen!" which jerked every slumberer awake. Once
the whole consistory was dozing. He whacked the pulpit and shouted
"Aufmerksamheit bitte!" Whatever had preceded it, the "Amen"
seemed to confer a shower of blessings. He supported the college like
granite, and while he and the college lived, Calvin College was eclipsed
in thought and contributions.

Henry's brother William was a fellow at the University of Chicago,
where he obtained his doctor's degree for a dissertation on the Book
of Job. He was a striking man, physically impressive, of noble appearance. He could have been a warrior among the Visigoths; he was
a powerful saint amongst the East Frisians. He was a spiritual warrior
in a life tangled by dreams, disappointment, and tragedy. He had an
excellent mind and a magnetic personality, but he lacked administrative skills. He poured his heart, mind, and spirit into a vision without
an adequate base. He was cruelly caught between his dreams and
reality and to achieve the former he miscalculated and sometimes
evaded the latter, hurting both himself and others. He had a heavy
load to bear; his older son was badly retarded, his younger son, a
bright, sunny boy, whom I had in class, was drowned while swimming
in a little Iowa lake, leaving a wife and baby. He was conquered, but
he never capitulated to despair. I am happy to honor his memory and
I still remember watching him preach because his gaze was always

over the audience as if he were reading from a distant script or engrossed in a vision.

Professor Diedrich H. Kromminga was an unusually gifted man,
burly, tall, with dark hair and magnificent moustache. He was a typical German, intellectually full of "eingehenden Bemerkungen." As a
boy I was impressed by the fact that this exceedingly masculine figure
would from time to time wipe the tears from his cheeks. As a young
man at Calvin I was impressed by the massive content of his sermons.
His sheep had a solid fare. For some time he would come regularly
to our home. I would then hear the rumble of talk in the study, and
the blue tobacco smoke would drift into the hallway. The meetings
ceased abruptly. He had tried to convince my father of the validity of
the premillenarian vision, but changing my father's convictions was
as difficult as biting a billiard ball.

My father was the third member of the seminary faculty. He was
a rather short man, immaculate from tip to toe, precise as a Swiss
watch in every thing he did. He was the soul of method and neatness,
somewhat of a health faddist. He had no vices except smoking, if that
be a vice. It interested me that he always smoked a mixture of Revelation and Serene tobaccos. His main intellectual foible, if it be a
foible, was a mystical interest in the numerology of the Scriptures.
My father came into the Christian Reformed church from the Silver
Creek Deutsche Reformierte Kirche near German Valley, Illinois. First
he went to the Missionshaus in Franklin, Wisconsin. He was dissat-
isfied with the theological emphasis there and when, after his objections, a professor told him that "die Reformierte Kirche kann sich
ihretwegen nicht aenderen," he went to the Theological School in
Grand Rapids, where he studied under one of the two of his lifelong
heroes, Dr. Gerhardus Vos. The other was a Dr. Stephens of the German Reformed church, who interestingly baptized my father in Germany and officiated at the service when he made public profession of
faith in Illinois. My father was, as Dr. Beets said at his funeral service
"a wonderful exegete," a lifelong, arduous student of Scripture, whose
studies were enriched by a deep mystical strain, more common among
the East Frisians than the Dutch he served most of his life. He had
an exceptional memory. I heard him preach a sermon from a text of
eleven verses which he quoted throughout the sermon without notes.
His masterfully crafted sermons enriched many members of the
churches he served.

The women who taught at Grundy College were Miss Lylas King,
of whom my father thought highly, and Miss Schutte who taught
music, an art in which Germans have shown much talent and by

Faculty of Grundy College and Seminary, 1920: L to R, seated, John Timmerman, W. Bode, D. H. Kromminga; standing, J. B. Strack, Lylas King, C. Hayenga, M. Schulte, A. Cleveringa.

which the musical organizations of Grundy College achieved much good will. The sciences were taught by Mr. Cleveringa. Considering the time, 1916, I think most would agree that it was an able faculty.

During the brief eighteen years of its existence, Grundy Seminary and College had on its staff a number of able people. The unusual gifts of Professor Henry Schultze, later President of Calvin College, and Dr. and Mrs. William Radius are well known in the Christian Reformed church. Dr. Fred Wezeman, later principal of Chicago Christian High, and the focus of one of our recurrent hermeneutical imbroglios, was a suave and literate gentleman of uncommon ability. Meindert De Jong, later world famous as a writer of childrens' stories, taught there for a few weeks, but slunk away on the midnight train. Dr. William Rutgers, later professor in Calvin Seminary, and a popular, gifted preacher was its second president. J. William Kingma was the third and final president of the college where his rare plenitude of natural ability could not save the floundering ship.

After an auspicious beginning storm clouds soon began to gather. On Good Friday, April 6, 1917, the United States declared war on Germany, a fact the Germans in Iowa thought bitterly ironic since they had voted for Wilson on the slogan "He kept us out of war." Germans and even the German language became suspect. Bismarck, North Dakota, became Pierre. High schools and even colleges in senseless rage threw out the study of German. The anti-German feeling in Iowa was exacerbated by the signal idiocy of a flag-waving chauvinist who decreed that German sermons should be immediately followed by a summary in English, which among other inconveniences stretched the services to more than two hours; and it was uncommonly hard on some German preachers. Billy Sunday, breaker of chairs and thumper of pulpits informed God in a prayer before the House of Representatives that the Germans were "a great pack of wolfish Huns, whose fangs drip with blood and gore." Grundy Center was not immune to this spirit. Reverend Mr. Drake's parsonage was for a time guarded by guns. As a German boy I was taunted by my classmates. Though the college was never molested it was under a heavy cloud and the future of Grundy Seminary as an institution for training German-speaking pastors received a savage and lethal blow.

The second blow came from the good brothers in Grand Rapids. The Board of Trustees, then known as the Curatorium, and the Reverend Mr. Hiemenga regarded Grundy with undisguised hostility. They wanted no brothers near the throne. They convinced Synod to order the Seminary closed in 1920. Synod in its magnanimity, and in insufferable impertinence, allowed the Junior College to survive. It canceled the $2000 a year rebate of Synodical subsidies, which it had never paid in the first place. Then they returned, every man to his tent. Grundy College never recovered from these blows. Neither Bode's idealism, a good staff, fine musical programs, nor the gifts of Classis, friends, and town were enough. The base of support was and always had been too small. By 1931 the staff had dropped to five, the students to sixty, and the Board had become an inept caricature of its former self. It recruited some members who had no Reformed moorings, a maximum of inertia, and a minimum of brains.

Since the Seminary was to close in the Spring of 1920, my father, the Reverend Mr. John Timmerman accepted a call to Paterson IV, New Jersey, where our new neighbors were Pasquali, D'Orio, Granito and Geminetti. It was a Dutch church in an almost solidly Italian neighborhood, Sicilians not Florentines, but gifted in song as well as combat. When the kids disobeyed, the father slipped off his belt and the whacks were resounding. I saw Mr. Geminetti bolt out of the house with Mrs. Geminetti in pursuit, finally throwing a bucket of suds over him. Mrs. Pasquali pressed the juice out of their grapes by stomping them barefooted in a barrel. The kids were tough and I managed to achieve some status by telling them about the wild west where the church members stacked their guns in the lobby while Wiersma and Cupido, two of the fastest guns east of the Missouri, stood guard at the doors. These youngsters didn't know Idaho from Iowa, and when I rode with Nandi and Tony Damato to the World's Fair in Chicago in 1932, Nandi asked me "What is it, Michigan Detroit or Detroit Michigan?" Yet I have only good memories of these neighbors, excitable, generous, quick-tempered, and amazingly gifted in music and street warfare.

After twelve years I returned to Grundy Center as a teacher in the shriveled Junior College that survived into the bleak, dark Depression. The Depression was at its wrecking, discouraging worst. The big bonanza had become a bust. Thirty percent of the labor force was idle. Able men lost their jobs, their savings, their homes, and their hearts. Passenger cars emptied and freight cars filled up. American citizens rifled the garbage cans behind the Palmer House in Chicago. Anybody who said that a man who wanted a job could find one was nothing more than a callous nincompoop. No one starved in Grundy Center, but the fare was sparse and the clothes were frayed. Nobody froze in Grundy Center but two of us guarded a gift of a carload of coal for the college with shotguns through the night. Corn was eight cents a bushel and people were singing "Brother can you spare a dime?"

The town seemed shrunken and wan, enveloped in oppressive shabbiness. Its spirit was eroded as well as its streets. The college building still had its fine lines, but in cold weather the boiler sounded as if it were about to blow up. For several days before school opened I accompanied the President, Dr. William Rutgers, as he went through the countryside trying to recruit students, inviting them whether they had cash or not.

Sixty students enrolled on opening day. Though largely from the town and neighboring farms, some came from Illinois, Minnesota, South Dakota, Kansas, and even Montana. Since the dormitory, erected with such hope and pride in 1917, was a wreck with warped floors and broken plumbing, the students roomed about town; they were an unsophisticated lot. There were no romantic egotists, no soulful, hyperesthetical young men or women. There was no Peter De Vries, urbane, chic and articulate; no DeJong brothers swelled with emotional elephantiasis. There were no geniuses but no cranks or crackpots either. They worked hard for and at their education. They had an openness and a Christian idealism one had to go far to equal.

The faculty numbered only five full-time teachers. A local pastor from the German Presbyterian church taught Bible on a part-time basis. Dr. Stratemeier was an able, inspiring gentleman. The Board had lost its vigor and the replacements did not fit. It included a fanatical premillenarian Baptist preacher, who a few years later was caught up in a rapturous indiscretion with his organist. There was little money to begin with, but in the first week of school the Austinville bank where the college kept its few funds, snatched the bulk of the money, so that for the balance of the year we were paid, when we were paid, from the personal account of the Reverend Mr. Joling, a loyal and fine friend of the school. I taught seventeen hours a week. It cost me $75 which I had to draw from a savings account in Paterson to stay afloat. From time to time I lent money to William Kingma, who had a wife and child and whose family at the end of the month were practically penniless. At the end of the year Dr. Rutgers received a call from Cicero, Illinois. I remember his saying after taking a long walk that he had been pondering his decision. He left.

I would not have returned in 1933 but for two reasons. There was no appealing alternative — even the army had crowds of applicants; and I did not wish to do nothing at home, though I would have been most welcome. The other reason lay in the fact that William Kingma had been appointed President. He was a singularly gifted man, encumbered by his versatility. He was a connoisseur in all the arts from painting to Chinese vases. He was a superb conversationalist; he had rhetorical plenitude. I heard him preach a sermon in Wellsburg on fruit bearing; he bore fruit for an hour and a quarter. He was an individualist, an eccentric, an imaginative maverick, just not made for a professional escalator. Furthermore, like Dr. William Harry Jellema of Calvin, he had the gift of inspiring confidence not only in himself but in your own self. He had great faith; he actually believed faith could make the dead bones live. That he was unsuccessful is no reflection on his remarkable gifts and personality.

Even though the enrollment was even smaller, ridiculously smaller, economically things were better; they were not good, only less bad. Meals were served free to the faculty at the college cafeteria, to which many kind people in Grundy Center and farms from Wellsburg to Kanawha contributed. The college car went out regularly to haul in canned vegetables, meats, fruits, and above all pumpkins. I counted the pumpkins, over seven hundred of them, heavy, round and energizing. We ate more varieties of pumpkin fare than anyone could imagine. One student worked his way through college by contributing the milk of his cow. Later on, the cow took time out to calve, and then we had so much veal we looked like vellum. Enough money came in so that more than half of our salaries were paid.

During this year I was treasurer, and I will never forget one experience. An elderly man came to the office. He had once pledged money to the college, but hard times had kept him from paying. Now he had eighty dollars in his shaking hands which he gave with great dignity and satisfaction. I often wondered how much he gave up, how much he sacrificed to pay that money.

Though the student body was small, a good spirit of hope prevailed, but in the spring of 1934 the dust from the Dakotas sifted over Iowa. It lay in huge drifts along the roadside; sometimes a hovering haze, so dense that car lights had to be turned on, spread like a blanket over the state. The drought began early; the corn drooped in the fields. In late May a devastating storm ripped off a great deal of the slate roof. I did not return in the fall. The college did open but only fifteen students enrolled, and the college closed. The three teachers still there taught some courses in town for a government program. What was left was the land, three buildings, and many debts.

Dr. Henry Beets once said to my father, "Don't invest in Christian causes. Give to them. I invest in General Motors." It must have paid off because he has to be one of the few ministers who never tapped the minister's Pension Fund. My father, however, anticipated the Depression by buying Grundy College bonds. I helped by investing some of my money earned at Cramer and King Silk Company in the same cause. First, our interest stopped coming. Then the bonds became worthless. When my father died, I had to get a statement from Classis Oostfriesland to the effect that they were junk; promises not kept — five thousand dollars of junk. They had apparently never been legally backed by anything. Apparently, if the college would fail the property would revert to Classis Oostfriesland. It did. Classis sold the land, the boys' dormitory, the girls' dormitory, the bricks of the college and every chair, typewriter, and test tube in it. They put the proceeds in an educational fund for the benefit of people who had never invested a dime in the institution or worked for its welfare. I have never disputed the legality of all this; what bothers is the lack of ethical sensitivity. I asked one of Calvin's curators from Classis Oostfriesland about this. "Well," he said, "We could only have paid ten cents on the dollar." When I asked him, "Whose dollar?", he walked away. Thirty-thousand hard-earned dollars totally lost to the people who loaned it. It has the odor of overripe Brussels sprouts rather than violets.

One sour note does not ruin a symphony. Grundy College did a lot of good. It prepared German preachers; it gave valuable experience to a half dozen Calvin College teachers; it trained educators and future clergyman, and it graduated many devoted Christians who served as a leaven in their communities. In the life of the Christian Reformed Church, Grundy College is a footnote; in the life of American culture it is not even that. The Lord doesn't judge as we do. I am sure Browning was right when he said

> All I could never be,
> All, men ignored in me,
> This, I was worth to God, whose wheel the
>   pitcher shaped.

It was all over long ago, but the echoes abide with me still. I will never forget our family's leaving Orange City where most of the congregation was at the small yellow depot singing "Des Herren zegen op u daal"; Valentine's Day in the third grade when the only valentine I got was from Sarah Slosky, the Jewish rag picker's daughter; the portly Dr. Beets dedicating the new dormitory at a time of high hope in the hot August sun; Dr. William Bode, President of the college, selling pencils in the college bookstore; Catechism classes with William Masselink, a student at this time, a lovable man as long as I knew him and a member of a great family who meant so much to ours and the Christian Reformed church; Dr. Lukas, the elderly German physician forced to stumble in patriotic pride at the head of the parade to the point of exhaustion; Bank Holiday in 1932 when I received thirteen dollars in dollar bills and small change for a month's work; the last days of Grundy College in the drought of 1934; the final commencement, when Dr. William Bode watched his son Julius graduate from Junior College as destiny sounded taps to his dreams.

Es waer' so schoen gewesen
Es hat nicht sollen sein.

7

"Sight of that Immortal Sea"

MEDITATIONS

Meditation: *the word suggests pondering, reflection, setting something aside for contemplation. It is a worthy activity, this leisurely and thoughtful reflection, one which helps order the busyness of daily life. Many people are inclined to reflect on losses and missed opportunities as did Wordsworth in these lines from "Intimations of Immortality":*

> *Not for these I raise*
> *The song of thanks and praise;*
> > *But for those obstinate questionings*
> > *Of sense and outward things,*
> > *Fallings from us, vanishings;*
> > *Blank misgivings of a Creature*
> *Moving about in worlds not realised. . . .*

The following meditations differ markedly from Wordsworth in their consideration not of what we have lost but of what we have gained by Christian faith. They are songs "of thanks and praise" for the treasures that are ours.

The Never-Ending Journey of the Wise Men

The Banner (December 15, 1972)

There are many travelers in the great journeys of literature and they seek very different objects. Don Quixote rides along the bare, sun-baked roads of Spain in search of an impossible dream. Captain Ahab sails the lonely Southern seas for vengeance. Aeneas, watching the burning city of Troy, remembering his wife under flames and rubble, puts his old father on his back, takes his little boy by the hand and seeks a home. But never before or since have astrologers, following a brilliant star, traveled many miles through rough country and hard weather to find God in the body of a baby.

They found Him, as tradition has it, in a manger, lying where oxen fed. But there was a wondrous glory about this, as Southwell says:

> This stable is a prince's court,
>   This crib his chair of state,
> The beasts are parcel of his pomp
>   The wooden dish his plate.
> With joy, approach, O Christian wight
>   Do homage to your king;
> And highly prize his humble pomp
>   Which he from heaven doth bring.

Mysteriously led to this crib and having worshiped Him with gifts and adoration, the astrologers fade from history with the light of the Maker of all the stars upon them. They had paid homage; they must in some sense have known that they had seen "the word within a word unable to speak a word," that in this birth, God had become man. They returned home, having found the way to an everlasting home.

This birth occurred in a stable on a petty side-street of the ancient world but it changes the meaning of life for everyone who sees the Son of God in the helpless baby. He knows now that God is neither an impersonal force or an unknowable mystery. Here was seen the beginning of the earthly manifestation of the love of God which led through years of selfless service to terrible sacrifice at Gethsemane, Gabbatha, and Golgotha. The coming of the child made it possible for Karshish, Browning's Arabian physician, to say:

> The very God! Think, Abib; dost thou think?
> So, the All-Great were the All-Loving too —
> So, through the thunder comes a human voice
> Saying, "O heart I made, a heart beats here."

How undeserved this coming was! After the crimes man had committed, after the knowledge of our waywardness and rebellion, after indifference and disobedience, such forgiveness and reconciliation! Not the vial of vengeance but the cup of blessing. How unexpectedly too were the old prophecies fulfilled. Though He was God He did not come in a royal palace, but His coming made a king tremble.

There was no public rejoicing, but there was unforgettable music from heaven. Later on His disciples witnessed a death instead of a triumph and a resurrection instead of a death. He moves that way still, but we know that He is the Lord of the unexpected and we can say with Whittier:

> Yet, in the maddening maze of things;
>   And tossed by storm and flood,
> To one fixed trust my spirit clings:
>   I know that God is good.

The birth of Jesus severed once for all the web of purely natural forces in which man is increasingly finding himself. This web is dark and thickly woven and there is no exit. If there is religious vision, it often seems but a reflection of man's hopes and fears. The birth of our Lord reveals to us a God who entered the natural process and delivered us from it forever.

Our Lord came to us as a babe. The great Christian poems, theologies, and magnificent cathedrals celebrate the fact. The soaring Gothic spires are founded on a crib, and the little child carries the keys of the kingdom. He brought a new, everlasting force into the world. What Arnold said is still true:

> And centuries came and ran their course,
> And unspent all that time
> Still, still went forth that child's dear force
> And still was at its prime.

That force, like the burning bush, is not consumed.

The astrologers brought the Christ Child expensive presents, but to repeat a trite phrase, they also brought themselves. In the case of the Wise Men this really meant something: discomfort, peril, and, I believe, some form of persecution. The journey to the crib was a long one over hard terrain, through alien country on camels. They were exposed to robbery and murder. The inns were often questionable, and I suppose there was cheating enough. Furthermore, theirs was no vacation on fringe benefits. They probably lost a good deal of income. When they returned they had to adjust to a pagan society. Was their strange report believed? Were they not regarded as unscientific quacks? Did their old customers still come for horoscopes? Were they still honored in kings' courts? Or did they have to choose between a lot of money and esteem and following the vision?

I think it altogether likely that there was no easy, bland accommodation between their new faith and the old practices. I do not believe there ever is.

The Dimensions of a Home

The Banner (February 26, 1971)

The title and theme of one of Thomas Wolfe's novels is *You Can't Go Home Again.* In a very profound sense this is true. The physical house may have been sold to strangers. The family is scattered, and if still largely there, often greatly changed. In another sense, it is not true. I am sure that you also have experienced the unexpected moment when the past flashes upon your mind with brilliant intensity, and the ghosts of the past come startlingly alive. Familiar voices call your name, and the home, church, schoolroom, and baseball field pass through your imagination with sharp vividness. The past is irrecoverable only in fact, not in effect or influence.

Home is one of the oldest words in our language, and it has been on the lips of generations. It always refers to more than a place to live and that is why it suggests so many layers of meaning. To some it is an abiding center of loyalty and love; to others it is a prison, a place

to flee. Some see in it little more than shelter and food. To one of
Frost's characters,

> Home is the place where, when you have to go there
> They have to take you in.

No one who has had a home can ever escape it, and there is nothing
trivial in rejecting it. To Christians a broken home is still a tragedy,
and to those who are not, it is still a matter of profound and often
unsuccessful readjustment.

I should like to examine a poem by an unfairly neglected poet to
show what a home can mean and in fact did mean to the poet Whittier.

Whittier is admittedly a minor poet, a fact that does not rob his
poetry of permanent charm, meaning, and value. He also had some
very old-fashioned ideas about the function and value of poetry. He
said, for instance, "The uses of poetry are to hearten the courage of
men and make meaningful their struggles." He believed, as did most
of the great poets and critics before the twentieth century, that literature has both a moral intention and a moral dimension, that it could
give delight both through art and thought. He succeeded in writing
poetry that touched ordinary men and women through a convincing
portrayal not only of the color and life of New England but of his
religious faith and prophetic vision. At the heart of that vision was
his utter reliance upon the providence of God, or as he put it:

> I know not where his islands lift
> Their fronded palms in air;
> I only know I cannot drift
> Beyond his love and care.

That vision is most memorably expressed in *Snow-Bound*, which is
both a regional and universal poem with unusually good characterization, narrative skill, lively description, and a classic expression of
the meaning of home.

The poem itself is a picture of the living past, of a day long gone
but imperishably etched upon the memory of the poet. On that "brief
December day" years past the "chill embargo of the snow" filled the
air with a white whirl, roared through the night to a morning leaving
strange patterns modeled by "the mindless wind." The blizzard continues through the next day, and in the evening the scene shifts from
the raw, outdoor weather to the hearth, the center of the family life.
During the evening an even earlier past is narrated by father and
mother and a visiting aunt, a past reaching to Indian camps, Quaker

history, and the Holy Land. Whittier sees the family as part of the stream of time, which though always passing is never really past, since "Love can never lose its own." The next day the poem opens up again to outdoor life and new duties.

The heart of the poem is the hearth, and here the family enjoys the timeless values of

> Food and shelter, warmth and health
> And love's contentment more than wealth.

What transfigures the simple, provincial life shown here is the symbolic dimensions of this home, the religious overtones, the fact that the home is welded not only by earthly ties but divine concern. The dead are indeed now gone but "Faith will trust" and look "to see the breaking day" of a permanent home. As Whittier has said elsewhere, "The only real and permanent joy is in finding ourselves in harmony with the Divine will and trusting in the 'Divine Goodness.' " The hurts and tears of time cannot destroy those who know "the Immortal Love, forever full," because this love binds them together here also.

These moving pictures were written not merely in transient recall or sentimental nostalgia. Whittier was trying in his own way to deal with the problem of time and the timeless. The old days do not drop futilely into a vast, meaningless void; they not only live in the present, they nourish and mold the present. The old hearth is not a bucket of ashes, but ever-living embers. The family members will always:

> Stretch the hands of memory forth
> To warm them at the wood-fires blaze.

The moral and religious values of this home live on, not in isolated, sporadic pictures, but they give an ineffaceable dynamism to all the lives affected by them. Even in faraway separation, even in the alien metropolis where life seems an endless encounter of swirling particles jarring each other without communion, even there

> The worlding's eyes shall gather dew
> Dreaming in thoughtful city ways
> Of winter joys his boyhood knew.

The firm values of this home consciously and subconsciously influence its members throughout their lives. Home is a place you can't leave even when you want to.

Whittier, thus, in a sense, answers the loneliness of the people in

Winesburg, Ohio, a book of stories by Sherwood Anderson, in which the characters grope about trying futilely to find meaning and understanding in life in a world where family life has disintegrated and one of the characters "began trying to force herself to face bravely the fact that many people must live and die alone, even in Winesburg." In this world, George Willard broods on:

> the countless figures of men who before his time
> have come out of nothingness into the world, lived
> their lives and again disappeared into nothingness.

Whittier saw the home as a place where man develops a sense of belonging, not only to the present but also the past and not only to the world of time but that of eternity. Even the most inconspicuous and anonymous member of the family inherits a long tradition, carries it on and adds to it. Furthermore, since it is a Christian home, its spiritual dimensions rest in the heart of God, whence no earthly turmoil can dislodge it.

Such a home as Whittier describes is not hermetically sealed off from human trouble. The strength of the love in the home and the love of God which made it possible turned Whittier's efforts to the broken, suffering world outside. He was no selfish escapist. He was jeered and jostled; he was pelted with rotten eggs; he was hooted at and hated for his service on the side of the rights of man. He was an ardent abolitionist. If Whittier has become the favorite of sentimentalists, it is because others have neglected the record. The Christ that he honored in his home, he served in the world. As he put it:

> But here amidst the poor and blind
> The bound and suffering of our kind,
> In works we do, in prayers we pray,
> Lord of our life, He lives today.

A true home has a heart for the homeless.

The home and family are among the oldest human institutions. Experience has proved their value and divine mandate has sanctioned them. Today, however, both are under attack. Recently, I listened to a television debate in which a local clergyman violently abused the institution and in which his opponent offered only feeble resistance. In the early nineteenth century the novels of Dickens come to a successful climax in marriage and the prospect of numerous children making merry at Christmas. At the close of the century, the novels of Hardy view marriage as a trap. Ben Hecht, in the 1920s, sees marriage as a post-graduate course in pessimism, and the recent *Couples* by John Updike gives us a dismally revolting picture of disintegrating family structure. The divorce and marriage announcements in the *Grand Rapids Press* are often about equal in number, and many of the names are familiar in sound. If this trend continues, a greatly enlarged percentage of Americans will not be able to go home again in any healthy sense.

One does not need to sentimentalize a home to appreciate its values. The most ruthlessly realistic appraisal would validate a good home, especially a Christian one. But a good home is not built by spineless whiners, egomaniacs, or people interested in their own introverted idea of happiness. The good home is built on the love of God and the love of man.

Love is a moral value without horizons; if it is real it offers only increase. The members of any family are sinful and sometimes wearing, even unlovable. But Christ loved the unlovable and in so doing changed them. I am not impressed by people who wave peace signs and plaster love symbols all over and make no effort to love the family, or those who show incredible tenderness to outsiders when they cannot tolerate the failures of one's father or mother or brother or sister. The family is the right place to begin loving and to keep on loving even when it is difficult. When we fail, we can also think of Whittier's words:

> And if my heart and flesh are weak
> To bear an untried pain,
> The bruised reed He will not break,
> But strengthen and sustain.

The more I think about it, the Christian home appears to be the right place to begin almost everything.

Antiques and Our Heritage

The Banner (September 29, 1972)

One need not travel far on the highways of our country to notice and finally become overwhelmed by the number of shops that sell "antiques." Hardly a village on a sideroad but has its share of old things. After a while one almost suspects that there is somewhere a hidden assembly line grinding out faded banners, tarnished Lucky Strike tins, old lanterns, battered license plates, thousands of pots and pans, and above all spoons. Some of it looks like junk but a great deal of it is not only old but beautiful and shockingly expensive. Anything worthwhile seems to start at $37.50. In the country of the young, the material relics of the past are big business.

One wonders about the motives energizing all this frantic collecting, storing, repairing, polishing, arranging, and selling. Some people doubtless have a genuine interest in the cultural and human drama behind all these objects. A washing board of the early 1900s is a rather graceless object, but it is also a monument to endless toil. Some are probably instinctive collectors "squirreling-up" antiques whatever their worth. Others are primarily interested in the real beauty in many of these artifacts. There is also the lure of money, because there is much money made here; in fact, in the swank shops the atmosphere is full of money. None of these motives is really wrong and some are noble and eminently praiseworthy.

The word *antique* has strong overtones and is applied to more than old objects. In a neutral sense it simply means old. In the shops, however, it has associations of value, beauty, and history. In poetry, as in Shelley's line "I met a traveler from an antique land," it suggests awe and mystery as well. But it may also have sharply critical overtones as in Eliot's "The Wasteland," where the wife of Albert "looks so antique (and her only thirty-one)."

It may be offensively critical when one refers to a human being or an idea as antique. In this article I use the best sense only — something old, precious, and beautiful. I believe that our heritage has such beliefs, values, and institutions that they are worthy of the honor of pious memory and pervasive influence. I shall refer to five such "antiques."

The awareness of an antithesis between believers and unbelievers

Antithesis is an old word among us. It was frequently used in classrooms, journals, and sermons thirty years ago. It has been one of our key words, followed by *commitment, integration, relevance,* and now *thrust.* These words seem to cluster together in distinct groups. *Antithesis* and *commitment* were often used together; whereas *integration, relevance,* and *thrust* seem closely related.

All are valuable words and I have no quarrel with any of them, but the most important and most forgotten word seems to me to be *antithesis*. Citizens of the kingdom of God have a distinct supernatural birth, a peculiar God-given task in the world, and a divine destiny. At the center of life is the Lord Jesus and His Word to which we owe our deepest commitment in love and in service. We try to make this commitment relevant without compromising our identity, or washing out our distinctiveness. In this type of thought the Christian was meant to be different from the unbeliever in reflection, language, critical judgment, and manner of life. There was to be no bland adjustment to the relativism of the day; no easy blending with modernity. The word is no longer in fashion, but the reality should be. If Christians become hard to detect, they are not strong Christians.

The sense of sin and human limitation

Sin is almost an obsolete word in our culture. We have criminals and lawbreakers, people have guilt feelings, often considered unjustified, but what newspaper would accuse the would-be assassin of Wallace as a sinner? The word would sound medieval. The exuberant religious movements don't talk much about guilt. *Sin* as trangression of God's law, as a cause of corruption, alienation, and human tragedy has very limited circulation.

In the face of the most massive evidence of human greed and callousness, man seems to view sin as a myth. There is little talk about the endless, thorny battle with sin in our ordinary lives, little feeling of the enormous distance between the ethics of the Sermon on the Mount and our daily existence. I remember vividly the almost monotonous prayers to keep us from sinning in thought, word, and deed; prayers, however, that rose from hard and inescapable experience. I am not stressing the morbid preoccupation with sin that one finds in Puritan diaries, which approaches sickness of soul and exhibits ingratitude to our Lord's redeeming power, but I am stressing the importance of a realistic and honest appraisal of the dark side of our daily lives and measureless need for daily forgiveness and daily repentance. Indeed Jesus has saved us once and for all, but He also saves us everyday. Nobody wears robes of stainless white this side of Jordan.

The priority of the sermon
in our Sunday services

I wrote about this before and have since found neither in practice nor rebuttal any reason to alter my convictions about the immeasurable spiritual benefits of good sermons. I use the word *good* because some of my friends pointed out that I was really assuming that the sermons I was talking about were good, but that fact does not invalidate the importance of the sermon; it only points up the lack of talent or preparation in the minister. The sermon is still a rhetorical instrument of great and abiding power to willing hearts and minds.

The importance of Christian education

The present Christian school system is a monument to severe early sacrifices and stellar devotion, a genuine attempt to provide an education that tried to apply the best Reformed tradition to the manifold problems of life. I have known men who walked a long way to work all their lives, who denied themselves and their families a car to provide a Christian education for their children. I have known gifted teachers on all levels of teaching who declined prestigious and lucrative positions to serve this cause. I have known board members who spent almost as much time in working for their schools as for their business. All was done in the belief that God would bless a distinctively Christian training for their children and a sound *factual* and theoretical knowledge of Scripture.

So it is with acute dismay that one sees a gradual erosion in attendance and support of these schools. They have given our children something to give the world; when they vanish, much of this unique knowledge of Scripture and interpretation will also disappear. Particularly distressing is the fact that only about 20 percent of our college youth attend one of our colleges. There may be good reasons why 20 percent should not attend these colleges; I can conceive of no good reasons why 80 percent should fail to do so — unless one calls indifference, apathy, or hostility to these uniquely excellent institutions good reasons.

The idea of an abiding city

The poet Sandburg once said, when he was young and didn't know any better and before he had written six fat volumes on Lincoln, that the "past is a bucket of ashes." When the past is over it is finished, burnt out — ashes to blow with the winds to anywhere. All the past is done, including human life. But the Christian believes that the past in the deepest spiritual sense is the beginning and determines the future.

I was poignantly reminded of this when I visited the country grave-yard where my grandfather is buried. There was a remarkable differ-ence in the gravestones. The newer ones bore merely a name and a date, a terse statement of transitory existence now finished. But the older graves had upon their frail and fading headstones a constantly recurring text in a language I heard so often in boyhood: "Selig sind die Toten, die in dem Herron sterben" (Blessed are the dead that die in the Lord), and I thought "This is it," a trust that defies the last humiliation with infinite hope; on the eroding stones covering re-morseless decay were words of profound promise. The later graves in Gray's words "Implore the passing tribute of a sigh," but the earlier ones gave rise to a thrill of hope and meaning and victory in the face of apparently utter defeat.

Emerson and Our Permissive Society

The Banner (October 23, 1970)

The editor has asked me to write some articles on the usable past in American literature and culture — that is, those events, ideas, and personalities which have a broad, human meaning for our times. This is a risky undertaking in an age which often re-gards the past as a "bucket of ashes." Tradition, for many, whether spiritual, moral, or economic, is as irrelevant as the pony express or the Erie Canal. The ancient landmarks are being obliterated whether by attack or mere neglect, and the morally and physically rootless American feels like an alien in his own land. The past has made him what he is, and if one wishes understanding as well as feelings and happenings, he will have to examine the past that made him.

Unless we are very insulated indeed, we can see growing rankly about us a new culture of the youth, which in its more violent forms threatens to modify American history. The more dramatic patterns of this culture shock many of us almost every day: the disheveled young-sters sprawling about in public parks, the weirdly attired youth slouching through the store with a tinkle of little bells and the reek of incense or merely unwashed accumulations, the wildly swinging rock sessions full of living and loving in ways that offend our moral sense. When we look at the college campuses, the formerly sedate halls of learning, we note that in the first half of 1969, there were 215,000 students on 232 campuses that took part in three hundred protests, some ending in fire, blood, and death. How did this come upon us? What have society and the parents been doing? At least one of the answers lies in American literature and American cultural history.

Whether we like it or not, whether it conforms to our simplistic ideas of the American way of life, much of this behavior is in the American grain. Rap Brown once said, "Violence is as American as apple pie." We cannot simply dismiss this statement by saying as a preacher once did, "This is a truth we do not accept." This nation has fought twenty-two wars; Americans own more guns per capita than any nation in the world. We have done a lot of shooting since 1607.

We have also had very influential and elaborate statements justifying extreme individualism and erratic personal behavior. Emerson and Thoreau propounded theories which, when they came to full flower many years later, would have chilled their thin New England blood. But the children of dissent both peaceful and violent would thrust Emerson's creed in his face. Here are some key statements:

"What have I to do with the sacredness of traditions if I live wholly from within? . . . No law can be sacred to me but that of my nature. The only right is what is after my constitution. The highest revelation of God is in every man. Make your own Bible."

This is the ultimate in permissiveness. Trust your own instincts, trust only your own conscience, and make your own Bible. Emerson's ideas were enthusiastically embraced and often debased by the young of his day. They fitted quite naturally with the free-wheeling life of the frontier and the general repudiation of Puritan morality.

We often think of the nineteenth century as an age of birch-rod discipline, but there is much evidence to the contrary. In 1849, an acute foreigner, Adam de Guronski, came to the United States, to Harvard. He was an eccentric who said "I can abuse everybody," and he did. He was a shrewd observer and said of the young people in the 1850s, "In America children generally lead and regulate their parents . . . in most of the relations and modes of life." The surge of youthful rebellion rose and fell during the century, but in the 1920s it reached a new peak of freedom and liberalization of moral and religious codes. Progressive education further weakened parental authority. But the really big change has occurred in the last twenty years, when many of the young reject American society. While the parents were busy making it, the young were being prepared for breaking it. Authority is waning, and there are few if any heroic figures to stem it by attraction to a new ideal. Today Margaret Mead, a famous anthropologist, says, "it will be the child and not the parent or grandparent that resents what is to come."

Into this progressively youth-centered culture, a product of a long tradition of dissent, individualism, or even violence, our parents and grandparents immigrated from the tight, authoritative societies of the Netherlands and Germany. For many years we maintained this authority sanctioned by scriptural precept in the church, home, and school. No one can deny that big fissures have appeared and that our domestic and educational harmony is being broken. The fences our fathers thought made good neighbors are crumbling, and the overwhelming pressures of American life are changing the attitudes and actions of both children and parents about the sedate ways of the past, and many parents worry over maintaining the authority of Scripture and their convictions concerning the Christian life. Can the pillars of the temple be sustained?

Our new youth-culture insists upon permissiveness; if this is not forthcoming it hurls out demands, and if these are not met the violent fringe practices destruction. We are still far from this fanatical fringe. The college students I know are overwhelmingly pleasant, well-mannered, and respectful; they are serious and openminded, but they face head-on a social and moral challenge which we would like to help them conquer. This cannot be done by adopting Emersonian individualism in which each man does his own thing as seems right in his own eyes. Moral and social anarchy will result from this. We have to transcend personal conscience; we must find an objective law to which young and old can submit, a set of sanctions which we find in Scripture.

The cogency of this answer will depend upon the value we place upon Scripture and the way we interpret it. If the Bible is a book whose historical accuracy has to be established by extra-biblical documents, if we have to find its meaning through highly sophisticated mythological approaches, if we see in the biblical stories recurrent archetypes, symbols or images whose origins lie in a shadowy evolutionary past — then we are, it seems to me, destroying the uniqueness of the book. If we disregard the testimony of traditional Christian experience as it has been illuminated by the Spirit through generations of Christians, if the main lines of scriptural truth are no longer plain over the ages and have to be reinterpreted by each generation, we will wonder just how valid our temporary interpretations are. I do not believe that my grandmother, who was a life-long reader of the Bible, or that my father, who was a gifted student of the Bible, came to basic convictions about the creation of Adam and Eve, redemption, grace, and Christian duties without the guidance of the Spirit. If basic interpretations have constantly to be changed instead of being rooted in the past and developed in conformity with it instead of repudiation of it, then Emerson was right when he said "God speaks," not spoke once for all.

Dr. Johnson's Thorn

The Banner (September 3, 1971)

One of the best tests of character is the kind of behavior revealed in the inevitable encounters with the thorns of life: personal weakness, frustration, physical disability, hostility, all the troubles none escape. One can whine in high poetry, as Shelley did, "I fall upon the thorns of life! I bleed!" Hemingway tried to dominate disaster through an iron code of courage and failed. Twain in his bitter last years fruitlessly barricaded himself in grim humor and looked at misfortune and life itself as a fated dream gone sour. However, the Christian like Paul faces the thorns of life with prayer and faith, knowing that God's grace is sufficient even though the thorn be irremovable. This Christian way Dr. Johnson tried to follow.

Dr. Samuel Johnson, the eighteenth-century poet, critic, biographer, and brilliant conversationalist, is one of the great literary figures whose work and memory have given pleasure, insight, and spiritual nourishment for many generations. Despite his accomplishment and fame, he had a lifelong thorn in the flesh, and I believe it is worthwhile today to see how he dealt with this nagging sore, since none of us are without some such burden.

Johnson was one of the world's greatest men. His physical courage approached recklessness; he once trounced four London thugs who attacked him; he swam in the Thames in mid-winter. He was strikingly independent; he never flattered or begged though he was often miserably poor and never well-to-do. His manners could be rude and movingly tender. When he was arguing for victory, he gave no quarter. His learning was precise and immense. As a talker he has hardly been equaled because of his vast knowledge, wit, reasoning power, and sheer nerve. On hearing a musical performance that was difficult, he said, "I wish it had been impossible." Of Mr. Foote he said, "Foote is impartial, he lies of everybody." He once settled an argument between the poetic merits of Derrick and Smart by saying, "Sir, there is no settling the precedency between a louse and a flea." Despite the rough manner, his generosity was unparalleled; he practically ran an almshouse of his own with quarrelsome inmates indeed. When he died, his friend Boswell justly said, "He has made a chasm."

Johnson was a devout Christian and the Bible was to him "the sacred volume in which are contained the revelations of God." He did not compartmentalize his life or hide his candle under a bushel. The implications of Christianity are expressed in his poems and criticism, but especially in his talk. He was articulate about his faith among unbelievers. When Dr. Adams asked him. "What do you mean by damned?" he said, "Sent to hell, Sir, and punished everlastingly." Human wishes may be vain, but human life has eternal meaning. A writer's duty is always to make the world better, not merely to report it; and his critical principles were based in order of priority upon revealed religion, truth to nature, and the examples of the classics.

Johnson's great gifts and achievements did not shield him from lifelong pain. From an early age he had a strong tendency to depression of spirit, what he called "a vile melancholy." Its effect made him say in *Rasselas*, "Human life is everywhere a state in which much is to be endured and little to be enjoyed." His depression took the form of obsessive thoughts, fits of indolence, and especially a fear of the fact of dying itself and "the final sentence and unalterable allotment."

Despite the gloom and even in the last years of illness he said, "I will be conquered; I will not capitulate." His faith in God gave him that courage, and prayer was his chief exercise of it. Time and again we meet such sentences as the following in his recorded prayers: "Let Thy Holy Spirit so purify my affections and exalt my desires that my prayer may be acceptable in Thy sight, through Jesus Christ." Johnson found in prayer his greatest weapon against melancholy. He also found a strong weapon in work, and despite his complaints about indolence, he did an enormous amount of work in his life.

One of the great scenes in biographical literature illustrates at once his spiritual courage, his faith, the power of prayer, and the healing value of work. On August 17, 1767, Johnson, the most famous man of letters in England went to the humble bedside of Kitty Chambers, the dying maid of his mother. He did this despite his intense and morbid fear of the act of dying and of the fact of death. He knelt beside her bed and prayed for her salvation. After she expressed the hope that they should "meet again in a better place," Johnson writes in his notebook: "I expressed with swelled eyes, and great emotion of tenderness, the same hopes. We kissed and parted. I humbly hope to meet again and part no more."

Faith in God destroyed all fear, all social and intellectual barriers, as a man of unbending intellectual pride knelt with a poor, unknown woman before the cross of Christ.

Johnson's thorn in the flesh was an oppressive melancholy, which could have caused even greater trouble had not God given him the grace of prayer and the powers to work. The thorns that oppress us vary, but no one escapes them. The Christian cannot escape the misery of man. Who lives through a single day wholly free from worry, fear, disappointment, envy, evil thought, or pain? Sometimes it seems that Emily Dickinson is right when she wrote:

> The Heavenly Father
> Leads the chosen child,
> Oftener through realms of briar
> Than the meadow mild.

I knew a Christian woman who had eight children, seven of which were born dead, and the one surviving child proved to be mentally retarded. She cared for that child tenderly and loved her deeply. I wonder how often that poor woman prayed and asked why. The answer God gave her was not a logically defensible system but amazing grace. That is what He gives His children, and we know it will always be sufficient even in the bitterest and inexplicable need.

We seem also to live in an age of thorns, an age in which images of disaster abound — atomic warfare, a polluted globe, unsupportable populations, racial antagonism, giant poverty in the midst of plenty. Coleridge seems to have the right words:

> We listened and looked sideways up!
> Fear at my heart, as at a cup,
> My life-blood seemed to sip.

The problems mankind faces often seem insoluble, and men run to and fro in bewilderment as they confront what look like inoperable cancers. Human ingenuity and intelligence and above all human nature is not enough. When was it ever enough?

It has been said that the early Christians turned the world upside down, but a more honest appraisal would limit this statement to the western world, and even in that world human greed and human sin were always everywhere present. We live in a lost Eden, and we are grossly fooling ourselves if we imagine that we can restore it. Only God can do that in a new heaven and a new earth. Here, even though we pray faithfully and work intelligently, thorns will be our human lot; yet we know that the Great Husbandman has His eternal loving purposes even through them.

Some Notes on Magnanimity

The Reformed Journal (August, 1979)

C. E. Norton, formerly a professor of Fine Arts at Harvard, once began a class on the idea of a gentleman by saying, "None of you, probably, has ever seen a gentleman." This sounds like the last word in rude snobbery, but if one knew, which I don't, how he went on to define a gentleman, the quotation might be less absurd. If one means by a gentleman simply external polish and impeccable etiquette, it is absurd. If one means by a gentleman the inclusion of a corresponding disposition, it becomes less so. If one includes in the definition, the notion of magnanimity, it begins to sound like truth. If one examines one of the best definitions I know, Norton becomes almost right. The definition comes from Chaucer, and ironically and characteristically, it is spoken by that boisterous rollicking sinner, the Wife of Bath. She says that the gentleman is one who is most virtuous at all times, both publicly and privately, both in intention and act, a person who tries always to do the deeds of courtesy in imitation of Christ. Such ladies and gentleman were rare in Norton's time when, he said, there was almost no barrier to "modern barbarism and vulgarity." In our age when barbarism and vulgarity parade their crudity on every television screen, when greed, powerplays, rudeness, and violence are common, Chaucer's gentleman is not an American model and infrequently a fact.

In his fascinating book of reminiscences, *Remembering Poets*, Donald Hall makes a remarkable statement about Ezra Pound, poet, translator, critic, booster, and traitor.

> In the history of literature, no writer equals Pound in accuracy of
> taste, or in energetic magnanimity.

He supports the first assertion by adducing Pound's early and generally unshared enthusiasm for writers as diverse as D. H. Lawrence,
Joyce, Eliot, Hemingway, Ford Madox Ford and Robert Frost, whose
literary practice broke Pound's poetic creed and whose excellence forced
his praise. He supports the second by many instances of Pound's
unparalleled generosity to poor poets and his fulsome praise for potential rivals. Both qualities are rare among critics and poets whose
taste is often determined by their own theories and practice, and
whose vanity stifles praise for others. Many writers excel more frequently in acidity than they do in magnanimity. They are often like
Disraeli, who when a fellow novelist asked him to read his new book
replied, "I shall lose no time in reading your book."

Writers are often thin-skinned, jealous, even vindictive. Hemingway
brutally parodied Anderson who had befriended him and denigrated
Fitzgerald who had championed him. Frost wanted to be on top of
the steeple and resented any other poet who approached it. "I've got
a book coming out that's going to drive Wilbur and Lowell into the
shadows," he said. That's where he preferred his fellow poets to be.
Alexander Pope poured verbal vitriol on many of his rivals and Dryden
tells us that the current poet laureate never ever "blunders into meaning." Ezra Pound, on the other hand, cajoled and pressured publishers
into giving his rivals a hearing. Pound was, whatever his later aber-
rations, a magnanimous man.

Pound's "accuracy of taste" was a product of genius and unflagging
labor, the kind of excellence which one marvels at rather than emu-
lates. His magnanimity, however, can serve as a model since it is a
virtue found in a share-cropper's hut as well as in a poet's study or a
prince's palace. Magnanimity despises manipulation, as common in
our country as smog. It undercuts vanity and expresses the Christian
ideal of preferring another. Like Portia's mercy, it blesses both the
giver and the receiver.

Magnanimity is enlarged courtesy, its second mile. When I was a
boy of eleven, Dr. Henry Beets, a man of talent and prestige, visited
our home in Paterson. He was friendly and pleasant—that was courtesy. He also took me on the bus to the city library to acquire a card
to begin good reading—that was magnanimity. That he drew out three
volumes of Sir Walter Scott was simply a magnanimous evaluation of
my ability. Thomas Carlyle worked long and hard on his history of
the French Revolution. He also complained loud and hard about working so long and hard on it. When a maid accidentally burned the large

manuscript, he neither vilified or fired her — and that was magnanimity.

C.S. Lewis liked argument, "a shooting war," but in his debate with Professor Leavis about "The Personal Heresy," he gives his opponent full credit for talent and weight of argument. Magnanimity always does that.

I was brought up in and have belonged all my life to a church where argument and debate are in everlasting flower. We don't believe in a fallow field, and our cultivation of the soil is so remarkably successful that though in some seasons the flowers may be slightly less lustrous, they never fade. As a matter of fact if sparsity of argumentation and debate should occur many would be alarmed by this sign of spiritual ill health. In one of his stories Peter De Vries portrays a father at the breakfast table, sternly slaying heretics. His son says, "Why can't we stop this endless debate and quarreling?" To which the father abruptly replies, "Don't be a crackpot." We batten on controversial issues. The notable scholarship in many of our Synodical reports attests to our seriousness. But we do not always or even often, engage in debate with magnanimity. As a little boy, I watched the blue tobacco smoke eddy out of my father's study and down the stair; I heard the low rumble of voices as my father and another minister engaged in a profound debate about millennialism, an issue that led to sporadic defections and is now as thoroughly buried as its advocates. Suddenly the discussions ceased as did the visits. The other minister was a brilliant man, but after the discussions he became a prickly pear. To differ sharply with civility and magnanimity has been hard for us. It is hard for everybody. Even when we can have the dubious pleasure of dancing about the pyre we have made of an opponent's arguments, we should at least congratulate him on having provided good material.

It is easy to be tolerant about what means little to us or to be patronizingly magnanimous when we have argued for victory and won. To retain a generous disposition toward one who seems like a termite gnawing successfully at the pillars of your temple requires grace as well as largeness of mind, because magnanimity is not a benign sentimentality flooding the mind. It cannot operate in a dunce or an emotional caryatid. It will not evade sharp debate or refuse to make a fool of a fool in a kindly, civilized way, but it will always honor sincerity, scholarship, clarity of expression, the diversity of human experience, and the limitations of human intelligence. I have no illusions about the difficulties. I have seen too many lost causes and outmoded loyalties go down the drain not to know how hard it is to praise and love the wreckers. Sometimes, unfortunately, I do neither.

8

"The Unextinguished Hearth"

LITERATURE

*P*rofessionally trained at the University of Michigan and Northwestern University, Professor Timmerman is a respected scholar of literature. In his career at Calvin College he taught nearly every literature course in the catalog, but is probably best remembered for his courses in American Literature and Chaucer. The following section includes selections from his many critical appraisals of literature. But these are more than just critical appraisals in the common sense of that term. Critical theory often suggests an arid investigation in a language that only specialists can understand. Such is not the case here. The reason for that lies in Professor Timmerman's insistence upon seeing the literary work as a living thing produced by lively authors. In each work discussed below, Professor Timmerman locates the enduring human significance, the common appeal, and the spiritual meaning of the work. Under his hands the covers of the book are opened, finally, to disclose us to ourselves. We see a bit of ourselves on each page, and the book lives on long after the pages have stopped turning.

This section represents only a very small segment of Professor Timmerman's many writings about literature, but in its divisions provides a sampling of that larger work. Included first are two essays which reflect his personal love for literature, "The Books in a Boy's Life," and "The Joyful Critic." Second, in two essays he discusses that enduring classic Pilgrim's Progress and specifically considers the message of this book to our age. In the last group of essays he considers several literary topics such as the nature of the popular novel, the task of the Christian artist, and Calvinism and literary criticism.

The Books in a Boy's Life

The Banner (October 5, 1973)

Although there was much love in our family and although my parents were moderately well-to-do, I looked forward to and received with delight one major gift on my birthdays — a book. This pattern of giving was general then, although the nature of the gifts might vary. I cannot easily think of a boy and his parents who would not feel uneasy about such giving today, since the book cost only a dollar. Yet those books were gateways to splendor.

When one is young the shadow line between fact and fiction is as thin as paper. One does not yet know enough about life and human nature to doubt the goodness of Sir Galahad; the dwarfs and fairies, so difficult to believe in a play, are easily assimilated by the imagination; animals talk, plot, and philosophize; the strong Norse gods parade their power. To the child this is as real as talk over a back fence. Alice in Wonderland could be the girl next door.

Early in life, my mother read books to me in Dutch and English. I don't recall the stories, but I remember the fact with immense gratitude. I do remember a picture, a little boy lost in a huge forest where the sunlit trees produced only fear. About him were these unending trees. How worried that boy and I were in all those silent trees. I remember distinctly also a picture of Jesus instructing the learned men and how strange that seemed. The first books I remember greatly admiring were the beautiful volumes of a German encyclopedia which I might look at after Sunday afternoon service. The art work in those volumes was, and still is as I look at the volumes now, spectacular: vivid pictures of undersea life, exotic flowers, bleak arctic wastes. I did not pause long with an illustrated edition of Dante's *Divine Comedy* because I would be haunted by the drawings of the lost: punished forever by flames of fire, up to the neck in slime, pressed into tight sepulchers.

Until its demise, my parents subscribed to a magazine, *Die Abenschule*. Every year they received a complimentary hard cover book with stories, colored pictures, and very funny cartoons with a whimsical German humor. One old German professor met another, who asked him, "Was that you who died or was it your brother?" To which the latter replied, "It must have been I because my brother is still living as far as I know."

The first books I remember reading myself were about a courageous, courteous, and remarkably canny goat, called Billy Whiskers. He was a gentleman and a hero; he took care not only of his wife but all his friends. He was a pillar of integrity and foiled many a villain. He performed a function very similar to that of the big stag that protects the interests of the holders of Hartford Life Insurance Company. I was also very fond of the stories of E. T. Seton's *Wild Animals I Have Known,* and other remarkable fictional recreations of the psychology of animals.

Quite naturally books about boys were most important to me. For some years I was engrossed in the Rover boys, serious Dick, fun-loving Tom, and practical Sam. I followed the brothers from the academy to the jungles of Africa and the roar of the Klondike. A librarian with a keen interest in children recommended the historical fiction of Joseph Altsheler, who had not only great narrative skill, but poetic language and historical imagination. The first book I read was *The Forest Runners,* and I can still feel the awful immediacy of death as Henry and Paul in a lonely cabin fought off the attackers. The vastness and mystery of the primeval forests engulfed a young reader, and the steel, courage, and intuitive woodcraft of Henry Ware dazzled him. I read all in the series about Ware and his friends as well as the fine stories of the French and Indian wars and the great plains. They are, I believe, unrecognized minor classics.

The little town in which I read most of the books of my boyhood was marked by rigid social law and structure. Our classroom was quiet and when it became very quiet there was danger. Fresh kids were not listened to; they were smacked. With a pervasive rigidity at home, in school, and in the church, what a relief it was to live in the goodly company of Penrod and Sam, and the funny fat boy Mark Todd. They broke rules without cruelty or viciousness. When Huck Finn came down Main Street swinging a dead cat, it was like reveille without the army. Tom and Huck never worked. When Tom had to work he conned his friends into doing the job. They borrowed watermelons and other good things freely. They enjoyed a leisure and freedom which a boy hoeing long rows of beans or picking them greatly envied. What I enjoyed in Twain then was the laughter; it took quite a few years to appreciate the tears.

With the inconsistency of youth, I also enjoyed and devoured the stories of Horatio Alger, devoted wholly to hard work and success. Whether the title was *Making His Way, Helping Himself, Facing the World,* or *Bound to Rise,* the pattern was the same, but the stories were still interesting. Alger, whatever his faults, was a storyteller of genius. The hero is either orphaned or left as an only son to support a widowed mother and her family. The home is usually dishonestly mortgaged and the mortgage overdue. The boy goes to the city, where by luck and pluck, honesty, thrift, and courage, he rescues the mother, achieves the boss' daughter and moves toward wealth. The fabulous and, to the cold realistic eye, sentimental stories, had an incalculable effect on many Americans, since they sold in the millions and expressed basic American ideals: the good *poor* boy, the dignity of the common American, the values of hard work and the importance of material success. Alger, who wrote so many success stories, died alone in a dingy room with the outline of another story on his desk. His works enriched everybody promoting them except the author. What Alger both in fiction and life got across was the indignity of the handout.

As is abundantly clear by this time, I was in no way a precocious reader, no Jonathan Edwards, who at twelve read Locke's *Essay on the Human Understanding* with the joy of a miser gathering gold. Dr. Henry Beets, a classmate and close friend of my father sought to introduce new dimensions. He was occasionally a guest in our home. He had a superb gift not only for making himself important, but of being important and of making others feel important. He had hardly arrived in our home, then in Paterson, when he telephoned Senator VandenBerg in Washington, D.C., to arrange for his opening a session of the U. S. Senate with prayer. When he returned he took me to the Paterson public library, arranged my possession of a card and drew out Scott's *Ivanhoe* and several other hefty novels. I was eleven and I found *Ivanhoe* rough territory. Sir Walter takes a long time to crank up his stories, and I gave up before the novel was really rolling. It was, however, a remarkable thing for him to do and for me a lasting tribute to his good heart and good literary taste.

The aforementioned incident, however, warned me against forcing a child's reading. Unless you have a child like William Cullen Bryant, who knew the alphabet at sixteen months, began Greek at fifteen years of age and after two months of study read through the New Testament, and at seventeen wrote sixty of the most famous lines in American literature, be thankful if your child likes to read. Greet any good reading with enthusiastic delight; great reading will probably come later.

I am always happy when I hear of parents who take the time to read to little children. I know the patience it takes to read *The Little Lost Lamb* over and over till you and your child both know it by heart, but in doing so you will share and guide the imaginative life of your child in love. It is so easy to delegate entertainment to the television set, but in so doing you and your child lose much.

God has given us many blessings and among the best are great books. He has given us His book, unexcelled in beauty, variety, grace and saving knowledge. He has given superb gifts to the writers of the classics. These books clarify the chaos of experience, interpret it with vision, and permit us imaginatively to share the manifold glory, wonder, mystery, and pain of life. The child who learns to read good books develops a resource that can only increase.

A Book for All Seasons

The Banner (April 23, 1971)

One of my father's favorite books was *Pilgrim's Progress* by John Bunyan. It was a vitally transforming book for me, and I have often wondered why so few Christians read it. It is certainly not a dull book unless one finds a superbly imaginative treatment of the crucial Christian experiences dull. The characters in this spiritual adventure story are not ideologically manipulated puppets, but are as real, fallible, and believable as your neighbors. The theology in the book has been felt in the pulses and the feelings come through. The long, hard journey from the city of Destruction to the eternal city of God is a violent battle every inch of the way. I believe this book is good for us today and deserves more than respectful neglect and an honored place on a list of the hundred best books.

Pilgrim's Progress was popular in the past. The Puritans read the book eagerly, and it was found on the rude shelves of their homes in such numbers that an unprecedented American reprinting was necessary three years after its publication in England in 1678. Bunyan, a Baptist, could say that the colonists regarded it with "a much loving countenance." The book was never so popular again.

Why has this book which so tellingly and touchingly records the awesome experience of Christian, its main character, been so neglected? I can understand the reaction of a former high school student of mine who wrote: "*Pilgrim's Progress* is more for grown-ups because it's all about sin and living righteously." This he considered the business of his elders and a dull business at that; for him it was a book one has to totter into.

But the grown-ups haven't been reading it either, however seriously they may be concerned with sin and living righteously. There are, of course, minor obstacles. The language is somewhat archaic, but then many of the same elders insist on the supremacy of the King James version of the Bible, which is somewhat archaic too. The hero, Christian, is a bit fanatic; his clothes are odd; his disdain of comfort and possessions annoying; and his rejection of his family disturbing. Christian strikes the modern Christian as an escapist. He flees the doomed city; he does not wish God to destroy it as Jonah did, but he is not intent on rescuing it either. Finally, Christian takes sin with uncommon seriousness; he really believes he is a bad man in himself. This is not for him a ritualistic description but a terrifying, inescapable fact. Christ took an unbearable burden from his back and saved him from a sharply visualized hell. Unless one shares this conviction, the book loses much of the power it has for one who does.

That John Bunyan wrote it is a miracle of grace. Bunyan was an uneducated tinker, a mender of pots and pans, an abysmally poor and anonymous man. All he had was genius and God used it marvelously. After a series of shattering spiritual crises, described with great power in *Grace Abounding*, release from ghastly fears and obsessively foul thoughts came through the love of Jesus. His seminary was the Bible. The grace of God freed him from terrors commonly associated with madmen. Consequently Christian's battle with Apollyon, his struggle with the Giant Despair, the wrestling through the Slough of Despond are concretely real. He called the book a dream, but it was a dream come true.

Like all great books it has levels of enjoyment and meaning. There is the level of action and plot. In plot the book is sensational, full of stir and tumult, battle and smoke, beatings, chase and escape. Little-Faith is attacked by three sturdy foes. He is "white as Clout."

> With that, Guilt with a Great Club that was in his
> hand, strook Little-Faith on the head, and with that
> blow fell'd him flat to the ground, where he lay
> bleeding as one that would bleed to death.

In action it has the punch of a chilling shocker.

Distinguished characterization is essential to fiction. Mere action should not dwarf the plot as in the average detective story. Great fiction adds a dimension to our friendships. Certainly, Christian, Faithful, Evangelist, and the Giant Despair are convincing and unforgettable. But many of the minor characters are shrewdly, even bitingly portrayed. The jury in Vanity Fair has such redoubtable characters as Mr. Live-Loose, Mr. Heady, and Mr. Money-Love. Lord Fairspeech, Mr. Two-Tongues, and Mr. Facing-Both-Ways are known to us all. And we have heard of Mr. Gripe-Man, a schoolmaster, in Love-Gain, a market town. The characters are inherently interesting as well as typical, and often amusingly British.

Good characters rise from a living social context and live on a real terrain. Bunyan abounds in faithful local color of the English countryside. Rural England becomes the setting of cosmic drama. When Christian stumbles through the valley of the Shadow of Death, he is struggling through an English bog. Vanity Fair is any English market. The Giant Despair is a typical English landlord growling out English custom:

> "You have this night trespassed on me, trampling on and lying on my grounds, and therefore you must go along with me."

The imagery of Scripture fuses with that of the English countryside in the final scenes of the book.

The prose of the book has always been praised. Its dialog may occasionally appear distressingly didactic, but granted the overwhelming conviction underlying the book, its fitness can be argued. The language is homespun yet colorful, suggestive yet precise. It is purified common speech, often redolent of the majestic rhythms of the Bible. It is lively, not prim. The pilgrims are put into a dark dungeon "nasty and stinking." Temporary Christians are described as "hot for Heaven, so long as the flames of Hell are about their ears." It is full of quotable sayings.

> "If a man would live well, let him fetch his last day to him, and make it always his company keeper."

It rises to memorable beauty in the ecstatic descriptions of Heaven, "for in this Land the shining Ones commonly walked, because it was upon the borders of Heaven."

But the greatest reach of the book lies in its meaning. It is our best allegory because of the precise relation between symbol and idea, sense and story. Vanity Fair, Doubting Castle, the Slough of Despond, the Valley of Humiliation are recognizable states on the spiritual journey. The symbolism is never baffling or chaotic. It is all picture, and it is all meaning.

Pilgrim's Progress is a classic of universal Christian experience. Christians are all way-farers and burden-bearers; we must all run the same hazard to the City of God. Bunyan knew sin and despair, almost to madness; he knew what it meant to be lifted from the miry clay, and the battering struggle to God's other kingdom. He put it all down in a book Christians should read.

I say even today because the way to heaven has not been altered, macadamized, or streamlined. There is, as Hawthorne pointed out, no celestial railroad with plush accommodations. There is no effortless journey at reduced rates. Sometimes it is good for us to read a book that brings such a truth smashing into our complacent lives, startling us with a sense of our lostness and need. We need to know again the price of rescue and where we stood before the hand of the Lord grasped us. Aged believers do not weary of an ageless story.

Bunyan's Christian, struggling along under his heavy pack, strikes an odd note today because he is burdened by his own sins, not those of others. He was intent on the beam in his own eye, not on the motes in the eyes of his neighbors; for him depravity began at home. If one has the acute awareness of personal sin that Christian had, the fact will surely modify the spirit in which we make our criticism — often necessary criticism — of others. The self-appointed genius of twenty who, often in the name of love and concern, attacks with merciless militancy the faults of other individuals and groups, might have greater modesty about his own saintly intentions if he looked inside first. Older people would do well to remember the burden on their own backs as they criticize the young and each other.

The Bible tells us that we should not think more highly of ourselves than we ought to think, and only in so far as we are moved by the Spirit of Christ does this advice amount to much. A solemn sense of the presence of pride, avarice, sloth, and wrath on our own backs will temper the judgment of both young and old. As fellow believers in Christ we need to follow the truth as God reveals it; we need to contend for the faith, and we must correct each other, but in so doing we should never forget the love of Jesus which alone can save us from our sins.

The Popular Book

The Reformed Journal (December, 1955)

What makes a popular book? Many suppose that a dubious title on a brash and suggestive cover will insure enormous sales. The garnish and tasteless displays of gunfire, mayhem, and sex which are found in almost all drug stores regardless of neighborhood or ecclesiastical association are misleading. People who thrive on such swill can find it in sections of *Life* or in television. At any rate not enough of them read books to make best sellers in the United States. Popular books are usually more than one-dimensional; they sell because of varied appeal.

It is true, of course, that very, very few books are broadly popular in a really extensive sense. *Gone With the Wind*, a phenomenal best seller, has sold over four million copies to a potential public of two hundred million people. The sale of a hundred thousand copies of a novel in the United States is amazing and few ever reach it. A sale of fifteen thousand copies of a book puts it in the best seller class. Zane Grey, a fabulously popular novelist, wrote sixty-three novels by 1947, which sold to the number of nineteen million. Considering the potential market, even that figure is relatively unimpressive. Books just aren't in a class with beer, not even the thinnest and most frothy of them. The gory, so-called comic books are estimated at selling forty million monthly; they are obviously popular, but no sane man would call them books.

The popularity of a book varies with the times, of course, there are no longer many Americans who, like Samuel Sewall, read Calvin's *Institutes* while their wives are picking raspberries. *Pilgrim's Progress*, once an enormous best seller, is hardly read today, possibly because, as one of my students once put it, it deals too much with sin and living righteously. In Puritan New England sermons outsold all other types of books. Some Christians still buy volumes of sermons for decorative purposes, but Americans generally do not. When Samuel Sewall was courting Widow Ruggles, he gave her as a splendid present Mr. Moody's "Election Sermon." Those times are gone, yet its echoes live in the sale of the sermons and prayers of Peter Marshall. When times change, tastes change. In the latter part of the eighteenth century, taste became sentimental and novels became sentimental and novels became damper and damper, an uncontrolled revel of the emotions, a bath of tears. The nineteenth century liked morality and sentimentality and produced battalions of reform novels from the mawkish *Ten Nights in a Barroom* to the superb *Adam Bede*.

Some strains last. The sentimental strain has proved much tougher than the Puritan or even the reforming urges. There has been for centuries an enormous appetite for fiction as sweet as chocolate. Syrupy sentiment, synthetic sunshine, and idyllic naivete have delighted millions in the tearjerkers of Mrs. Porter whose books have almost become a national institution, as Pollyanna as *The Reader's Digest*. The strain of adventure and exploration has been equally enduring. Mary Rowlandson's narrative of her captivity by the Indians sold furiously. The early dime novels had enough adventure to terrify Leatherstocking himself. Folksy, homespun books have attracted readers over many generations.

Some recent varieties of popular books have proved feverish moneymakers. The happiness books are an example. Dale Carnegie with his booster shots for the inadequate; the *Life Begins at Forty* books (when everybody knows that is the beginning of the expanding abdomen, false teeth, grey hair or none at all); the "kid-yourself," *Be Glad You're Neurotic*, and "Don't Worry" books — all sell in numbers. The creaking and the scared read the fairy tales of the pseudopsychiatrists and go home rejoicing, sicker than ever.

Norman Vincent Peale has hit the jackpot lately and now bids the middlebrow not to fret and to be sure to shine with a clear, pure light. Dr. Peale desperately wants to be a sunbeam, and some people think he is. Today, books about doctors, who have now reached the apogee of the hero-in-white "golden-calfism," are rousingly popular; clergymen are less so; and the teachers make best sellers only when they are knifed and beaten as in the lurid *Blackboard Jungle*. Humorous books are selling, and publishers like to go *Inside Thurber*. But the really popular book today is about the Civil War. Any book about the Civil War. I am eagerly waiting the posthumous autobiography of Robert E. Lee's horse "Traveller." We have had about everything else.

The genuine best seller fills the cultural needs of a wide audience. Sometimes this audience includes intellectuals but not frequently, for the popular book and the classic rarely coincide. William Faulkner and Margaret Mitchell are both Southern novelists, but there the similarity stops. All of Faulkner's books together have not sold like *Gone*

With the Wind. The intellectual novelists of our day present a criticism of our culture, the popular novelists offer an escape. That is the need they fill. Even many of the notable volumes on the Civil War are for many Americans a form of retreat into a glorious and unassailable past.

Is there a formula for best sellers? There is no *one* formula. The secret does not lie in literary art; ordinary adequacy of style or technique is ample. *The Robe* sold because of its religious appeal, its sentimental notion of brotherhood, and its vague mysticism. The historical romance when combined with love and adventure is always surefire. Pure adventure seldom fails. Humanitarian books from *Uncle Tom's Cabin* to *The Grapes of Wrath* enjoy steady popularity. Books as diverse as *The Story of Philosophy* by W. Durand and *We* by C. Lindbergh have been best sellers.

To illustrate the impossibility of a single formula, let us run over ten of the all-time best sellers in the United States. They have sold from two to eight million copies each. *Alice in Wonderland* takes us to dreamland. *One World* by Wendell Wilkie is hard-headed realism. *Ben Hur, The Last of the Mohicans,* and *Ivanhoe* are romantic historical novels. *In His Steps* is an illustrated sermon. *Tom Sawyer* and *Treasure Island* are boys' books adults enjoy. Shakespeare is on the list partly because of English teachers. *A Tree Grows in Brooklyn* is there too. These books do not have a great deal in common; but on greatly varying levels of literary skill, they share one trait — human appeal. They deal with people and their problems.

There is really no single formula, but if one thinks about the best sellers of the last twenty-five years, one can suggest certain promising recipes. Age cannot wither nor habit stale the custom romance. A person with moderate talent would do well to use the American past, unfurl the flag, parade the patriots, demolish the villains, and marry the hero and heroine before they set out into the golden west. An equally wide though different audience responds avidly to the religious novel in which bibilical or ecclesiastical characters are reinterpreted, humanized, and sentimentalized. Popular mental health books have a brisk sale; use your weaknesses and catapult to serenity on your failings. Spicy autobiography, racy journals, sports stories are all good possibilities.

Most popular books are middlebrow. Highbrow novelists like Joyce or Faulkner do not reach a mass market. Popular books reflect the influence of a mass culture which seldom uses books. The wonderful reprints in various editions of paperbacks are selling largely in academic centers and often in proportion to academic requirements. By and large the American reading public is not reading the best. Of the ten best sellers I previously mentioned only Shakespeare is a classic of the first magnitude; four are unimportant, and the other five minor masterpieces. Popular books are not the best, but very much better than many people think.

It is arresting, however, to notice how well religious books sell in the broad American market. The most popular book in American publishing history is *In His Steps*, a fictional sermon. Religious books satisfy a basic need of a wide segment of our public. Deeper than the materialistic surface lies the loneliness and the fear. The important contemporary novelists offer a criticism of our times; they picture man in his miseries, but they have little or no religious faith. They feed disillusion not hope. We often talk about making an impact upon American life. Here is one place a man with gift can do it.

The Unextinguished Hearth

The Reformed Journal (September, 1961)

The past for many Americans is a bucket of ashes. This library, so rich in holdings, so admirable in service, so generous in expenditures, tells us that the past is an unextinquished hearth. The past and present meet on the walls about us and crowd the shelves with splendor. These books are a tangible evidence of Emily Dickinson's statement:

> A word is dead,
> When it is said,
> Some say.
> I say it just
> Begins to live
> That day.

The shelves are crowded with silent people who talk most admirably, with characters who have acted nobly or abominably in fact or fiction. In that book you will find Benvenuto Cellini, equally expert

in carving medallions and people; in this one Cesare Borgia, who
served with confidence and poisoned with pride. Aaron Burr stops
casually to tell you about "My friend Hamilton, who I shot." Sidney
Smith informs us that "gout is the only enemy I don't want to have
at my feet." In that great poem the twisted dwarf form Twickenham,
Alexander Pope, condescends to immortalize a lord as a "mere white
curd of asses' milk." Smiling through Paine's biography you hear
Twain drawling that he resigned from the Confederate Army because
he did not wish to shoot anyone to whom he had not been introduced.
In his *Autobiography* you hear Gibbon, plump and satisfied, say, "I
darted a contemptuous look at the monuments of antiquity." Coleridge's ancient Mariner grasps your lapel to weave a magic spell as he
makes dead men row a spectral ship upon a rotting sea. In term-paper
time you sigh with Huckleberry Finn as he says, "A person's conscience just ain't got no sense." In these books you find the glitter and
the glory, the humor and the pathos, the faith and the despair of the
pageant of man.

The writers of these books have been of all faiths and no faith.
They have seen man as noble in reason or as lice on a space-lost bulb.
Some have seen him with the light of another world in his eyes; others
in Fitzgerald's words have seen him "standing at twilight on a deserted
range with an empty rifle in my hands and the targets down." Unfortunately, in the production of literature the sinners have a considerable
edge over the saints. Byron is more interesting than Cotton Mather,
and the bulk of published sermons have all the captivating charm of
conventional textbooks on education. Though John Donne flames across
the centuries with undimmed splendor, most Puritan literature is read
by isolated scholars. However, I have been greatly influenced by both
the saints and the sinners. To make these remarks relevant to the
occasion, I have chosen authors who greatly interested and influenced
me in my college and university years.

John Bunyan's *Pilgrim's Progress* may, as one of my former high
school students put it, be too "full of sin and righteousness" to influence young people today, but that is no reflection on Bunyan or his
classic.

Bunyan was an uneducated man who wrote a great classic because
he had poignantly memorable experiences, creative imagination, and
an amazing saturation in Biblical rhythms and phraseology. His agonizing, sometimes hallucinatory experiences, made him feel as if he
were a brand snatched from the burning — which, in fact, he was. The
world for Bunyan was Vanity Fair, a place to deny and to desert.

Christian is intent upon escape from the city of destruction; he runs a hard race through great dangers, battle and smoke, beatings and cold water. He passes through Vanity Fair, that great booth of the lust of the eye and the pride of the flesh, but he sees no values there. He hurries on to the land where the shining ones commonly walk.

Pilgrim's Progress is a classic of universal Christian experience. We *are* wayfarers and burden bearers; we are adrift on a slender spar in an infinite sea, where there is but one Lighthouse. The authentic experience in the precise allegory enables us to share the hard journey through Vanity Fair, Doubting Castle, The Slough of Despond, and The Valley of Humiliation. Yet I feel an unconvincing Anabaptistic strain in the book; the world must indeed be denied but it must also be won. There is something a bit warped and fanatical about Christian. Flight and denial are preludes to Christian conquest.

I was first attracted to Samuel Johnson by Carlyle's magnificent portrait in *Heroes and Hero Worship*. Carlyle, whose acidity spared few but Scotchmen, who called J. S. Mill "the most unending ass in Christendom," and in a bad moment said that his friend Tennyson was a lifeguard wasted on poetry, thought Johnson one of the world's great men. Fortunately, Boswell agreed with him many years before and wrote the magnificent *Life of Dr. Johnson*, which I have read through in its entirety twice and many times in parts. It is the best bedside book in literature. Johnson's personality, comments, poems, essays, and *Lives of the Poets* have been a major influence in my life.

Samuel Johnson once said that it was the biographical part of literature that he loved best. Boswell has given us a speaking likeness of that burly, dominating figure, as he thunders his "Yes Sir, No Sir, Why Sir?" over the "dark backward and abysm of time." Through Boswell's magical gift the real man emerges, and when that booming voice settles an argument in an elegant eighteenth-century drawing room concerning the respective merits of the poets Derrick and Smart by saying, "Sir, there is no settling the precedency between a louse and a flea," we feel the living man among us. Since Boswell refused to make a kitten out of his tiger, we get the full Sam Johnson, burly, slovenly, uncouth, bolting his tea by the quart, sweating over his pork, and yet presiding in the most dignified literary circles with the imperial dignity of the prince of letters that he was.

Johnson was one of the world's great men. He was strikingly independent; he never truckled or flattered or begged. He bowed to the authority of Scripture but to no man. His manners could be revoltingly rude and movingly tender. When he was engaged in arguing for victory, he could toss and gore opponents. His generosity was unparalleled; he practically ran an alms-house of his own with complaining inmates indeed. His learning was precise and enormous. His published prose rolls and heaves along in rhythmic sweeps and surges; but his conversation sparkles. As a conversationalist he has hardly known a peer, because of his vast learning, remarkable wit, clear reasoning, and imperturbable nerve. On hearing that a musical performance was difficult he said, "I wish it had been impossible." Angling he described as a process with "a stick and a string with a worm at one end and a fool at the other." Of Mr. Foote he said, "Foote is impartial, he lies of everybody." He once said, "If I did act Hamlet as Garrick does I should frighten the ghost." When two ladies came to him expressing their satisfaction that the naughty words had been omitted from a piece, he exclaimed, "What, my dears! Then you have been looking for them." He was the tyrannical dictator of the most brilliant literary club of his day and when he died Boswell justly said: "He has made a chasm."

Johnson was a devoutly religious man. Suffering from a lifelong and vile melancholy, obsessed by thoughts of madness and death as extinction into a white silence, haunted by a sense of guilt and sin, he was driven to God by despair. He saw the vanity of merely human wishes and looked to eternity. His *Book of Prayers* and his meditations reveal his need of commitment to Jesus Christ as Savior. The Bible was to him "the sacred volume in which are contained the revelations of God." He accepted the cardinal doctrines of the Christian faith. He did not bury his light under a bushel. He did not compartmentalize his life. He expressed the wish that *The Rambler* would be conformable to the precepts of Christianity. The implications of Christianity are in his poems and prose; but he was especially articulate about his faith in intellectual circles. When Dr. Adams asked him in an illustrious company of eighteenth-century rationalists, "What do you mean by damned?", he said, "Sent to Hell, Sir, and punished everlastingly." He believed in an objective, eternal moral order and said so. He believed in the vanity of human wishes but not of human life because at lane's end lay the gateway to fulfillment.

Literature was not in Johnson's opinion to be severed from religious and moral considerations. His critical principles were based in order of priority upon revealed religion, truth to nature, and the classical tradition. A writer's duty is always to make the world better, not merely to report it. Shakespeare's truth to nature is illustrious, but Shakespeare fails because "he seems to write without any moral purpose." The criticism is unfair, but the principle is true. Literature for Johnson fuses pleasure and truth to make men better, and men are at the best when they are Christian.

But one cannot study literature and remain with the saints. The writer who really made me feel starkly the predicament of man without God was Thomas Hardy. Hardy was my first real experience with the well of loneliness. His works are an attempt to find an answer to the pain and terror of life, an explanation for the mystery of "infinitely gentle, infinitely suffering things." Hardy gets no answer from the heath. Life is controlled by an automatic natural principle "loveless and hateless," a blind irrational force, which operates

> like a knitter drowsed
> whose fingers play in skilled unmindfulness.

This vast energy stunts the trees, darkens the heath, stokes the passions into disaster, blinds the eyes of good men, and weaves life's little ironies like the collision of the iceberg and the Titanic.

Hardy's major novels pit largely passive men and women against massive internal and external forces. Tess of the D'Urbervilles, instinct with tenderness and conscience, is opposed by her father, her mother, Alec, Angel Claire, society, nature, hereditary tendencies, and chance. Everything goes wrong everywhere. The gentle girl goes to the gallows after the "President of the Immortals had ended his sport with Tess." Eustacia Vye, so "beautiful exceedingly," becomes fatally attached to the fatally different Blym Yeobright and ends in darkness in a black pool in rain and storm. Marty South in *The Woodlanders* is last seen at the grave of Giles Winterbourne, crying, "But he was a good man," as if *that* made any difference. Poor idealistic Jude in *Jude the Obscure* seeks light and learning and finds his three children hanging from the rafters with the note "Done because we were too many." The wretched bondsmen sweat at their oars and then walk the plank into a shoreless sea. Looking at life Hardy asks:

> Has some vast imbecility
> Mighty to build and bend
> But impotent to tend
> Framed us in jest and left us to hazardry?

It is no good to come back from Lyonesse with magic in your eyes because "Crass Casualty obstructs the sun and rain."

I was young when I first read these books and poems. I did not see all their faults, although I knew the dice were always loaded. I knew that an unconscious will could not have "dark designs." Yet the books left a dull, stunning grief. I felt what it meant to be without God. I felt also an enduring pity for all suffering things. I realized too what later experience confirmed, that complete naturalism is impossible for a sensitive mind, because if it were, it just couldn't care.

I went to college early enough to care for Matthew Arnold. I was moved and still am by both Arnolds, the Arnold of the poetry and the Arnold of the critical essays. The former Arnold is the disenchanted intellectual, sick of his age, lamenting the loss of faith, the elegist of impossible loyalties and sombre memories. The Arnold of the essays is urbane and impales the Philistines, and enjoys being dogmatic because he knows he is right.

Arnold's *Essays on Criticism* are superb reading; even Eliot admits that, although he calls him "an undergraduate in philosophy and a Philistine in religion." There is first of all the suave and impeccable prose with which he so deftly scissors opponents with sweetness and light. There is the relevant sense of tradition. There are many concrete bits of wisdom as well as big bits of blindness as in the judgment of Shelley as "an ineffectual angel beating his luminous wings in the void." Shelley was far from an angel and anyone who tries to keep up with Shelley's scholarship will doubt the term "ineffectual." Arnold helped me most in two ways. The first was by his distinction between the personal, historical, and real estimates of literature. There are books we value highly because we fulfill ourselves in them. Maugham's *The Moon and Sixpence* was such a book for me. It is not great literature, but it was an imaginative realization for me. The historical estimate accounts for Anne Bradstreet's poetry in Foerster's *American Prose and Poetry.* It isn't nearly as good as much of the *Literary Review.* The real estimate is what one should always aim at. Briefly it is simply a fusion of perfect form and truthful and serious substance. Such a fusion constitutes a criticism of life. By a criticism of life Arnold meant that great literature presents heightened experience as a test for ordinary experience, wise experience as a judgment on ordinary living. The experience Arnold prefers is humanistic rather than Christian, but the formula can readily be used for Christian purposes.

T. S. Eliot, the last writer whom I consider, has exerted an enormous and paradoxical influence upon contemporary poetry and criticism. Eliot, the classicist in criticism, as he calls himself, has written some of the most symbolic and suggestive poetry of our time. His influence in poetry has been largely technical; the Christian spirit that informs the best of it has had few echoes. Modern formalist criticism, with its lemon-squeezer technique, its emphasis upon close textual analysis, upon the poem as organism, upon psychological rather than logical unity, owes much to Eliot; but it has largely rejected his more mature value judgments. Eliot as a Christian critic has been an outstanding exception in the maze of modern critical outlooks. Where is the center of that judgment and what is its value to us as Christian students?

Eliot maintains that formal criticism though indispensable is never enough. It is necessary to determine whether the work we judge is literature, but it is inadequate to offer a final evaluation. Formal criticism must always be completed by criticism from a "definite ethical and theological standpoint." Man is a whole being and the writer moves us wholly. At the center of our being is our religious commitment; one cannot be concerned solely with technique; one absorbs ideas, images, emotions which involve the centrality of our being. A Christian reader must judge the total impact of a work of art by moral and religious standards. Hemingway's masterpiece *A Farewell to Arms*, though obviously literature, is not great literature because its morality is naturalistic. Since Eliot judges from this viewpoint he is hard on contemporary literature, which he feels on the whole to be degrading. He quotes with approval Maritain's observation on "the unconcealed and palpable influence of the devil on an important part of contemporary literature." Modern man's life and art are in the wasteland, the dry land, and are spiritually sterile. This does not mean for Eliot a retreat from culture, a closing of Hemingway and Jeffers, but rather a keener awareness of their grave defects.

These Christian criteria Eliot has been privileged to disseminate through much of Western culture. Though his theological criteria have been generally dismissed, yet the fact that he has been widely taught and read in every American college has, at least, made many college students aware that an insistence upon moral and religious standards is something more than a Puritan anachronism. He has given light and leading to many of us.

Before closing, I should like to mention a few other books that have meant a great deal to me. There was that model textbook, Stace's *A Critical History of Greek Philosophy*, so admirably lucid in its handling of profound ideas. There was Galsworthy's *Forsyte Saga*, that brilliant story of beauty and greed in aristocratic British circles. I like such books. I like books about cultivated human beings; I prefer their company to poor whites, perverts, heroin addicts, and New York cafe society swine. There was Henry Adam's *Education*, the epigrammatic and incisive account of the development of a mind, the prelude to naturalism, the convincing demonstration that the course of history from Caesar to Coolidge can hardly be called evolution. There is the great poetry of Browning with its continuing Anglo-Saxon heroic strain "I was ever a fighter."

Is there any moral or lesson to be drawn from all this? Of course, literature is enjoyable and enlarging. The books you reluctantly blast your way through will hardly help you. Yet we must always be critical as well as appreciative readers and, if God gives us the gift, creative students. Not one of us can by industry, will, or desire become a genius, but we can all purposefully and realistically use all the talents we have. Avoiding pretentious and naive assertions about Christian scholarship and Christian art, we can hope to do something more than merely record with scrupulous accuracy the influence of Goethe upon Matthew Arnold or the incidence of the word *purple* in Emily Dickinson's poetry, however commendable these activities may be within their province. Though we can hardly hope to solve the problems connected with Christianity and culture that have haunted the Christian mind for nearly two thousand years, we can at least create an atmosphere in which gifted minds are free to work out original solutions.

Mr. F. O'Connor has a fine little story about two boys. The older boy, supposedly sophisticated and knowledgeable, invites his young friend to an evening of attic window peeping on a neighboring husband and wife. O'Connor skillfully develops an attitude of prurient expectation, but all the boys see is two people praying at their bedside. While watching thus ignominiously, the younger boy feels someone else watching them, somebody from beyond. He felt he could never after that be sophisticated like his friend, because, as he says, "Always beyond the appearances I would only see eternity watching." Thus the Christian sees all things, thus he reads and thus he writes — with eternity watching.

Calvinism and Literary Criticism

The Banner (June 26, 1959)

John Calvin died in 1564, the year in which Shakespeare was born. Though there have been varying opinions about this exchange of genius, no one has doubted the genius. The problem consists in fruitfully uniting the Christian vision of the former with the artistic splendor of the latter and the tradition of modern literature. Literary criticism follows literature; it does not create it. Calvin had a wide primary acquaintance with Hebrew, Greek, and Latin master-pieces; he could not take into account the new drama of Shakespeare, the flaming lyrics of romanticism, grim, naturalistic fiction, and the dizzying varieties of contemporary literary art. Calvin's literary criticism is, of necessity, partially dated.

Calvin's critical outlook has often been modified and distorted by a Calvinistic climate of opinion. Calvinists have often tended to exalt subject matter and to minimize technique, to want literature that has a "palpable design upon us." They have forgotten that successful art fuses significant content with commensurate form. Calvinists have often judged art biographically and personalistically, evaluating the novel or poem in terms of the life of the author; whereas the work of art remains an independent creation to be understood but not judged by an author's life. Calvinism, with its emphasis upon control, mea-sure, and balance, has had a particular difficulty in appreciating the roll and surge of romantic art, the literature of the untrammeled ego and the dream.

Calvinism has also, however, provided certain conditions and at-titudes favorable to artistic achievement. In freeing society and the state from the church, it has also to an extent freed the artist. By its insistence that this is God's world, Calvinism has counteracted the Puritan distrust of the sensuous and the concrete as trivial and sinful. Calvinism with its feeling for common people has stimulated a respect for the dignity of man so essential to literature. Finally, however spe-cific communities may have provincialized or massacred the idea, Cal-vinism has been characterized by a love of liberty; and intelligent liberty is what every artist needs — liberty but not the trough.

Calvin was not a literary critic. He never made such a claim; neither do his followers. He gives us theological insights, penetrating com-ments and a certain outlook, but no sustained body of critical writing. What do these comments come to?

Calvin finds the source of the beautiful in God, the great artist who made the fathomless universe with its unending delightfulness. God is glorious; His glory fills the world and is marked by clarity, harmony, and purity. Man must continue the creative effort on the human level. When he uses the materials of the universe to make art, he should do so according to the Word and Spirit of God. What does that mean?

Calvin believes this to be a rational universe, patterned by God, full of observable harmonies. These patterns the writer reproduces. In doing so the artist submits to the nature of things, and by submitting to the nature of things he discovers the law of artistic integrity. Through the influence of the Holy Spirit both Christian and non-Christian afford insight into the nature of things. This remains true despite the divisive and dissonant influence of Satan. Homer's characters are true to life. The purples and silks of Donne's sermons, the homespun beauty of Bunyan, the imperial drama of Shakespeare, the meticulous realism of Trollope, the moral insight of Hawthorne, the pity of Steinbeck constitute authentic art. These men portray truth even though some of them portray the world without the Word, because the truth is according to the Word and Spirit of God whether one knows it or not.

Calvin's specific literary principles have been succinctly summed up by Dr. Wincelius. They are: (1) a sense of the correct idea of the object; (2) an invitation to the writer to efface himself when he is confronted with the greatness of his task; (3) an appeal to simplicity and sobriety; (4) an appeal to a well-balanced view of reality; (5) a desire for clarity and purity.

These principles show clearly the influence of classical literature and French humanism. Great literature has been written under this banner but not romanticism. The habitual tendency of romantics to color the universe with their own psychological dyes and to beat out their metre in organic and frequently in very free patterns needs a different sanction. Furthermore, contemporary literature with its dissonance and disjunction, its preoccupation with myth, symbol, and suggestion, its concern with the unconscious, is at variance with Calvin's sense of balance, measure, and restraint. For some that means disapproval; to others it suggests a narrowness in Calvin that should be widened to make use of the principle of organic form and a fuller range of imaginative and subjective.

Calvin preferred a simple, clear style. He believed that the prevailing style of the Bible was simple, rude, naive. Such a style best expresses the majesty of God. The occasional variations simply suggest that God does not consider Himself bound by a plain medium. We are not bound to a plain medium either, though Calvin clearly prefers it. Such a style is admirably fitted to the *Institutes,* but it would ruin Melville's *Moby Dick* or Hart Crane's poetry. A good style is an appropriate one; and the complex, ambiguous experience of *Moby Dick* would be flattened by an expository diction.

If one were to translate Calvin's principles into contemporary preference, he would, it seems to me, prefer a soberly realistic literature, a typical and objectively verifiable report of life. He would regard naturalism false in its philosophy and hopelessly biased in its report of human experience; he would be ill at ease with a stream-of-consciousness novel; he might find Eliot's Christian vision admirable but be baffled by the technique; he would find Graham Greene demonstrating the doctrine of total depravity with a vengeance. If he had to write a "Christian" novel, he would probably prefer to write a new edition of the *Institutes.*

Five Travelers

The Reformed Journal (May, 1956)

Many of the world's great fictional characters have been travelers. Don Quixote rides along the sunbaked, straggling roads of Spain pursuing his broken dreams. The Ancient Mariner and Captain Ahab were lost in eerie Southern waters. And we, landlocked and envious, watch them from the pierheads of our quiet lives. The voyage is, of course, admirable narrative structure, but it is also good technique for symbolism, since life has from time immemorial been called a voyage, a journey; and around this central metaphor allegory, myth, and meditation quite naturally cluster.

I wish to discuss five travelers who travel by lane, railroad, the river, and the sea. Taken together they represent five major aspects of the American vision, five outlooks upon reality. The travelers are Christian in *Pilgrim's Progress*, the protaganist of Hawthorne's "Celestial Railroad," Ishmael in *Moby Dick*, Samuel Clemens, and Huckleberry Finn. In knowing them one gets to know something of the

> American muse, whose strong and diverse heart
> So many men have tried to understand.
> The pure elixir, the American thing.

Christian, as we all know, appears in an English book, but he had, nevertheless, an immense part in the information of the American mind. With his archaic speech, odd clothes, hurried passage, and transcendental ideal, he seems at first remote. He is fleeing Vanity Fair, where we like to have a good address. A bit warped, fanatic, and

Anabaptistic, he wants to get through the narrow gate with the scantiest baggage. Christian travels to heaven on English lanes. Rural England becomes the setting of cosmic drama. When Christian stumbles through the Slough of Despond, he is struggling through an English bog. Vanity Fair is any English market; the Giant Despair any English landlord. The imagery of Scripture fuses with that of the English country-side. But we know he is traveling another road too. Vanity Fair, Doubting Castle, the Slough of Despond, the Valley of Humiliation, and the River of Death are recognizable stations on the Christian's spiritual journey. Bunyan is recounting a common spiritual odyssey without writing a tract.

Pilgrim's Progress was on the rude shelf of many a rough cabin in colonial New England. It did not serve as decor to impress the visiting clergyman, but it, together with a few other books, formed the core of Puritan reading which, in turn, formed the core of the Puritan mind. Christian was both hero and vision. Although the book has subsided into little more than an unread conversational counter, it remains a permanent statement of a distinct American vision.

Years later, when Nathaniel Hawthorne lifted his pen to write, eight generations of New Englanders looked over his shoulder, and the ghost of Judge Hawthorne who hanged the witches roiled the black ink into which he dipped his pen. He grew up in Salem where the echoes of Puritan sermons were not yet silent. There was a blackness in him and a grim realism that made him see that "the depravity of the unregenerate man is no myth." He had no taste for the catch-penny wisdom of a worldly-wiseman like Poor Richard, nor could he accept the religion of Christian. A friend of the transcendentalists, he could not accept their vision of life. He found fault with Emerson's perpetual smile because "he ought to wait for something to smile at." The vague, cloudy, transcendentalism of Emerson seemed to him a misreading of life.

Neither could he abide the booming affirmation of Whitman with his indiscriminate acceptance of everything, his romantic expansiveness, and his blindness to the problem of evil. He disliked Whitman when he said:

And nothing, not God is greater than one's self is

or:

Clear and sweet is my soul, and clear and sweet is all that is not my soul.

Hawthorne simply could not understand the man who could say to Traubel that it was a comfort to him that the Lord finds a place for all, for the bedbug, the rat, the flea, even for Matthew Arnold. He used his sense of humor to ridicule the transcendentalists' position; and he did this most effectively in the story "The Celestial Railroad."

In the story the protagonist visits the city of Destruction, where he is pleased to discover a railroad to the Celestial City. He puts his burden in a baggage-car, settles down in a comfortable coach and rolls to Zion. The cars slide smoothly through the Slough of Despond, knife easily through the Hill Difficulty in a splendid tunnel on to Vanity Fair. The city has now many churches served by such admirable clergymen as Mr. Clog-the-Spirit and Dr. Wind of Doctrine. After a happy, dawdling sojourn, he resumes his journey on the commodious train. When he arrives at the dark river, a ferry boat awaits to carry him over. But the boat, he now discovers, leads to perdition. In attempting to escape this dark doom, he awakes rather tritely to find it a dream. But the point has been made. The transcendental way is a misreading of life; it is an illusion.

The protaganist appears under many names in many stories. He may be Ethan Brand, Goodman Brown, Aylmer, or Giovanni. Whoever he is, he soon discovers that evil is real and that there is no hope for a better world until the human heart is regenerated. In "Earth's Holocaust," the reformers burn up all impediments to virtue, but a cynical bystander reminds them that nothing will avail unless they cleanse the human heart, "unless they hit upon some method of purifying that foul cavern." Hawthorne's vision is a vision of the evil in men's hearts. It is a vision that will be deepened and intensified by James and Faulkner. Henry James wrote book after book to demonstrate the insatiable egoism of the human heart, man's inhumanity to man, his emotional cannibalism whereby he devours other people to advance himself. The work of Faulkner is a tremendously complex saga thick with the evidences of man's depravity.

When *Moby Dick* appeared in 1851 it was unhonored and unsung; yet today the great white whale haunts the imaginations of men as it flashes its malevolent whiteness through the Southern seas. When the good ship "Pequod" "blindly plunged like fate into the lone Atlantic" the greatest voyage in American literature began. Melville wrote the book for many reasons, some of which he knew and some of which only his critics know. In the criticism of this book, if anywhere, "Freuds rush in where angels fear to tread." The interpretations of *Moby Dick* are legion and complicated. I am no Melvillian, but I do believe I see

194   *"The Unextinguished Hearth":* Literature

something of the vision of the book, and the vision lies not in Ahab but in Ishmael.

Moby Dick is a dramatic narrative with philosophical implications. It is a blast against Emersonian optimism. Emerson for Melville is a "Plato who talks through his nose," who thinks that "pain is a tickle." Captain Ahab is obsessed with pain; he is larger than man. Ahab, says Melville, is above common; he is the ungodly god-like man, the dreamer of the avenging dream, and, unknown to himself, "Fate's Lieutenant." He sees in the great whale the incarnation of all that cracks the brain, an "intelligent malignity." For Ahab the whale becomes a symbol of the mystery of evil whether he be agent or principle, and in attempting to destroy the whale he destroys himself and his crew — all but one — the protagonist of the story, the wanderer Ishmael. For Ishmael the meaning of the whale lies in its whiteness, and whiteness is an ambiguous symbol. Moby Dick is the source of light and heat as well as demonic, destroying power. He is a symbol of an ambiguous universe. And what does a man do with an ambivalent symbol of an ambivalent universe? There is only one thing to do — accept it. Ishmael is an agnostic. Ishmael accepts the whale as an unfathomable mystery. When man comes to the final questions, he cannot get beyond the ambiguous whiteness toward which his feelings will be ambivalent. Ishmael is the herald of Henry Adams who said that whether man investigates religion or science

In neither case does — or can — the mind read anything but a different reflection of its own features.

And Henry Adams was a prophet to E. A. Robinson who said, "We are children in a spiritual kindergarten trying to spell God with the wrong blocks." And Robinson is echoed in Fitzgerald, who felt "that I was standing at twilight on a deserted range, with an empty rifle in my hands and the targets down." All stare into the same gray mist, but with each writer the heart grows sadder. The evil Hawthorne saw in man's heart now permeates the heart of the universe itself.

But the nineteenth century had other visions. There was the raucous, boastful, superbly self-confident voice of the frontier, manifest destiny, America unlimited. And that brings us to the incomparable redhead, Mark the Double Twain, whose Missouri drawl caused a cataract of laughter for many years. The sunny laughter changed into a biting snarl over the years but we want first to look at Twain, the traveler, the Tom Sawyer in him as he went to Europe and wrote his chipper book, *Innocents Abroad.* The book was written from the viewpoint of a cocky Missouri philistine, who reports things honestly, who feels that Wagner's music is better than it sounds, who comments on Raphael's paintings in terms of yardage and square inches of color, who estimates cathedrals by the pound, who finds Palestine a dreary, sun-baked, tight little land where the inhabitants need passports to stretch out for a nap. Mark went through the Near East jibing left and right. Seeing a picture of the Queen of Sheba visiting Solomon he says, "I shall say to myself, you look fine, Madame, but your feet are not clean and you smell like a camel." He finds the gondolier in Venice "a mangy barefooted guttersnipe." So he travels through Europe puncturing fakes and exposing exploitation. Mark does praise some of the fine things in Europe, but the mood is one of ardent Americanism; there is no doubt where this traveler stands and for him America is promises. Mark Twain in this book is an inverse symbol of the American booster, of the American belief in progress. In Boston a little old lady was asked why she didn't travel; to which she replied, "Why should I travel when I am already here." The mood of *Innocents Abroad* is "Why should I travel when I am already here."

Mark's early faith in the democratic experiment was never as robust or intense as Whitman's. Whitman actually hoped by means of his poems "to institute the lifelong love of comrades" and "to plant companionship as thick as trees along the rivers of America." Twain never hoped for as much and so his faith was more realistic and typically American. Twain never rejected democracy; what he rejected was human nature. He never rose to the beatific vision of Whitman; he believed with Lincoln that all men are equal, especially in their orneriness. Yet although he got to see with Sandburg that

> The big fish eat the little fish,
> The little fish eat shrimps
> And the shrimps eat mud . . .

he also always felt with Sandburg that somehow

> The people will live on
> The learning and blundering people will live on
> You can't laugh off their capacity to take it.

That kind of chastened democratic faith is close to how most Americans feel; and it remains today articulate in American literature as one can see by reading Sandburg, Steinbeck, Saroyan, and even MacLeish.

Mark Twain's sunny spirits were successively eroded by the gilded age of General Grant, personal disaster, and the dog-eat-dog capitalism of the 80s and 90s. The romantic Tom Sawyer in him was displaced by Huckleberry Finn.

Huckleberry Finn is a realist before he floats down the Mississippi; when he comes back he is a cynic. He has never trusted civilization; when he returns his distrust has been proved to him. The last sentence he says is:

> But I reckon I got to light out for the territory ahead of the rest, because Aunt Sally she's going to adopt me and civilize me, and I can't stand it. I been there before.

He can't stand it. Not only because he wants to be an idler, unwashed and drifting, not only because he hates grammar and Sunday school, but because he distrusts the whole alluvial civilization through which his raft has floated.

Huck and Nigger Jim float down the Mississippi. He says, "You feel mighty free and easy and comfortable on board a raft." That is right, but you better not get off. When you get to shore you meet the Shepherdsons and the Grangerfords and the utterly murderous and insane feuding. When you get near the shore, you meet the iniquitous frauds, the Duke and the Dauphin. By the time they finish a few performances, Huck is "ashamed of the human race." Deeper in the South an accident occurs on a boat. Huck asks:

> "Anybody hurt?"
> "No'm. Killed a nigger."
> "Well, that's lucky; because sometimes people do get hurt."

The river of life flows on and the shores are inhabited by the scum at Pokeville, the feuding pseudo-aristocrats, and the greedy charlatans. The shores are full of pestilence, but the river is not safe either. Floods come and houses float by with dead men in them; animals float by dead, distended, and foul.

Huckleberry Finn is on an open river after all; he is in an open universe where nothing seems certain. He can be loyal to Nigger Jim only by being disloyal to his people. Huckleberry Finn is traveling in a naturalistic world; and his book is a prelude to the literature of the naturalists.

Ernest Hemingway once said, "All modern American literature comes from a book by Mark Twain called *Huckleberry Finn.*" Though

Hemingway had in mind particularly technical matters, the statement holds in relation to philosophical outlook or vision. Man is nothing in a naturalistic world. Values have been lost. After Clemens, who still had an innate and unextinquishable kindliness, come the grim prophets of disaster and meaninglessness; Crane, to whom men are lice clinging to "a whirling ice-locked, disease-stricken, space-lost bulb"; Dreiser, to whom the world is a stinking mess; London, to whom man is at best a crafty animal. What has man to return to after disillusion: he has, as Eliot says:

> The stale food mouldering in the larder
> The stale thoughts mouldering in their minds,
> Each unable to disguise his meanness
> From himself, because it is known to the other.

If there is no image of God in man, if there is no contact with a divine order, if man is only an intelligent beast and has no tomorrow, if the sacramental dimension is lost, then one may get a literature with pity but it will have little nobility. After all, as Larry says in O'Neill's *The Iceman Cometh*, "You can't build a marble temple out of a mixture of manure and mud." That is the dead end of Twain's naturalism.

Christian, the protagonist in "The Celestial Railroad," Ishmael, Mark Twain in *Innocents Abroad*, and Huckleberry Finn suggest, though they do not exhaust, the range of American literary vision. The basic visions are there. Bunyan's faith, though remarkably refined and deepened by Eliot, is the same faith at bottom. Faulkner's world of dense and insoluble evil is a darker version of Hawthorne. Ishmael's agnosticism is still a living option. There is not much of Emersonian optimism or Twain's early jauntiness left in American literature, but the coming political platforms will show that it is still alive. There is indeed a new note of tenderness and mysticism in Hemingway's *The Old Man and the Sea*, but the tenderness is toward the marlin whom the old man regards as more noble and able than man. The story is still powered by the law of the jungle. The traveler is still in an open boat on a cruel sea, and the winner takes — nothing.

Thomas Wolfe, another traveler, sought the future in the past, but looking homeward, he found he could not go there. Yet he had a vague faith in America and its people. He concludes his last book with the memorable words:

> A wind is rising and the rivers flow.

Wolfe based his faith upon the unextinguishable spirit of man. In our world of measureless spaces, crowding peoples, and mammoth bombs such a faith seems ungrounded. The traveler needs a hand from heaven.

Prudes and Savages

The Reformed Journal (March, 1973)

Brit19ritish and American literature in the nineteenth century was predominantly restrained, genteel, and at times, prudish. When Walt Whitman sang the body electric and the splendor of the flesh, he was violently attacked by literary critics and also fired from his government position. Rossetti and his friends received contumely for serving "the fleshly school of poetry." Even Thackeray complained that the public would not permit him to portray a man. The formula for popular fiction in America was "a little history, a little courage, a strong measure of lawful and pure love, a dash of rattling adventure, and a happy marriage to come out of it all." In the early years of the twentieth century, Dreiser's *Sister Carrie* was withdrawn from publication because adultery was obvious, even though never dwelt on or described. Sex was handled gingerly and tangentially. Coarse language was very rare. Most novels could be read by the entire family, and magazines that couldn't were short-lived.

Over the years, however, the reaction to this restraint and sometimes excessive delicacy has reached the point of blatant overkill. What began as an honest attempt to portray life has frequently abandoned reason, good sense, and balanced perspectives for gross and uninhibited candor. The lily of unattainable virtue has been replaced by the tarantula of animal passion. The novels, the plays, and even the poems teem with barnyard imagery, bedhopping fornicators, slithering gay blades, and panting Lesbians. Martha Foley's *Best American Stories* portrays a seedy world of cloacal themes and grotesquely immoral characters. The characters devour themselves and others in a haze of alcohol and drugs. There is little effort to portray a balanced view of man, to see life steadily and to see it whole. One gets the raw savagery in human experience as if this were the whole of it. In plays like *The American Dream,* by Albee, this savagery is raised to the level of the absurd; and in *Who's Afraid of Virginia Woolf?* one sees two intelligent people destroying each other in a miasma of alcohol and recrimination. There is in many gifted minds, as Fiedler put it, "a weariness with striving to be men." The downward comparisons have become downward actions.

I am keenly aware that moralistic and theological criticism is painfully irritating today to many writers and readers even though critics like Johnson, Eliot, and Lewis practice it. The hoary chestnuts of originality, creativity, and esthetic skill are used to bombard the hostile critic. What seems to me mere prurience and voyeurism, an adolescent urge to shock, or an utterly wrong celebration of sexuality, is supposed to be redeemed by artistic savvy. It stinks but it is beautiful. I would go further. Even when the author writes from a profound sense of ironic despair and portrays an utterly crummy world as Beckett does, he is engaged in flagrant misrepresentation. The grotesque distortions exceed credibility, and whatever satirical legitimacy there may be is ruined by unbelievable excess. I believe that every important literary work has an intrinsic moral and theological dimension, that this dimension cannot be antiseptically separated from flawless execution, and that, when a novel falsifies life, corrodes the imagination, and attenuates the spiritual life, it should be courageously judged. One may need to know such works to understand the mind of the age, but one should observe that they reveal a fever that indicates appalling spiritual illness.

I hold no brief for an imaginative world that disregards the fearful moral and psychological lesions of life, the evil, the sin, and the unhappiness. But one does not have to choose between opulent garbage and witless primness. Henry James often gives us a profound sense of pervasive evil without clinical and detailed analyses. Robert Frost gives us, as he said, real potatoes but with the dirt off. Willa Cather saw the greed and barbarism of man, but placed it in a framework of honorable tradition and human dignity. *King Lear* teems with animal imagery; man can hardly sink lower than in this play, but there is in the play the Christlike gentleness and love of Cordelia as well as the vicious barbarism of Regan; the perfidy of Edmund is balanced by nobility, and, at the play's end, promise. As in *Moby Dick*, life had its unfathomable mysteries, but there is in life both good and evil, and Ishmael has the wisdom to see and accept it. Neither work ends in savagery, and both suggest a wise maturity and ripeness.

Romans 1 gives a fearful picture of a culture destroyed from within and the words have a startling appropriateness today. The "fierce faith undying" of the Puritan past is almost out in our culture, and the impressive words of Eliot in *Thoughts After Lambeth* are, it seems to me, sadly true:

> The world is trying to experiment of attempting to form a civilized but non-Christian mentality. The experiment will fail; but we must be very patient in awaiting its collapse; meanwhile redeeming the time: so that the Faith may be preserved alive through the the the dark ages before us; to renew and rebuild civilization, and save the world from suicide.

Pens, Pennies, Patrons

The Reformed Journal (November, 1957)

A writer writes; he fills notebooks, cartons, a trunk, a room. He writes till he is boxed in between unsubmitted and rejected manuscripts, and if the room should go up in flames he would be savoring the phrases with which he will immortalize his tragedy. A writer writes till he grows fat and flabby on public incense or until he is hanged as a disturber of the peace. He composes until success, antagonism, the failure of his shaping imagination, or death stops him. And just before he dies he will probably make a striking remark or compose an epitaph.

Unfortunately such literary compulsion, such a seething urge to verbalization, does not always reside in genius. It is shared by Zane Grey, who wrote sixty-three novels with a sale above 19,000,000 copies. It is shared by Mrs. Sigourney, who wrote edifying effusions on such subjects as "monody for the Death of the Principal of the Connecticut Retreat for the Insane." It is shared by the poetess of the Ladies' Aid gurgling a long-rimed poem on the pastor's twenty-fifth anniversary, and it is shared by the bard of Woden, Iowa, singing "Man on the Tractor."

The good and the bad; there are thousands upon thousands of them in the United States dulling their pens, blurring their pencils, shredding their typewriter ribbons. A few are worth our consideration; for the rest we reserve a kindly irony and the comfort of Browning's Andrea del Sarto:

> Ah, but a man's reach should exceed his grasp,
> Or what's a heaven for?

Theirs be the glory of the imperfect and the earned rejection slip.

Now, the poet, the dramatist, the novelist, the original essayist, the gifted biographer — all face large problems in our country. I shall treat five major problems and try to give you the facts. These problems are economic, cultural, linguistic, personal, and spiritual.

Economic Problems

The writer, like everybody else, needs money, but he has often had to get along on very little of it. Genius has always known poor pay. Edmund Spenser yearned for security; Milton received a pittance for *Paradise Lost;* Coleridge was a pensioner on other men's purses all of his literary life; Browning was supported by his parents till he was thirty, after which Elizabeth Barrett assisted in the project; Poe lived in shanties, whereas his characters live in mansions of unparalleled splendor; Stephen Crane was almost a Bowery bum. Indeed there is truth in Coleridge's statement that the literary life is but bread and cheese by chance; and in the lament of John Ciardi, contemporary poet and teacher, who has said, "I get my crumbs in books and my bread from student themes." The making of literature has often required a pachydermatous hide and a spartan digestion. And even rich men like Henry James wished the psychological support of sales; he hoped, he said, to grow "in his temperature garden some specimens of rank exotic whose leaves are rustling checks."

Do not be misled by the klieg lights shining on the fortunes of Fitzgerald, Twain, and Marquand. Most writers today need to supplement their literary incomes. Do not think of Mark Twain, who made and spent $100,000 in one year in the nineteenth century. Forget Harold Bell Wright and let Margaret Mitchell go with the wind. Forget George Eliot, who earned $1,500,000 — no income tax, and no literary agent. Remember that our poets of distinction have earned less than $500 a year from their poetry in the last thirty years. Remember that the average writer's income is today, in the words of Kenneth Roberts, "scrawny and having a rank odor." The men in the grey flannel suits riding the New Haven from New York to Connecticut are not poets.

Cultural Problems

Our culture on any intellectually significant level is multiple and splintered. Possibly on the level of decent mediocrity, the United States does not have a kind of soulless industrialized culture living on, with, and for things. Pragmatism, our dominant outlook, has made an instrument of the mind, and truth a matter of adjustment. The large public wants the cozy soul, safe from womb to tomb, in an expanding economy from whose technological cornucopia pours an endless stream of shining gadgets. It seeks success from sorrow in the movies, the slicks, sports, and tranquilizer pills. But who would call its authors writers? Above the level of the detectives, westerns, and slicks there is only the tangled skein of multiple commitment, conjecture, and agnosticism. In religion there is the vast range from the sentimental slush of Norman, "Millicent" Peale to the complex Anglo-Catholicism of Eliot and Auden. The man who reads the fatty jargon of the typical educationists does not die of death, he dies of vertigo. In philosophy there are at least fourteen categories of intellectual dissonance as well as the latest school of genteel spectatorial analysis. In literary criticism, there are the impenetrabalists like Mr. Kenneth Burke, the moralists like Van Wyck Brooks, the humanists like Babbitt, the formalists like Cleanth Brooks, and the literary historians in numerous universities. Whirl is King. Maybe it is best like Ezra Pound to mutter to oneself.

The significant American writer has no unified culture to grow out of and to speak to, no unified medieval world in which a monk writing in Rome could be understood by a monk reading in York. There is no common faith, no common symbolism, no great common apperceptive mass of reference and allusion, and so the great authors sometimes seem even to an educated person to write of matters as abstruse as astrophysics in a language as obscure as Sanskrit.

On the one hand, then, we find the learned, or esoteric author, on the other a vast public that has lost its reading nerve. Vitiated by television, "athletomania," and newspapers, the average reader regards the literary genius as an impenetrable stranger if not as a nut. The gap is profound, and since the great poets do not write for Burma Shave, the ordinary public may as well read the timetables on the Chesapeake and Ohio.

Linguistic Problems

Part of the trouble is a matter of language and its use. The creative writer, as Allen Tate has said, is concerned with communion rather than with communication, with shared experience rather than with paraphrase. A work of literary art always tells more than it says. Communication means getting your meaning across. For communication, paraphrase is enough, for communion it is never enough. For communication an author can move on the level of denotation; for communion he must share experience; he wants to strip the veil of familiarity from the commonplace, to present a brave new world. That means in the words of the Imagists "death to the cliche," war on the trite phrase, "war," as Viereck says, against "lush adverbs and senile rhymes in tattered gowns." The creative writer wishes to electrify language. And so he uses jarring colloquialisms, arresting figures of speech, strange juxtapositions, unconventional syntax. He tries in the words of Pound "to resuscitate the dead art of poetry." Eliot tells us in Prufrock:

> I should have been a pair of ragged claws
> Scuttling across the floors of silent seas

Hart Crane that:

> Down wall, from girder into street noon leaks,
> A rip-tooth of the sky's acetylene.

Cummings tells us that spring is "puddle-wonderful," Sandburg points to "that pig-sticker there in the corner."

All these devices are meant to give us the feel and tone of experience rather than a shorthand transcript. They are a head-on assault upon the malfeasance of metaphor by ad-men, detective, and romance writers. We say, "All must die." The poet says with an eye to heightening experience:

> Beauty is but a flower
> Which wrinkles will devour
> Brightness falls from the air
> Queens have died young and fair
> Dust has closed Helen's eye
> I am sick, I must die
> Lord have mercy upon us.

Since the literary artist deepens experience both intensively and extensively, we have to work to share that experience; and in less traditional poetry than that which I have just quoted one may have to work hard. If we refuse to learn the great language, the poetry escapes us. Often, however, there is neither great language nor poetry; that also takes intelligence to discover.

Personal Problems

The artistic temperament has always had its burden of personal tensions. The genius, whether real or self-appointed, does not easily mesh with society. He is often a troublesome knot of contrariety to himself and to others. Profounder sensibilities, intellectual snobbery, unmitigated conceit, neurotic imbalance, and just plain orneriness all play a part. Sometimes his difficulties result from a noble and serious effort to share a superior vision; after all, as Emily Dickinson has said, "Much madness is divinest sense." Brilliant people are seldom humble. As Keats has said, "I feel in myself all the vices of a poet — irritability, love or effect and admiration." Socrates may have been right, but I have known many smart people who knew a lot of things that weren't so. Making overwhelming demands upon themselves and especially others, burning for appreciation and reward but meeting with apathy and misunderstanding, the life of genius tends to be warfare upon earth within and without. For every well-ordered life of a Browning or Emerson, there are half a dozen Poes and Hart Cranes; and even a model of conventionality like Lord Tennyson, wearing the white flower of the blameless life, was an inveterate hypochondriac oozing melancholy and

> Tears, idle tears, I know not what they mean.

In any society, particularly in a philistine society, the genius seems somewhat odd; and when he bursts, red-haired and loudmouthed upon the placid Victorian scene like Algernon Charles Swinburne, he strikes the public as something demonic. Tortured within, acidly critical of what is without, wanting public support and not getting it, the poet like Hart Crane does not unexpectedly jump into the Caribbean Sea, because for him there is not

> the world dimensional for
> those untwisted by the love of things
> irreconcilable.

Spiritual Problems

Frequently, all the preceding problems are exacerbated by the lack of faith. The great writer needs unity and is oppressed by severance. He above all needs a staying center to his life. The writer like the rest of us needs wholeness, and a man made in the image of God cannot find wholeness without Him. The Christian religion is irrelevant to most of the great writers of our time. St. Michael may be on his heights on Mount St. Michael, but for them he is guarding a stone-cold and empty church. The ghost of eighteenth-century deism has never been laid, the web of fate lies heavy still. The romantic heresy which tried to force a personal emotional unity upon the universe through empathy has been blasted for an irridescent if enchantingly beautiful dream. Wordsworth's violet by the mossy stone no longer enjoys the air it breathes and has been replaced by Hart Crane's "tarantula rattling at the lily's foot." The writer has to go it alone, as Coleridge anticipated the modern mood already in 1797:

> Alone, alone, all all alone
> Alone on a wide, wide sea
> And never a saint to take pity on
> My soul in agony.

And so we get a literature of sadness, a literature of sick souls; the dim thicket of evil in Faulkner, Fitzgerald's jazz age vampires; Hemingway's tough guys and their code of "Don't whimper." There is little nobility in it, and sometimes a sense of bitter despair. Tomorrow is gone. Between man and man, and man and God, there is only "the unplumb'd, salt, estranging sea."

In this wider world of our time we are in some respects an island and in others most decidedly a part of the main. Our writers share the lean and hungry look. The man who writes in *The Reformed Journal* or who wrote for *The Calvin Forum* has or has had the pleasure of seeing himself in print and paying for it. The man who writes for *The Banner* treads with a wary linguistic and cultural foot. Only on the personal and spiritual level is our problem less severe.

Yet we have had and do have men of letters, stimulating writers with gift, insight, and imagination. We have had creative writers also, although they have left us. What can we do to keep what we have and to cause the creative writer to flourish among us?

Writing the Christian Novel

The Reformed Journal (December, 1957)

The Christian poet, dramatist, and novelist need public support. Possibly the poet can create for long years with very little of it: Whitman and Frost are examples of long, lonely creation. But the dramatist needs the attendant public to make his art live, and so, I think, does the novelist. Therefore in discussing the fostering of creative art among us, I shall consider the novel, the one genre that has some chance of reaching our public. I shall tell you what I hope for in a Christian novel, its genesis and reception. That I who cannot write novels do so is but another example of occupational effrontery.

The novel, would, of course, be a work of art; its Christian significance would in no sense atone for shoddy craftsmanship. In art one can neither cheat nor fake and no Christian writer would want to. A Christian novel would therefore be a fictional example of significant verbal form whose angle of vision is Christian. All art is selective. Every novelist chooses his detail from a philosophical point of view however crude or naive that may be. The body of life, the contained experience in this novel would be patterned by Christian vision, and it would be the integrating spirit of the latter that would make it Christian.

There can certainly be no Calvinistic literary technique. There are no sectarian lines, colors, or tones. John Calvin had a style, but Calvinism cannot have. The sonnet, blank verse, rime royal, Spenserian stanza are contentless forms. Realism, stream-of-consciousness writing, even surrealism as techniques are neutral. Neither is there a Calvinistic subject matter. What could it be? A man reading the Bible? The life of a Calvinist? A study of Calvin's ideas? The history of Calvin College? If there is to be a Calvinistic novel it will have to express itself neither in form specifically nor in subject matter specifically but in tone, spirit, vision, total impact.

Let me illustrate. *Tess of the D'Urbervilles* is one of Hardy's greatest novels. When one finished the sad life of Tess one is moved to agree with the author that the "President of the Immortals" had finished his sport with Tess; when one finishes *Jude the Obscure* one oppressively feels the weight of the Hardyean world, a world of capricious, irrational force, a world of Hap, in which one can well ask with Hardy:

> Has some vast imbecility
> Mighty to build and bend
> But impotent to tend
> Framed us in jest but
> Left us now to hazardry?

When one finished a typical Dreiser novel life seems a stinking game. In the earlier Hemingway novels the struggles of man seem about as important as the "struggle of ants on the burning log of a campfire." Coleridge's "Rime of the Ancient Mariner" concretely presents a world of passivity, a world in which the entire action and personal reaction are moved from the outside. In all these authors there is no mistaking the vision. In that sense one can certainly have a Christian novel, if not a Calvinistic one. A Christian novel would leave the reader with the full conviction that events have moved in God's world, a world where God's providence is naturally and organically operative. The world and vision of Dante, of Chaucer, of Milton, of Bunyan, of Greene, of Paton have this Christian spirit.

I do not pretend that such a novel will bridge the cultural and religious gap between the Christian and non-Christian. A novelist is neither an apologist nor an evangelist. His first duty as novelist is to form his experience as freshly and movingly as possible. As novelist he has no mandate to demolish existentialists or manhandle naturalists. It is his duty to give an authentic vision. But my hope is, of course, that this novel will be so soundly rooted in reality, so richly regional that it will not be provincial. It may well deal with Americans of Dutch descent, but they will be human; if you prick them they will bleed, if you oppress them they will rebel, if you beat them in business you are very smart. Furthermore their religion is no obscure hole-in-the-corner aberration; their spiritual life is in the main line of Protestantism. They emphasize man's guilt, severance, and woe — watchwords of modernity. If the people and their lives are presented with brilliance, if the novel is a conspicious esthetic triumph it will be studied by intelligent men of alien vision; it will work its way into critical appraisal as significant art and may be used by God as a transcendent tract.

An important question concerns the nurture and support of letters and men of creative genius if such should appear.

For genius one must, of course, wait. Genius is notoriously whimsical in its appearance. Since, however, it has come in the person of
Burns to a Scotch hut, in the person of Keats to a London stableman's
home, in the person of Twain to a Missouri store, and in the person
of Henry Adams to a Massachusetts mansion, there is nothing incredible about its possible appearance in Clara City, Minnesota, or Lodi,
New Jersey. Prospective men of letters will doubtless appear. How can
we stimulate the maximum fruition of whatever talent God gives our
little group?

We must give our writers roots, a sense of belonging, an anchorage.
They must possess the world of nature and man as well as judge it.
The artist works through concrete detail; and the biography of literary
genius convincingly evidences the necessity of a rooted childhood and
adolescence and an appreciation of the senses. He must feel one with
his family and group; he should not have, as Crane, to "shoulder the
curse of sundered parentage." He should have a father on earth and
in heaven. He will then have the security that permits regarding judgment rather than a wail of despair. A writer brought up feeling that
he belongs in this world because he belongs to God to whom the
world belongs will have proper groundwork for proper vision.

One of the reasons why Puritanism has been so sterile in a literary
sense is precisely that the Puritan felt so uneasy about the world of
the senses. One feels the fear, the distrust of the overwhelming beauty
in leaf and landscape, in the panorama of clouds, in the haunting
witchery of spring. Puritanism often felt nature as an enchanter.
Therefore Puritan poetry is generally thin, spare, and bloodless. One
must go to the Anglicans and the Catholics for poetry, because they
saw nature as redeemed, the sensuous experience as legitimate, and
when realized in art, a form of worship. One must feel this to be God's
world if one is to write like Hopkins:

> Glory be to God for dappled things —
>   For skies of couple-colour as a brinded cow;
>   For rose-moles all in stipple upon trout that swim;
> Fresh-firecoal chestnut-falls; finches' wings;
>   Landscape plotted and pieced — fold, fallow, and plow;
>   And all trades, their gear and tackle and trim.
>
> All things counter, original, spare, strange;
>   Whatever is fickle, freckled (who knows how?)
>   With swift, slow; sweet, sour; adazzle, dim;
> He fathers-forth whose beauty is past change:
>   Praise Him.

As the writer matures he needs a congenial atmosphere in which to flourish. Such an atmosphere grows out of a realization that art is not a product of formulas. Even a classicist like Pope realized that a good poem "needs to snatch a grace beyond the reach of art." A Christian novel will not aim at a series of do's and don'ts; it does not cramp the experience and observation of the Christian consciousness within a set of external imperatives, neither does it channelize vivid experience into a mechanical and obvious thesis. Rather it gives us the honest vision of a sensitive Christian soul, and it gives that with the restraint and delicacy characteristic of the Christian mind and heart. We have to let the Christian artist find his own form and express his own experience in his own way. As Keats has said:

> The genius of Poetry must work out its own salvation in a man. It cannot be matured by law and precept, but by sensation and watchfulness of itself. That which is creative must create itself.

We must give our writers artistic freedom because literature cannot be written to order. What the artist expresses is his own vision of reality, his individual insight, his difference. That cannot be dictated. In the case of the Christian that difference will be rooted in Christian belief. It will come naturally, intuitively. Reason and intelligence will give it structure and form.

But as with all freedom, there are limits for decent men. Complete artistic freedom, freedom to say anything you please any way you please is surely a vicious thing. Both art and morality impose restraints. Certainly a Christian writer will dike some of his own stream of consciousness. What are just limits for the Christian? It seems to me that the famous phrases attributed to Saint Augustine have point here. They run like this: In the necessary things unity, in the doubtful things liberty, in all things charity. The Christian writer must respect Christian dogma and morality; he must be allowed freedom in form and taste; and he should always exercise charity.

The Christian novel we hope for may come as a sharp blow on the cheek. An uncritical vision is no vision at all. We all admit we have made but a feeble beginning of sainthood; if a writer is to portray us he will show us as sinners with touches of nobility through grace. Our growing materialism, our lack of interest in the free play of ideas, our straining at the gnat of an unpleasant word in a novel while we swallow the camel of bathing beach attire, our preoccupation with ecclesiastical trivia — all are fair game for the novelist. Don't be angry if he asks you to pay for the satire.

Since it is a writer's business to sharpen experience through the deft and illuminating word, we must allow a good deal of formal experimentation and we must be prepared to earn our enjoyment of his work. We cannot loll on our sofa while appreciating a fresh talent.

Our men of letters should also be encouraged. They should be instrumental in introducing a lively flow of ideas into circulation. Our intellectuals should create an atmosphere of living opinion and discussion. Philosophers, scientists, literary critics, theologians should all be making ideas available to the creative artist and to us. Our educated men and women should feel free to investigate, criticize, and report. They should make tradition contemporary and the contemporary relevant to tradition.

We have pens of one sort or another; their efforts may, if they are lucky, bring in a few pennies. I doubt, however, whether our group has produced a writer loyal to it whose literary earnings provide more than a pleasant bonus. Suppose you wish to be a creative writer today. What are your prospects? You cannot arrange to be born to wealthy and sympathetic parents, but you might find it convenient to marry a patron. You can make a living in industry as Wallace Stevens did, or in medicine as Wm. Carlos Williams does, and write with your excess energy. You can attempt to combine creative writing with college teaching as so many critics, novelists, and poets do today. You could run the hazard of trying to write salable pulp until you have money enough to write for art. But there are not many John P. Marquands. It remains true in art as elsewhere that "to the victor belong the spoils." Or you can live a long time on Poverty Lane like Faulkner and Sherwood Anderson or always like Fred Feikema.

Almost all these ways exact a high price. The rich wife isn't easily got and when got may not be easily managed; a divided career easily results in meager output. Poverty Lane is hard.

Now, I can feel for the person who says: "Let the writer take his chances — like the inventor. Struggle won't hurt him, and if his products do not sell, that is his tragedy. Society does not owe the artist a living." I can feel for that attitude, but I do not share it. I believe art is of such incalculable worth to a culture that if a genuine artist cannot support himself through his genius the public should aid him. I find the death, largely from poverty and neglect, of poets like Poe, Lindsay, and Hart Crane tragic; I find diminished creativity because of absorption in other tasks and wariness because of academic associations most unfortunate. Fortunately many Americans share this point of view because there are many grants, scholarships, awards, and prizes available today. Furthermore, some publishers have become much more adventurous and generous. However, these are really stopgaps. The writer eventually runs out of graduate-assistantships, *Hudson Review* Fellowships in Fiction, Fulbright and Ford fellowships. Finally, his books have to sell.

What can we do in our own circles? Patronage in the old sense is an anachronism today. It was a vital option in the days of chivalry when the poet had a wholly respectable place in a noble household. He was a court bard and proud of it; he accepted his pension and his cask of wine without servility. Today private patronage is both humiliating and impossible. Our support will have to be more objective. Promising chemists and musicians attain scholarships at Calvin. Promising seminarians are given a fellowship to the Free University. Why not emulate this in creative writing? The Eerdmans Publishing Company has for years given generous support to student writing. Others might go and do likewise. But one must be realistic, and these can only be temporary aids; in the last analysis, the best way to help a writer is to buy his book and to help sell it.

I wish to conclude by defining the role of the man of letters in our Reformed community. I trust that epithet does not sound too pretentious; I am fully aware that we do not harbor a Matthew Arnold, a T. S. Eliot, or a Douglas Bush. When I speak of the man of letters I refer to a man who is habitually and professionally concerned with reading and interpreting great literature and who from time to time evaluates his experiences in rewarding writing. I believe a person has a vital role to play in our group and that it differs sharply from the role of the typical university scholar.

I do not mean, therefore, a primary devotion to investigative research, the publication of articles for learned, specialized journals on the sources of Chaucer's astronomical references, or such an article as Edward Hungerford's scintillating account in *American Literature* of "Walt Whitman and his Chart of Bumps." There are more than enough talented scholars to deal with those matters. I refer rather to a thoughtful, Reformed, appraisal of literature.

Such appraisal should be esthetically competent, but it should go beyond formalistic criticism with its preoccupation with function rather than value. It should judge the moral, philosophical, and religious values of creative art. It should understand and interpret the cultural agony of our time. The great writers have always been moralists in the sense that moral judgment is implied within the contained experience of the work of art. Shakespeare's world is a world of judgment as well as sympathy. It is full of error, sin, ruin, and incalculable waste rising from the characters of men; it is also a world of humanity, understanding, and above all mercy. Even Faulkner's world in his own words "measures greatness by the distance between the dream and the failure." He too tried, in his own words "to catch the answer to the whole riddle." Consequently, the final value of a literary experience is determined not alone by esthetic but also by religious criteria. In great literature meaning and form are commensurate, the truest vision in the most adequate form is the greatest writing. It is our business to integrate our faith and our literary experience into sound criticism. That is difficult indeed. To do it we will need more talent, more time, more energy, and additional media.

Our Calvin alumni have during our brief independent existence as a college produced an unusual amount of good writing. Five of our alumni have reached national literary prominence. We may dislike some of their work as undistinctive, but that it shows talent of a high order is indisputable. Can the University of Michigan alumni equal it during the last thirty years? We have had, have, and will have gift; it is our business to promote its full fruition.

9

"The Higher Dream"

TWO ADDRESSES

Purportedly the twentieth century is the age of communication. Networks of satellites and wires strangle the globe with the sound and fury of a million voices.

T. S. Eliot wrote in Ash Wednesday:

> And the light shone in darkness and
> Against the Word the unstilled world still whirled
> About the centre of the silent Word.

One wonders if the still, small whisper is irrevocably drowned in our rage for communication.

Professor Timmerman's many addresses have reminded his listeners of the beauty of the just-right word, the well-crafted phrase, the finely tuned sentence, all in consonance with the revelation of the Word. Two such addresses are included in this section.

Do Not Let These Stories Die

Honors Convocation Address, Calvin College, May, 1972

Spark (September, 1972)

Some people do not read any stories; they look at "Hogan's Heroes." Some fear stories, and some dislike them, but they all miss something valuable. A story whether actual or fictional packs power. A college freshman was so moved by the biography of Lincoln that he wrote on his examination paper, "Abraham Lincoln was born in 1809 in a log cabin which he built with his own hands." Queen Victoria tried to immortalize her beloved Albert by sprinkling statues over England, but her efforts were vain because there was no story in her man. When Aristotle wrote his great work on literary criticism, he gave priority to the fable, the action, or the story. Much of our greatest literature from Homer to Hemingway has dealt with action. At the close of the Knight's long tale, all the Canterbury pilgrims, both young and old, said it was a noble story worthy of being remembered.

This is true of all good stories, because they provide a way of knowing, controlling, and evaluating experience. When the singer in Whitman's elegy on Lincoln walks toward the singing thrush in the "solemn shadowy cedars" and "the ghostly pines so still," he walks with the thought of death walking on one side of him and the knowledge of death on the other. What a story does is to change thought into a kind of knowledge. As a Christian, I can live with war, trouble, and the dying of honor because I believe in God's providence, but if I were Thomas Hardy, I should see the world as produced by crass causality and full of happenstance. If I read the poems and novels of Hardy, I know what it feels like to ask the question:

> Has some vast imbecility
> Mighty to build and bend,
> But impotent to tend
> Framed us in jest
> And left us to hazardry?

When Billy Budd is falsely accused by the insanely jealous Claggart, he is so shocked that he cannot speak but strikes Claggart dead. He had no language to express and control his savage indignation. I wonder how many stories have enabled both the reader and the writer to control their experience. The greatest story of all, the story of Christ's coming, determines how we look at all other stories.

I have always been greatly interested in the roots of great stories and as a consequence have read many literary biographies. The greatest of these is still Boswell's *Life of Samuel Johnson*, written by a man so strange and paradoxical that no novelist could have invented him, and about a man so vastly impressive that one cannot forget him. I have discovered, I think, two important facts. The first is that writers, even those with slender formal education like Hemingway and Faulkner, have been great readers of the very best writing, the classics, the genteel tradition if you wish. The second is that the writer, especially in the United States, is likely to emerge from a closely woven group with a real sense of tradition. Carl Sandburg once said, "The past is a bucket of ashes," but he soon repented and wrote six fat volumes on the life of Lincoln. Katherine A. Porter has said, "All my past is usable."

For years there has been a demand for the great American novel, but I believe there never will be a great American novel. America is too big, too multifarious to write a truly representative novel about. In our common life we tend to pare down the individual edges, to submerge our identities in our manners. The color and drama of American life lies in its pluralism, and our best writing has been rooted in closely woven groups with a unique and strongly felt tradition.

Mark Twain grew up in the Missouri heartland of America and its innocence and idealism, its cynicism and violence made him the writer he became. He wrote some of his best works in its dialects; the thoughts and imagery of the Presbyterian Calvinism of his youth haunt his works, and whether he calls Hannibal, Missouri, St. Petersburg, Dawson's Landing, Hadleyburg, or Eseldorf, Germany, it is the same little town seen from increasingly dark perspectives. Twain once said, "It's mighty free and easy on a raft," but he never found the raft to take him from that town. Robert Frost, on the other hand, is pure New England. When one reads his poems and is imaginatively meditating, watching a foolish white-tailed hornet, meditating in a disused graveyard or choosing something like a star, one is in New England. The voices are pure Yankee. The rhythms and rhymes are impeccably controlled and the great griefs are kept under. What a difference if one travels to Jefferson, Mississippi, Yoknapatawpha County — William

Faulkner, sole owner and proprieter. The great griefs shriek at us in deeds of blood and violence. The cleared land edges the dim, primitive woodlands, the heavy rivers burst into flood and waste. The curse of chattel slavery draws doom down over the land, and man's heart is in desperate conflict with itself, his fellowman and nature. The sinuous prose bends and winds, swirls and floods about us. Faulkner's fiction is vastly impressive and it owes much of this impressiveness to the life and legend of the unique culture, which it so magnificently portrays. Finally, even as international a writer as T. S. Eliot has said of his poetry, "But in its sources, its emotional springs, it comes from America." By that he meant particularly the Mississippi and New England.

Furthermore, these origins do not create provinciality; they create a concretely realized world. The poems and stories are organically rooted in a web of genuine human relationships and natural facts. Human beings are most alive and most themselves when they grow in a warm texture of human relationships and nature, rather than in a depersonalized and mechanized society.

Great writers are not merely spectatorial in their attitudes toward the world; they come or are forced to come to a perspective, a commitment, even when it makes them weep. Now such a vision or religious perspective is not a constriction for a writer, not if it is truly believed in. Then it becomes a deliverance from chaos, a stay against confusion, a principle of order. It is no strangling presence if the belief is part of him and comes as Hemingway said "from his head, from his heart, all there is of him." Philosophy is good to have, if, as Keats said, "it has been proved on the pulses." Vision is confining only when alien and imposed.

This is true of the Christian vision. Even in our fragmented, disorderly world, a writer of the stature of Flannery O'Connor could both say and prove this. She said, "I see from the standpoint of Christian orthodoxy. This means that for me the meaning of life is centered in our Redemption by Christ and what I see, I see in relation to that." She pictures a world where a good man is hard to find, where sin has produced disruption and destruction. To dramatize this point she uses the art of distortion, the grotesque. There is the conductor who "has the face of an ancient, bloated bullfrog." Ruby Hill is a "short woman shaped nearly like a funeral urn." She portrays characters missing an arm or leg, having a cast in the eye. There are mutes and morons. All symbolize a spiritual deformity. Even nature is often grotesque. The sun shone "like a furious blister in the sky"; men, trees, even animals are warped from something. They need something and what they need is the very person man has displaced. They need Jesus, the Lord, the healer of all deformity, the only one who can bear the troubles of the world away.

I should like to relate some of these comments to us and our tradition, realizing that tradition is a way increasingly less traveled by, but believing that neglecting it involves real loss. I believe T. S. Eliot is right when he said that one of the functions of poetry is to "retard change." He did not mean to rule our experimentation but to rule in the priceless values of the past.

I believe we have a tradition worth remembering, not only in a spiritual but also in a literary sense. It is a dramatic tradition in which unusual courage was common. Sod huts, blazing sun, and bitter chill in South Dakota. Lush crops at times but also drought, hail, and tornado in Iowa. The Reverend Mr. Van Raalte praying for parishioners dying of swamp fever. Lonely graves of little children dead in a new land. Long, hard hours, low pay, and acrid odors in Paterson. These were bitter struggles and our ancestors met them with robust, undying faith. That faith also created a tension, a sense of antithesis between the religious and secular life. There was for many years no bland accommodation to the surrounding culture. Real problems arose in trying to be "dead-hearted" to the world and yet implacably industrious: the divided loyalties of property and piety. Furthermore, there was real struggle in "mansoul," the heart. My youth was lived in the spiritual city of John Bunyan and the Puritans. Christian still had a heavy burden; he inched through the "Slough of Despond," fought the giant Despair, was immured in "Doubting Castle," and faced anxiously the dark river before journey's end. The baggage was then not dropped at the counter, and no smiling stewardess ushered the traveler in for the effortless journey to the celestial city. The chill desolation of death was not muted by mortuary rites. There was probably a surplus of quarreling and theological hair-splitting over the south and southwest side of an issue, too much iron and steel, but a writer like David DeJong shows plainly that he was not rebelling against foam rubber.

The last remark brings us to our writers and story tellers. I believe graduates of Calvin are admirably equipped to write good books for reasons implicit in what I have already said and for two others, one well known but not sufficiently appreciated, the other not well known and insufficiently appreciated. The first is the invaluable training our graduates have received in sound study of the Bible, not only in a spiritual but also in a literary sense. The Bible is a cultural storehouse of inestimable value. No one claiming to have a liberal education can be ignorant of it. It is not only great literature in itself but a major cause of great literature in others. Its rhythms echo in our poetry from Chaucer to Eliot. Its images, thoughts, and stories are woven into the fabric of much of our greatest American and English literature. Melville alone has 1400 allusions to the Bible; Faulkner and Eliot are deeply indebted to it.

In the second place, we have a literary tradition of real extent and substance. Anybody who thinks we have not been writing simply has not been reading. From my earliest youth the presses have been groaning. When I was a little boy, I regularly brought magazines and papers to my father's study in three languages and a dialect. Not only *The Banner of Truth*, but *De Grondwet, Der Reformierte Bote, Religion and Culture, The Calvin Forum*, and many others. We still have these magazines devoted to noble ideals, solid scholarship, and a limited circulation. The publication never ceases. Pamphlets buzz about us, and independent prophets, who can't publish, mimeograph, and

> Fire in each eye, and papers in each hand
> Rave, recite and madden round the land.

Obviously, some of this looks like literature only at a distance of four feet, but a great deal of it is good writing and some of it is important. Gifted scholars and essayists, graduated from Calvin, have written notable articles and excellent books. But five of our novelists have received national interest and reputation. We have had more novelists than poets. Several slender volumes of poetry have been published, of which the best, in my opinion is *Learning the Way* by James Den Boer. David DeJong produced a book of poems, many of which appeared in *The Chimes*. I could not understand them then; I cannot understand them now. Our novelists have been more voluminous. Wessel Smitter wrote a dramatic novel, *F.O.B. Detroit*, which was made into a fine motion picture. David DeJong has written two bitter books about us, and one superb novel, *Old Haven*, which, I was told, missed the Book-of-the-Month Club because of Clifton Fadiman's adverse vote. Meindert DeJong's children's stories have an international reputation. Two of our writers, Manfred and De Vries have had national attention. Their books are regularly reviewed in first-class magazines; they are discussed in scholarly journals, books or chapters in books. A master's thesis and a doctoral dissertation have been written on their work at two of our great universities. I saw their books in paperback editions in Amsterdam and London. Manfred's *Lord Grizzly* has sold over a million copies. Though I do not share the vague naturalism of Manfred or the stoical humanism of De Vries, I would be less than honest not to admit pride in the achievement of these class-mates and friends.

We are thus benefactors of a hundred years of hard struggles, monumental sacrifices, and solid achievement, a hundred years of dramatic history and a thousand stories. I should hate to see this past rejected in anger, wiped out through indifference, regarded full of illusory loyalties and capsizing causes. There must be a right way to memorialize this past whether through history, biography, or fiction. We want neither the Victorian biographer who edges in with the undertaker, writes with the tearful widow editing the script, and produces a plaster saint, nor do we want the biographer of the 1920s who used all the know-how of the F.B.I. to produce a rogue. What we want is the dignity of the truth; that is enough. Such a story would not be sheer sentimentalism; it would be appreciative without being idolatrous. There would be nobility in it as well as criticism. Satire would be legitimate if it follows Faulkner's dictum that "You must use the evil to try to tell some truth which you think important." It is my profound wish that such a story be written, because if it were truly told, it would demonstrate our deepest conviction that only that which is done for Christ is imperishable.

Saints, Sinners, and Satire
Retirement Address

Calvin College (May, 1976)

In her essay "The Fiction Writer and His Country," Flannery O'Connor says, "I see from the standpoint of Christian orthodoxy." That an American novelist should have made such a statement in the last half of the twentieth century is not only extraordinary but profoundly encouraging. Fitzgerald, a quarter of a century before had said, "I felt that I was standing at twilight in a deserted range, with an empty rifle in my hands and the targets down." A quarter of a century before that E. A. Robinson had said, "We are children in a

spiritual kindergarten trying to spell God with the wrong blocks," and
Frost had said

> We dance round the circle and suppose
> The secret sits in the middle and knows.

O'Connor did not write out of a naive unawareness of the spiritual
emptiness all about her. In her novel *Wise Blood*, Hazel Motes says
with tragic finality, "Where you come from is gone, and where you
thought you were going to was never there, and where you are is no
good unless you can get away from it." She, however, views human
experience from the fixed point of our Redemption in Christ and adds
"that what I see in the world I see in relation to that."

When Miss O'Connor says that she commits herself to a vision
that transcends time and place, an eternal perspective in which it does
not greatly matter whether the characters move slowly and merrily
from Southward to Canterbury, or slowly and painfully from the City
of Destruction to the land where the shining ones commonly walk, or
ironically on the Celestial Railroad in effortless ease to perdition, or
violently from Milledgeville, Georgia, to Judgment Day. What counts
is not clothes, times, and habits, but the awful choice of the right road
and the true country. Her problem was to make the choice and the
journey real to a culture that denied both.

Flannery O'Connor was a brilliant storyteller, whose Christian beliefs determined what she saw, how she saw it, and ultimately how
creativity and conviction were organically fused in her stories. She
knew her beliefs were a stumbling block to many readers, but she
wanted readers as every artist does. She had no wish to be like Swift
when only his servant appeared on a stormy evening to celebrate
Communion, and Swift began the form by saying, "We are met dearly
beloved Roger." She would agree with the Host in the Canterbury
Tales:

> For certainly, as that these clerkes seyn,
> Whereas a man may have noon audience
> Naught helpeth it to tellen his sentence.

To reach a large and often hostile audience, she had to domesticate
the supernatural, to reveal distortions in our culture as truly abnormal,
to assert as mystery what many of her contemporaries regarded as
mist. She had to do this to attract readers; she had also to do so
because it was the habit of her mind. She says, "to the hard of hearing

you shout and for the almost blind you draw large and startling figures." Consequently, her stories abound in the grotesque, the use of Gothic devices, and massive irony. There is Ruby Hill, "a short woman shaped nearly like a funeral urn," which in a spiritual sense she was. The Misfit and his ghoulish aides arrive "in a big black battered hearse-like automobile." And what could be more ironical than that Hulga Hopewell, Ph.D., should be taken in by a country charlatan. The fantastically ugly, the demonically evil, the weird turning of tables were not used as contrived gimmicks to ensnare a public that liked to look at the Munsters, but as revelations of spiritual want. They were part of a satirical arsenal jammed with deadly weapons. Flannery O'Connor was a master of many literary devices among which the use of satire seems to me the most spectacular.

Satire, the art of ridiculing people you don't like, beliefs you despise, and institutions you regard as corrupt is an art with well-defined limitations. Neither humor nor satire is effective without implied standards of what is expected to happen or what ought to happen. Neither humor nor satire is operative in your case if your security or identity is threatened. When a three-hundred-pound man goes through a reed chair to the floor you laugh if you are not personally involved in the consequences. In the late sixties, that era of portentous self-importance, when everybody was entitled to do his thing, there was little one could safely laugh at. If a child drew a banana that looked like a pumpkin, praise his creativity; if a poet peddled free verse that looks like shredded prose, consider it originality. When there are no fixed standards or the standards are tyrannically fixed, little humor surfaces. There was little room for laughter among the Nazis or the Students For Democratic Action. Flannery O'Connor is a hard-hitting satirist who at times threatens our security. Maybe she should.

Mark Twain said, "If a thing cannot endure laughter, it is not a good thing." When Shelley said of his literary critics, "I feel only a slight disgust and wonder that they presume to write my name," he reveals a vulnerability in the romantic outlook, an inability "to see ourselves as others see us." Humor and satire provide three major services.

Relaxation. O'Connor's stories are peppered with humorous descriptions and witty remarks. A young man is said to be bound to be a "Church of God preacher because you don't have to know nothing to be one." When Sulk complains to Astor, an old black employee, about Mrs. Shortley that "Big belly acts like she knows everything," the old man says, "Never mind, your place too low for any body to dispute it with you." Who can forget the conductor on the train to

Atlanta who "has the face of an ancient bloated bullfrog," or Mrs. Flood who has "racehorse legs," and "hair clustered like grapes about her brow"? To conclude: as Mrs. Pritchard, her hands "folded on a shelf of stomach" says, "All I got is four abscess teeth," Mrs. Cope replies snappily, "Well be thankful you don't have five. . . . I can always find something to be thankful for."

Humor and satire also provide *Revelation*, a penetrating glimpse of those truths, which a Christian Reformed pastor once said, we do not accept. In the story about her, Mrs. Turpin, a huge woman with sharp black eyes for others and head full of self-esteem and self-appointed sainthood for herself, visits a doctor's office. She is a good woman who keeps her pig pen clean and thanks God for not making her a nigger or white trash, for "having a little of everything and a good disposition besides." She feels like shouting, "Thank you Jesus for making everything the way it is. It could have been different." She has actually just done so, when a book crashes into her head, hurled by a sick Wellesley student, who has listened to her pious blubbering with increasing hostility, and finally whipped the book at her in a frenzy of disgust and calls her an old wart hog from hell. For once Mrs. Turpin is hurled into genuine self-awareness of her true spiritual condition, her bloated self-righteousness. She is plunged into painful self-examination, and at the end of the story in apocalyptic vision she sees souls ascending to heaven and "that even their virtues were being burned away."

Finally, humor and satire may induce *reformation*. Not all satire has such a noble intention. When Kerr describes Mr. Rutherford as "a shark about to feed on a brother," he is merely being catty, and when Carlyle described Rossetti, the poet, as "sitting in a sewer and adding to it," he was suffering from dyspepsia. The great satirists like Pope at times and Swift did write out of moral indignation, did stoop to truth and moralize their song to make virtue prevail. Flannery O'Connor, of course, is no writer of tracts, but she did want in her own words, "to show the operation of grace" and through satire she shows us our corruption and the need of cleansing power. She, like all satirists, had an abundance of material. One challenge the human race has never failed to meet is to make fools of themselves. This capacity is inherent, irresistible, and universal, and she gives us many telling examples.

Flannery O'Connor lived only thirty-nine years, the last fourteen of which ached with a disease or fear of its recurrence, lupus, a degenerative illness of the bone, which forced her to wear crutches for the last nine years of her life. Returning from a literary party in New

York, she said of the participants, "You know what's the matter with all that kind of folks? They ain't from anywhere," a strange comment by a resident of Milledgeville, Georgia, even though it was the state capital until sacked by Sherman. But Georgia is stamped like Braille over all her work. She was graduated from Georgia State College in 1941 with an A.B. in Social Science. Her literary gifts and her talent for drawing cartoons were clearly apparent then. Her stories abound in cartoon-like characterizations. Mrs. Bailey's face was "as broad and innocent as a cabbage." Mr. Buth's stomach "hung over his trousers like a sack of meal swaying with his shirt." Two of her college cartoons are interesting; in one of them two fish are angrily arguing in a pond and one says to the other, "Why don't you jump out of the lake?" In another a homely wallflower sits neglected at a dance and murmurs to herself, "Oh well, I can always be a Ph.D." After college she spent two years in the Creative Writers Program at the University of Iowa under Paul Engle, who says of her presence, "The dreary chair she sat in sang." Six stories earned her a Master of Fine Arts degree. Later, on a journey home from New York for Christmas, she became desperately ill with lupus. Upon her recovery, the O'Connors moved to a country home. Here she enjoyed the pompous behavior and startling beauty of the peacocks, which carry so much symbolic freight in some of her stories. She was able to travel and lecture. Her artistic development was steady and startling. In July of 1964, she died before her pen, as in the case of John Keats, "had gleaned her teeming brain."

Miss O'Connor belonged to two counties, Baldwin County, Georgia, and the true county of the soul; however, she consistently sees the former in the light of the latter. Both are brilliantly reflected in *A Good Man Is Hard to Find*. The red clay roads and the slow, reddish river, the flat weedy fields, the symmetrical forms edged by woods, the city nearby rising up "like an orchestra of warts," the country people blown up and distorted for emphasis, the slow and infinitely adjustable blacks, the noisy fundamentalism in little churches where blacks and whites speak in tongues, the thin manners torn by passion and sin — all are vivid and concrete, and all are seen in the light of the true country of the soul, which sees the good country people as the spoiled salt of the earth, and the cast in the eye, the wooden leg, the club foot, and even the sun shining "like a furious white blister in the sky" as signs of a world spoiled by sin. It is also a world mercy has not yet abandoned, and where at times "the trees were full of silver-white sunlight and the meanest of them sang." The two countries are not yet finally sundered, and therefore worth writing about. There is still room for mercy even if it comes through violent assault.

The nine stories in *A Good Man Is Hard to Find*, introduced to a friend with the words "nine stories on original sin with my compliments," together with the ten stories in "Everything That Rises Must Converge," constitute relentless and uncompromising attack on the life and attitudes of the fallen world it portrays. This attack, in my judgment, focuses on three illusions. The first is the idea of the natural goodness of human nature. The cancerous growth on Mr. Paradise's ear, Rufus Johnson's club foot; Mrs. Shortley's grotesque hugeness are signs of internal corruption. One may be able to find a good man like Mr. Guiza, but he and all others are poisoned and in need of the river of grace. The second is the idea that human evil is the product of heredity and environment, that the buck stops at one's antecedents, or that there is an invisible Player moving the pawns. Man cannot *blame* God for his inhumanity to man. Mother Crater knows the score but she is so eager for a son-in-law that she sacrifices her idiot daughter to Shiftlet who worships machinery, the old car, which her dowry will power. Mrs. McIntyre says of our Lord, "As far as I am concerned Christ was just a displaced person." Both Hulga and Pointer plan their sins. The third idea is that sin, if it exists, consists merely in breaking human laws. O'Connor calls sin "a responsible choice of offense against God which involves His eternal justice." The consequences of sin appear remorselessly in this life and the next. The Misfit now becomes a fiend. Mrs. McIntyre crumbles into invalidism; Hulga is reduced to a cipher of herself. In another brilliant story, Rufus Johnson says, "Whoever says it ain't a hell is contradicting Jesus." The illusion is the myth of human engineering, that man can unaided create a good society. As will become abundantly clear, only mercy can do that, the presence of the Holy Spirit.

A Good Man Is Hard to Find contains nine stories, seven of which are clearly religious. Though they are not contrived dramatizations of dogma, all have a religious core of meaning.

"A Late Encounter with the Enemy" is a stinging satire on Southern nostalgia and its pasty sentimental celebration of the past. General Tennessee Flashback Sash is one-hundred years old and knows it. A private in a Civil War he has forgotten, he is a General by gift of the media, kept alive by habit, vanity, and a disastrously educated granddaughter, Sally Poker Sash, who is about to graduate by courtesy of longevity. She wants her senile grandfather on the podium to bestow Honor and Glory of her graduation. He has eyes only for limelight and purty gals and dies while she receives a degree she doesn't deserve and he accepts honor he hasn't earned.

"A Stroke of Good Fortune" is a satire of Ruby Hill, a fat woman whose head is balanced "like a big florid vegetable" at the top of the sack she is laboriously carrying up a long flight of stairs. She is a "short woman shaped nearly like a funeral urn," and she has a persistent pain in her belly about which she has consulted Madame Zoleeda, a palmist, who told her, "It will bring you a stroke of good fortune." She is haunted, however, by the fear of cancer or a child, both repellent to her. She knows the truth but rejects it. She rejects the gift of a new life. She prefers sterility to her stroke of good fortune. She desecrates nature and the gift of God.

In a letter to Mr. Lytle, Miss O'Connor wrote, "There is a moment of grace in most of the stories, or a moment where it is offered, and is usually rejected." This moment is clearly apparent in the stories that follow.

The title story "A Good Man Is Hard to Find" is drenched in Gothic atmosphere and moves from a waveringly happy beginning to a grotesque and horrible end. The Bailey family, a good country family, are going on a trip to Florida. There are Bailey, a long-suffering man, two sassy young children, a baby, the naive mother, and a silly grandmother who sneaks a cat along in a basket. As they make a detour, on Grandma's request, to visit a place that isn't there, Grandma makes a sudden movement that causes Petty Sing, the cat, to leap on Bailey's shoulder, where she "clings to his neck like a caterpillar." The distracted Bailey runs into a ditch and the children in a frenzy of delight howl, "We've had an accident!" Grandma says, "I believe I have injured an organ." But the hilarious is soon displaced by the horrible. The ditch is bordered by deep, dark woods, and everything is still as death. Slowly down the road comes a "big black battered hearse-like automobile," containing the Misfit, a dreaded psychopathic killer just escaped from prison, and his aide Hiram and the soulless boy, Bobby Lee; Grandma, whose age has only made her more stupid, says to the Misfit, "You're the Misfit," and thereby seals the doom of the family. The story moves with agonizing slowness to its gory end, as the family is shot to death. Only the grandmother is left. She is praying to Jesus and urges the Misfit to do so, but he says, "I don't want no hep. I'm doing all right by myself." Both the Misfit and the grandmother face a moment of grace in these terrible circumstances. The Misfit says, "Jesus thrown everything off balance," and later he says, "If he did what he said, then it's nothing for you to do but throw away everything to follow him." He knows the truth, but "needs no hep," and is reduced to complete despair and finds no pleasure in his evil. The Grandmother, however, recognizes her identity with the Misfit in their common fallen nature; she reaches out to touch him and of this act Miss O'Connor has said:

> It is the moment of grace for her anyway — A silly old woman — but it leads him to shoot her. This moment of grace excites the devil to frenzy.

The Misfit shoots her three times, but not before in the very last moments of her life the Grandmother had related her true spiritual condition to Jesus Christ and showed love for her enemy.

This is frankly a grotesque and gruesome story, a holocaust of horror, but the point is made with reverberating resonance. The Misfit has rejected Jesus, the way of mercy, and when he rejects it, he falls into a despair which obliterates all tenderness and decency. Like Chillingworth in *The Scarlet Letter*, he has become a fiend and "It's no real pleasure in life."

The Misfit is the greatest sinner in these nine stories; at the other pole is Mr. Guizac, a saint in the simple sense of being clearly a Christian man, at once a follower and symbol of Jesus Christ, the displaced person who came to throw everything off balance and to redeem us. "The Displaced Person" is in my judgment one of the truly great American short stories. It is firmly rooted in Southern life; the characters, with the exception of Mrs. Shortley, are largely realistic; the plot is entirely credible; the style is unusually rich and poetic, and for O'Connor there is an unparalleled portrayal of beauty in character and physical objects. The second word in the story is *peacock*, and this exotic bird with its tail "glittering green-gold and blue in the sunlight" is a symbol of the beauty of Christ. For the worldly Mrs. McIntyre, the peacock is only "another mouth to feed," "Nothing but a peachicken" and "when the peachicken dies there won't be any replacements." To the priest, a genuinely spiritual man, the peacock is a symbol of the glory of the Savior. How one views the peacock makes all the difference in this story.

The story begins as Mrs. McIntyre, who "had on her largest smile," walks down the steps of her house to greet Mr. Guizac, a displaced Pole of World War II, his children, and his wife, "a woman in brown, shaped like a peanut." Mrs. McIntyre is a tightly-constructed woman of rigidly prudential habits. To her chagrin, she has to employ shiftless, slowly moving Negroes and undependable poor whites to keep her barn clean and her farm solvent. Jammed with energy, she has divorced two husbands and buried a third, a judge whose platitudes she quotes while he lies grinning under his tombstone. Mr. Guizac, the displaced person, is a human dynamo, a top-flight handyman who in a sense displaces everyone about him. Mrs. McIntyre at first says, "At last I've somebody I can depend on," and a little later in the story, "That man is my salvation." Guizac, however, unsettles everybody; he has neither social nor radical prejudices. He faults the blacks for petty theft, shames the indolent Shortleys, and is willing to wed his cousin, in Poland, to a "half-witted thieving black stinking nigger." Although his competence is saving everybody, Mrs. McIntyre is driven to say, "He's extra and he's upset the balance around here." She decides to fire him despite Father Flynn's reminder of "the ovens and the boxcars and the sick children — and our dear Lord." As she goes to the shed to give Guizac his final notice, he is lying under a small tractor with his trunk sticking out. Mr. Shortley backs out the large truck, brakes it sloppily, then jumps out. The truck rolls slowly toward Guizac lying on the ground. Neither Sulk, the Negro boy, Mrs. McIntyre, or Mr. Shortley yell as the tractor smashes Guizac into pulp. Mrs. McIntyre "felt her eyes and Mr. Shortley's eyes and the Negro's eyes come together in one look that froze them into collusion forever." In rejecting the displaced person, they doomed their farm and themselves, but they had rejected in clearly apparent allegory much more than Mr. Guizac.

There is no story by Miss O'Connor in which grace is so abundantly and bluntly offered and so consistently rejected. Mrs. Shortley, worried about the huge tract of land and Mr. Shortley's black market moonshine, feels savagely threatened by Guizac and rampantly poisons other minds against him, as does Mr. Shortley. She has false visions, regards herself as a divine emissary to testify against the whore of Babylon, and goes to her eternal reward via a stroke. But no one is so consistently confronted by the claims and mercy of Christ as is Mrs. McIntyre, the worldly-wise woman.

Mercy rains on Mrs. McIntyre but nothing sprouts in her stony heart. When Father Flynn remarks on the splendor of the peacock's fan and says, "Christ will come like that," she is embarrassed the way "sex had her mother." When she says of Guizac, "He didn't have to come in the first place," the priest replies on a higher level, "He came to redeem us." In the most revealing dialog of all, Father Flynn says, "When God sent his only Begotten Son, Jesus Christ our Lord, as a Redeemer to mankind, he. . . ." Mrs. McIntyre interrupts (in a voice that made him jump), "I want to talk about something serious like the management of a farm." At the end, broken in spirit and body, she still "Don't want no hep." Even during the priest's continuing ministrations, she remains obdurate, guilty as far as this story goes, of the unpardonable sin.

The moment of grace is a watershed in human destiny. In one way or another the words of the gaunt fundamentalist preacher haunt all the stories. "Believe Jesus or the devil. Testify to one or the other." The Reverend Mr. Bevel stands in the low red water of the river urging the good country people to lay their sins and sickness in the blood it symbolizes. Among the crowd is a shabby, perverse little boy, Harry Ashford, who is taken from his gin-soaked home to the baptism by his baby sitter. The young preacher is saying, "There ain't but one river and that's the River of life made out of Jesus' blood." The little boy, says O'Connor, "knew immediately that nothing the preacher said or did was a joke." The boy approaches the preacher who says to him

"Have you ever been baptized?"
"What's that?"
"If I baptize you," the preacher said, "You'll be able to go to the Kingdom of Christ; you'll be washed in the river of suffering, son, you'll go by the deep river of life. Do you want that?"
"Yes," the child says.

After he's baptized, the preacher says, "You count now. You didn't even count before." Harry Ashford is only a little boy, but something strange has happened to him. Small as he is he has been touched by something mysteriously splendid and compelling. When he returns to his home, his drunken mother puts him to bed; the next day as he prowls the empty house, examines the shriveled vegetables and old pork bone in the refrigerator, he leaves the house to find that Kingdom of Christ in the river. He walks slowly into the red water where the waiting current "caught him like a long gentle hand and pulled him swiftly forward and down. For an instant he was overcome with surprise; then since he was moving quickly and knew he was getting somewhere, all his fury and fear left him." Obviously, these are large and startling figures, but neither the psychology nor the theology is stressed to the point of absurdity. Obviously the little boy committed suicide, but in his own heart he was gaining life by losing it. This story is dense with archetypal overtones; the meaning of the rite of baptism as symbolical dying to sin and new birth in Christ is driven home by grotesque literalness.

Three important stories should still be considered, but I should briefly point out the impact of three others. "A Temple of the Holy

Ghost" makes clear that our bodies, however unnaturally misshapen, are still God's temples, so that a hermaphrodite can say, "This is the way he wanted me to be, and I ain't disputin his way." A preternaturally sharp little girl (there are various astounding little girls in her stories) "hears the giggling girls from Mount St. Scholastica laughing about Sister Perpetua's calling their bodies Temples of the Holy Ghost," but she felt "as if somebody had given her a present." "A Circle in the Fire" reveals the fact that callous inhospitality, an unwillingness to harbor the homeless, however repellent, makes even the angels helpless in ministering to the offender. There will be no protecting circle about Mrs. Cope in the fire. In "The Life You Save May Be Your Own," Mr. Shiftlet drifts into Mrs. Crater's place on hot air and a wooden leg. His hunger for the decrepit car is rivaled only by Mrs. Crater's yearning for a son-in-law. They arrange marriage between the innocent idiot daughter with her "long pink-gold hair and eyes as blue as a peacock's neck" and Mr. Shiftlet with his mouthful of religious mishmash, an eye only for machinery, and a heart fat with deceit. On their honeymoon, Shiftlet abandons the girl in "The Hot Spot," where she has fallen asleep, while the waiter says in awe, "She looks like an angel of Gawd." In a sense she was; she was the moment of grace for Shiftlet, his chance to save his life. As he drives down the road, a cloud "shaped like a turnip" blots out the sun and "there was a guffawing peal of thunder from behind and fantastic raindrops like tin-can tops crashed on his car." Shiftlet is fleeing to Mobile, while the heavens laugh in derision.

"Good Country People," with its heavily ironic title, introduces us to Manley Pointer, an abandoned hawker of Bibles "brimful of pardons," which ought, as he says, to be "in every room of the house besides in the heart of every man." "Believing nothing since the day he was born," Manley Pointer with the sharp nose, gaunt figure, "sticky looking brown hair" hanging disheveled over his forehead, collector of curios such as a woman's glass eye and a wooden leg, belongs to the same family as Chaucer's Pardoner, excelling him in cruelty as he falls far behind him in talent. He destroys souls with cheerful, amoral glee, an imp who revels in evil. On a certain morning, just before dinner, which his pointed nose has probably smelled out, Pointer, reeling under a heavy load of Bibles, visits the home of Mrs. Hopewell, who is always spouting optimistic platitudes, one of the good country people who don't know a thing about mercy because, like Mr. Head "she had been too good to deserve any." Her daughter, Joy, a misanthropic intellectual with a wooden leg and a sullen disposition, has changed her name to Hulga, a heavy chunk of sound, to express her disapproval of her mother and the universe. She has a

Ph.D. in Philosophy, which has taught her to see through everything into nothing and "has the look of someone who has achieved blindness by an act of will." Though she despises Pointer as an empty bubble from the Church of God, she agrees to go a-picknicking with him to see what "Mother Nature is wearing. O'er the hills and far away," in order to burst his bubble. During the night she dreams of seducing the lamb-like Pointer, and using his remorse as a step in his education. Never have the tables been more viciously turned. In a weird scene in a hayloft, she discovers that all the Pointer really wants is her wooden leg, which he manages to secure. In surrendering the leg she surrenders her identity, what makes her different. As Pointer moves over the meadow, she remains lying in the straw, utterly crushed with his words, "You ain't so smart. I been believing nothing ever since I was born," boiling in her mind. At this moment Hulga is probably the most pathetic figure in O'Connor's fiction — unable to walk, hoodwinked by a country bumpkin, really stung into nothing for the first time, her philosophy and psychology a shambles, his final taunt "You ain't so smart" destined to echo in her mind as long as she lives, she lies in the sordid straw, wretched and miserable, and poor and blind. Unlike the case of Mr. Head, the action of mercy does "not cover her pride like a flame and consume it." At the end of the story she lies in the straw in despair; the gospel had surrounded her life, unable to break her pride, and now there is no longer any mercy.

Our final story, "The Artificial Nigger," is an initiation story. Mr. Head is sixty, a time of "calm understanding of life" and "adequate credentials for being a suitable guide for the Young." He has "a long tube-like face" and a great deal of pride in its top. Mr. Head is going on a trip to Atlanta to educate his young grandson in the meaning of life. Immediately after they enter the train, at a whistle stop, it enters a dense tunnel of trees and they never emerge from a constricting tunnel of experience until they return. Mr. Head offers the boy a pompous guided tour of the train and begins to do the same in the city, but he is lost in the labyrinthine streets and terrified by the alien black faces. The boy feels as if "he were reeling down through a pitch black tunnel." They soon find themselves in a bizarre world, dense with mystery and threat. They are lost. Resting momentarily on their dark journey, Nelson, the boy, falls asleep and his grandfather wanders to the corner. When the boy jerks awake, his grandfather is gone, and he dashes off in terror, crashing into a Negro woman. When Mr. Head arrives she shouts,

You Sir: You'll pay every penny of my doctor's bill that boy has caused.

As the crowd turns angrily toward Mr. Head, the police arrive, and the hostile black women shove and stare, and then he says, "That is not my boy. I have never seen him before." The boy is transfixed by shock and even the hostile women stare in horror at such treachery and let him and his grandson walk slowly away. Both are eerily alone, helpless and lost.

What follows in the story is a strange miracle of grace and a detailed comment on the nature of mercy. As Head and Nelson walk along in cold bitterness, they see a weathered plaster figure of a Negro, leaning crazily forward on a fence, staring out of white eyes, with a piece of bronze watermelon in his hands. In a mysterious way this artificial nigger drains away the terror, suggesting that the hostile streets and black faces had been grotesquely distorted by fear, that as the two had experienced them, they were artificial, unnatural, teeming with unreal threat. Mr. Head then has a revelation and there were "no words in the world that could name it." Suddenly he realized that "he was forgiven for sin from the beginning of time . . . and since God loved in proportion as He forgave, he felt ready at that instant to enter Paradise," the ultimate true country to which the accepted moment of mercy opens the door. Mr. Head has been saved by grace freely flooding his soul in mystical vision.

Henry James, a realist, has said:

> There is no impression of life, no manner of seeing and feeling it, to which the plan of the novelist may not offer a place.

These nine stories constitute a startling vision of fallen man in memorable language. To make her vision real, O'Connor uses satirical exaggeration, sharp irony, ugly distortion, Gothic devices, and apocalyptic vision. Furthermore, William Faulkner has said, "You must use the evil to tell the truth which you consider important." This she does — to show the contour and quality of the true country of the soul.

Her impression of life has understandably alienated some readers hostile to the Christian faith and has intimidated and offended some others that accept it but who are distressed by her frankness, bold humor, and emphasis on the grotesque. Yet the stories at bottom deal with reality. I believe every evil act and thought could be supported by evidence from life; the difference lies in concentration. In real life evil erupts about us more loosely and its presence is mitigated by elements O'Connor ignores. Not a single person in her stories is beautiful and we all know that Fitzgerald did not describe the last of the Southern belles. The graciousness of Southern life, the decent godless people are largely absent; common grace is almost minimal. If, however, her selection had been widened and softened by Chaucerian compassion, the intense fabric of her vision would have been irreparably dimmed. The vision remains harsh throughout; even the Lord who came to redeem us "puts the bottomrail on top" and keeps it there; He throws everything off balance, and His all-demanding eyes insist on keeping it that way. He gives boundless mercy, but confronts us also with boundless claims. Few readers would deny her *originality*, however extravagant; her *humor*, however pungent; her *satiric power*, however acidly applied; her brilliance as a story teller; her strong, tough, and rapid style, at times shimmering in vividness. Neither would any sensitive reader deny the fact that the nine stories show us the meaning of life centered in our redemption in Christ.

In the end it is the old, old story: the fall, the desolate garden, the miraculous Birth, the drops of blood in another garden, the cursed tree on the hill, the resurrection in Joseph's garden — and because of it all the presence of illimitable mercy to those who believe, this story never ends as C. S. Lewis says in the close of *The Last Battle*:

> And as he spoke He no longer looked to them like a lion, but the things that began to happen after that were so great and beautiful that I cannot write them. And for us this is the end of all the stories, and we can most truly say that they all lived happily ever after. But for them it was only the beginning of the real story. All their life in this world, all their adventures in Narnia had been only the cover and title page; now at last they were beginning Chapter One of the Great Story which no one on earth has read; which goes on forever; in which every Chapter is better than the one before.

10

"Gladly wolde he lerne and gladly teche"

ON TEACHING

*I*n C.S. Lewis's The Lion, the Witch and the Wardrobe, *the memorable Professor Digory Kirke, first explorer of Narnia, ponders the incredulity of the older Pevensie children and finally explodes: "Why don't they teach logic at these schools?" What do they teach them in the schools anyway, he wonders. What they teach them is facts but not logic. What they teach them is hard nuggets of indisputable fact but not meaning. What they teach them is system but not wonder. The spirit withers under the reign of facts. As alternative in the* Chronicles of Narnia, *Lewis offers the theme of holidays. But these holidays are ordered.*

The following essays discuss both the holiday or festivity of education, but also the order which must inform such education to give it direction.

As did Lewis, Professor Timmerman demands order in learning. Education is not doing anything you like—and this applies to teacher as well as student. Education must be pointed toward enduring values, toward absolute meanings. Such education has a guide not in the world of fact, but in the world of the spirit.

235

Literature in the Calvin Classroom

The Banner (June 9, 1961)

The Complex Task

The teacher should acquaint the student with the major masterpieces and their relation to their own age, to each other and to the men who wrote them. He hopes to stimulate the ability to understand, appreciate, and evaluate works of literary art and to write competent prose. Since the great bulk of this literature has not been written by Christians, he and his students are immediately involved in problems of discrimination and discernment of uncommon difficulty.

The teacher of literature cannot simplify his task by an easy retreat from its difficulties. He cannot enforce an airtight immigration policy by means of which he allows only Christian writers into his classroom. That would make a farce of education. He cannot solve it by admitting disturbing secular writers and then confining himself to slashing them to bits. That would make a farce of the doctrine of common grace because the image of God, however tarnished, enables unbelievers to contribute both truth and beauty to the life of man. On the other hand he can certainly not adopt the usual impersonal, spectatorial attitude of the university teacher. A classic embodies a vision of life and therefore religious perspectives. The Christian teacher will regard a religiously unexamined classic as dangerous an inactivity as a religiously unexamined life.

Proper Understanding

The student must be taught to understand the meaning of poems and novels upon their authors' own terms in their own ages. Relying upon intelligence, imagination, sympathy, industry, and *Webster's Collegiate Dictionary*, the student earns his way to comprehension. Without such understanding on the part of both teacher and student the course will consist in a mere transfer of words without going through the mind of either. The process of understanding involves a measure of imaginative identification with the author's experience. In the case of Christian writings this is clear gain; in the case of non-Christian writings it often results in delight, wisdom, and spiritual enrichment even though the basic outlook of the author must be sharply challenged. However, in the case of some works, usually assigned only on the senior college level, there is a realism and naturalism, however honestly utilized by the author, that is spiritually distressing, even agonizing to a sensitive Christian.

It is the study of such writing, a fragment of our total offerings, which often puts the English departments in our colleges in the critical spotlight as it would other departments if their authors were more widely read. Should the student read books with hostile visions, and if so how should they be handled?

We at Calvin believe that such books should be taught if they are genuinely representative, authentic in experience, and superb in craftsmanship. The Christian student cannot afford to be ignorant of the deistic writings of Thomas Jefferson. They help him understand the very mold and pressure of the age which produced the Declaration of Independence and American democracy. He must read Thomas Hardy to know what happens when science triumphs at the expense of faith. He must know something about the rootlessness, irrationalism, and spiritual dryness of our time. He must know the wasteland to appreciate what he has and to bring it what it needs. He lives in a literary world of anxiety, preoccupied with the fact that:

> Into many a green valley
> Drifts the appalling snow.

Can we afford to close our eyes to the truths which these writers reveal about the nature and plight of modern man? But how does one deal with these books on the college level?

The teacher of literature should be decidedly outspoken about proper perspectives in reading. The Christian student cannot be a mere channel of experience. The student's mind is neither a blank nor a sponge. He should read in the light of faith, with controlled imagination, critical reserve and judgment ever awake. Reading in this way he can appropriate the psychological insight, the brooding descriptive power, the tender pity of Thomas Hardy and reject the soulless materialism at the heart of his dark vision. Merely depraved imagination has no place in our work. Portrayal of sin has, because man is a sinner. Writing novels about sinless men is flabby sentimentalism. But the work has to have a genuine moral concern, even though we may have to condemn the morality. Furthermore, reading lists are carefully explained because students vary in spiritual stamina, and assigned materials of clashing faiths are usually examined in class.

The Matter of Form

The steady exposure to the best words in the best order makes the student sensitive to style; much carefully marked writing makes him competent. The English Department does all it can to insure such competence, although a large number of college students are under its discipline for only a twelfth of their college careers. Furthermore, I may add that we do not supply able writers with all their publicly expressed ideas. Bright students hatch their own eggs.

Literature is meaningful form. Without meaning on some level writing is gibberish; therefore art for art's sake is merely hollow melody, or pleasing imagery without a centre. But meaning, however idealistic or noble, without adequate form is not literature whatever other good thing it may be in the way of edifying tracts. Purely formal matters concern sound effects, versification, choice of words, and structure. The formal elements must fuse with the content so that we experience a satisfying unity in which each part supports the whole. Upon technical matters our commitments have little to say. A sonnet is a precise poetic form which can be used by a Christian or a humanist. But upon the contained experience, the total impact of the work, the Reformed perspective has for us the last word to say.

The Final Estimate

The Calvin teacher never leaves his students in doubt about his Reformed perspectives, but he must treat his students with understanding. Students enjoy argument about basic issues, but they dread unrelieved unction. One can protest too much. Sometimes the poem speaks best for itself. Thorough and honest scholarship creates a respect which is moved by conviction. Then the student knows the critical judgment is neither affected nor superficial. "Tintern Abbey" by Wordsworth is an elevated poem which expresses in stately language and beautiful natural imagery genuine sensitiveness toward human beings, and a remarkable mystical experience. Wordsworth here crystalizes the core of his belief with moving skill. Having granted this, one is constrained to point out that his view of nature is mistaken in places, the mysticism misleading, and the theology false. God is not a vague, impersonal infinitude. He is absolutely transcendent and can be known only through Scripture through the operation of the Holy Spirit, and man can be saved not by some human idol but only through Jesus Christ, our Lord. Wordsworth is really worshiping his own mind. In some way as this the Christian teacher completes the purely literary judgment: thus he tries to integrate the values of a work of art with Reformed perspectives so that he is true to sound scholarship and serviceable to the spiritual life of the student.

A Lion Without

The Reformed Journal (January, 1960)

A college student is, of course, immune to no temptation, but his favored position makes him particularly vulnerable to the sin of sloth. Evidently even the Hebrews liked to loaf. Solomon tersely warns them that slothfulness casteth into a deep sleep, that the slothful man hideth his hand in his bosom, that the slothful man is brother to him that is a waster, and that the desire of the slothful man, killeth him. Solomon's targets may be sitting before me.

Sloth is laziness. The slothful student is the perennial goldbricker, the genteel idler purring her way through college, the relaxed epicurean, taking a motto from Omar Khayyan, "an hour we have, ah let us waste it well." He is the potential A student gracefully subsiding into B's, the potential B student comfortably accepting C's, the solid D student content to be himself. He is a waster, squandering not only money, but his most precious possession, his time, which is his life. Sloth is sin.

Sloth has myriad manifestations. There are the inveterate sleepers blinking their way into class and dozing after their arrival. Some sleep in the library; some sleep here. There are the dreamers, lost in pointless reverie, getting an A.B. in fantasy. There are the tireless babblers who measure their lives in coffee spoons. There are the academic armadillos thoroughly armored against the uncomfortable impact of new ideas. Sloth turns on WMAX and tries to read Thoreau on sounds. Sloth more than anything else turns in the disheveled mosaic of jarring syntax, doleful spelling, wandering modifiers, shoddy diction, and assorted howlers some students justifiably call their blue books. Sloth is a deadly sin.

I am talking about the waste of time. I am not arguing asceticism, or pleading for pale bibliomaniacs. I am strongly in favor of intelligent discussion, legitimate diversion, and animated romance. I am simply saying that the first business of a college student is study, that the normal amount of study the faculty recommends is thirty hours a week, and that a significant invasion of that quota is sloth. Sloth in this context is intellectual laziness.

The ancient Israelite whom Solomon is reprimanding is troubled with conscience. He knows he is slothful; he offers a powerful excuse. There is a lion without. Now, he is no Samson, no swordsman, no lion-tamer. So the only thing he can do is to hug his hearth. He wants no mournful obituary in the Gaza Post. No, he will wait for the National Guard.

But is there really a lion in the street? Or is this Israelite an honest neurotic imagining lions? Or is he just a liar?

Sometimes the slothful student is just a liar. He deliberately invents lions without; he malingers illnesses, he fakes the unobtainability of books and the necessary missing of classes. Such a student should be rebuked. Sometimes the slothful student is genuinely neurotic. He feels inadequate, he imagines grudges against him. He has real headaches. Such a student should be helped. Sometimes there is a lion in the street. The subject matter is difficult, the outside reading is laborious, athletics may interfere with his studies, his sweetheart may demand too much of his time. This student must get out and fight. The Calvin variety of the National Guard, the counseling service, cannot help him. Not to fight here is spiritual sloth.

There are indeed lions in the streets of life. One does not travel this life without risk and battle. Job said it long ago: yet man is born into trouble as the sparks fly upward. Sometimes the targets are down and there seems to be nothing to shoot at. The life of a student requires moral heroism. Wincing at difficulties, dodging assignments, carrying special consideration, seeking shoulders to sob on causes as many failures as mental incompetence. Often the only way is through. Retreat is the Beatnik way, bewailing the cruel edge of things, giving up moral questions in despair, writing ragged English — puff without powder — parade without performance — culminating in the poetic masterpiece called "Howl." What a travesty on man! I prefer the prayerful courage of the Christian who dares great things with the help of his Lord. I know that Browning sounds too cheerful for this iron age. Our poets specialize in images of despair, but Browning hit a noble note in his final poem written in the last year of his life.

One who never turned his back but marched breast forward,
Never doubted clouds would break,
Never dreamed though right were worsted, wrong would Triumph,
Held we fall to rise, are baffled to fight better,
Sleep to wake.

"The words of the wise are as goads," says Solomon. "Seest thou a man diligent in his business? He shall stand before kings."

A Noble Profession

The Reformed Journal (September, 1981)

A seminary professor I once knew spent a few weeks on an Iowa farm. He believed in physical fitness as well as in theological rigor, and, since this was before the era of jogging, he worked at haying with the farm hands. The farmer complimented him by saying, "I see you can work too." A colleague of mine was asked about his teaching load and answered "Nine hours," whereupon his interlocutor replied, "You sure put in a long day." Such misinformation is common, as is the notion that teaching is far from arduous and that excellence in it is a minor art. If one cannot refute this from experience, a new book entitled *Masters* (New York: Basic Books, 1981) will provide plenty of evidence.

During my years of teaching at Calvin College, I tried several times to give a student an A+. The registrar always cut out the plus. I suppose he was right. An A represents excellent work in terms fair to the class and subject matter, but from time to time one has students who transcend these standards of excellence. A similar situation is true of teachers. There are many good teachers, some excellent ones, but once in a while one is fortunate enough to encounter a teacher who transcends the standards of reasonable excellence. How does one establish or pinpoint the occurrence of such excellence? Through evaluation sheets hastily checked in the last ten minutes of a course by students who have never taught anybody? By peers and deans who never sit in class? By board members who sit in for half an hour during the discussion of subject matter they know little about? Jason Epstein, editor of *Masters*, has a good word here: "Proper evaluation can perhaps only be made after the spell of a powerful teacher has worn off, in the former student's maturity, when in tranquility he can recollect experience." Such persons have written the eighteen portraits in *Masters*, and formidable persons they are: Edmund Wilson, Sidney Hook, Kenneth Lynn, and John Wain among others. What is their consensus?

Before I mention their criteria, I should say something about student evaluations. They do indicate the dud with somber efficiency, and they do specify with gratifying accuracy the well-liked teacher. What they do not do, at least in compensatory result, is to give help to either one. A teacher may stop massaging his chin, jingle the coins in his pocket, or sniff continuously, but if he is judged as unclear, unorganized, and dull, how will the evaluations aid him to clarity, coherence, and brightness? How, as far as that goes, can anybody help such a person? He is a problem in elimination, not reconstruction.

Teaching is a performing art. Every performer has varying techniques that are noninterchangeable, but there is a consensus in the book on the qualities energizing the means. They are surprisingly obvious. A master teacher has a superb knowledge of subject matter, is always profoundly and zestfully convinced of its value, and is admirably able to communicate both the knowledge and the enthusiasm. He knows that every discipline has some dry ingredients, but he does not announce it by a public lament about its aridity. It is an integral part of the picture. *Masters* limits its portraits to college and university teachers at prestigious universities and that is its weakness. There is nothing in the criteria or the American educational process that necessitates such snobbery. There is nothing in the criteria that excludes high school and elementary teachers. Their lack is erudite scholarship, not extraordinary talent for teaching. The high school or elementary school teacher who is master of what he needs to know for his work, teaches it with belief and zest, and communicates it to where it is not easily dislodged meets the test whether he teaches at Thomas Jefferson High School or the fifth grade at P.S. 18 in Paterson.

The techniques of these eighteen teachers portrayed in this volume and all great teachers vary dramatically and in each case are closely interwoven with the magic of personality. That is why it is difficult to teach people how to teach. Imitation is often self-defeating: somehow the prospective teacher has to be helped to find his own rhythm. Yvor Winters, poet and professor at Stanford, relied on impersonal analysis of poems; I. A. Richards taught them in a dark room with the poem to be analyzed on a screen and made the lectures memorable by a remarkable placing of the poem in the whole history of great poetry through innumerable illuminating references. F. O. Matthiessen of Harvard identified himself so thoroughly with the Shakespearean characters he taught that they became as alive as the members of the class. Christian Gauss of Princeton made his classes lessons in morality and wisdom not by evangelical zeal, like Billy Phelps of Yale, but through low-key asides and comments. Morris Cohen, philosophy teacher of the College of the City of New York, employed the Socratic method with such brutality that one is astounded at the admiration Sidney Hook expresses. Cohen once went up to a group of students and said to one of them, "The trouble with you, Mr. A., is that you can't think." Cohen may have appealed to aggressive disputants like himself, but how about those who needed encouragement rather than intellectual flogging?

What enhanced the teaching of most of these eighteen men and women was their creative scholarship. To the stimulus of their spectacular knowledge, they added the excitement of discovery. Most of them were rigorous; though they enjoyed their popularity, they do not seem to have courted it. What is not emphasized in the book are two qualities I found in each of the great teachers I was fortunate to have: genuine interest in all their students and the selfless gift of encouragement. An encouraging word at the right time can spark a career or rescue a self-deprecating soul.

One reason for this lack of encouragement lay in the size of the classes these famous professors taught. I took two courses with a brilliant and distinguished professor at the University of Michigan. His lectures were models of rhetorical excellence and unfailingly interesting. There were over two hundred students in the classes, whose tests and papers were marked by an assistant. The student was neither a name, a number, nor even a grade to the teacher. He was always both elegant and somewhat statuesque. But high respect for his attainments was not suffused with the kind of spiritual love I had for my greatly gifted college, high school, and fifth-grade teachers. There is an irresistible lure and éclat to large audiences for a teacher and preacher, but both run the hazards of ministering to anonymous faces.

After over forty years of teaching, I have undiminished esteem and admiration for the profession. I am sorry to see its possible accomplishments being eroded by millage rejects and threatened by conditions that burn teachers out. Teaching is full of surprises: the shy and silent student who turns in the best term paper; the self-appointed genius who knows all the answers except those required on examinations; the Chaucer student who could read Middle English as Chaucer must have spoken it; the would-be poet who handed in a four-page poem composed solely of adverbs; the freshman who in deadly seriousness handed in as a prospective term paper topic, "The History of Mankind"; the young man who was obsessed by what he considered Poe's obsession with eyes; the plagiarist who defended his theft by claiming that he wanted the matter stated as well as it could be stated. One of my greatest surprises has been that I never encountered a repentant plagiarist.

One of my college teachers once said in class that he enjoyed teaching so much that he sometimes felt as if he should be paying for the privilege. I have never been seized by such euphoria. Teaching is no effortless joy ride. I have felt at times as if I were prodding a tortoise for fifty minutes. It is no cause for congratulation to watch the competition for interest waged between the reading of the "Ode to Duty" and the buzzing of a blue fly on the window pane. I do not, like Mr. Chips, look back on over forty years of teaching "with a deep and sumptuous tranquility." The teacher who is not slightly nervous before every class is uncommon. Yet it is a noble profession. In the mutual submission to, mastery of, and critical engagement with a tradition and discipline transcending everyone in the class, there is a heady mind and "heart-stretching" exhilaration. If one is a Christian teacher, he or she will at the right season and in the right way sow the good seed with the firm hope of harvest.

Mr. Chips Couldn't Make it Today

The Reformed Journal (November, 1977)

Mr. Chips, to whom James Hilton paid an eloquent if sentimental farewell in his novel *Good-bye Mr. Chips*, had in a long career as schoolmaster and Latin teacher only "slight and occasional discipline problems"; he mellowed into pleasing eccentricity, repeating old jokes with impunity year after year, and moved into legend before retirement and into myth after that. Of course, the book was published in 1934, and Chips ended his career near the close of 1918 — all now lost in the dark abyss of the irrecoverable past. When I read of the tribulations of teachers today, I recall Mr. Chips, musing at eighty on a tranquil past in which his harshest disciplinary act was the assignment of a hundred lines to a student who intentionally dropped the lid of a desk in class. How would Mr. Chips, a good man and a good and gentle teacher, fare in the Latin classes, if there are any left, in the violent schools we read about in the papers?

We usually associate casualties with football players, policemen, and the armed services. I have never heard of a clergyman trounced by a parishioner, a lawyer beaten up by a client, or seldom of doctors mending each other after being lacerated by a patient. During the past year, however, over 70,000 schoolteachers have been physically attacked by their pupils; one had her hair set on fire and some have died. Teachers in some schools suffer from battle fatigue, and many sweat with fear in classrooms, corridors, and playgrounds. At the same time, many Americans, including an hysterical journalist in *The New Yorker* of May 30, 1977, are violently angry because the United States Supreme Court refused to recognize proper paddling as a form of "cruel and inhuman punishment."

What does one make of all this? In the first place, after teaching over forty years in peaceable schools, one feels like an immigrant in one's own country. The stark and dramatic contrast between many contemporary schoolrooms and my own grammar and high school days almost defies belief. In my youth the student body was markedly different. At fourteen the disaffected and the stupid left school for the factory or the farm. The underachievers were flunked and the overachievers skipped grades. We all had homework and our parents usually hovered over us until it was finished. I saw more violence on the playground than I ever did in the classroom: the school pump was in regular use for rehabilitation.

I spent half of my grammar school days in a public school and the other half in a Christian school. Discipline was uncomfortably tight in both places; the ruler, the paddle, the stinging slap were in infrequent but always in potential use. Teachers were not worried about bruising the egos of smart alecks. My third-grade teacher, a Miss Graham, was a real cracker. When I was in the seventh grade, half a dozen older boys tossed a lavishly dressed sissy in a sizable barnyard puddle. After recess the six boys were ordered to the front of the class, made to bend over, and then soundly whacked. In a high school chapel, a minister given to lengthy and inexplicable pauses, saw a boy laughing in the front row; he reached out and smacked him soundly in the face (you could feel it burn) and then calmly went on with his speech and pauses. If discipline was reported at home, more usually followed.

The parents, whether they supported Christian or public schools, believed in orderly classrooms and refused to tolerate disruptive behavior. The children and the administration feared the parents, who feared nobody. Today, as someone said, the administration fears the parents, the parents fear the children, and the children fear nobody. Authority was genuine. I remember no unjustified punishment and no discernible damage. We didn't always love our teachers, but we had to behave and we did learn. The idea of attacking a teacher was simply unimaginable, though we sometimes felt like it. How we felt was largely irrelevant to what we had to do: the parents, the public, and the school system made sure we did it, and because of that ordinary teachers could survive and gifted ones could make a lasting impression.

In such a lost world paddling made sense. In contemporary schools supported by a unified community with similar values it still does. I assume, of course, that the paddling is administered in the proper place, in a proper amount, by a teacher who finds it disagreeable but effective. Is there really anything in this that common sense or the Scriptures can fault? I am old-fashioned enough to believe in punishment as well as rehabilitation, and naive enough to think that the former may promote the latter. I have no sympathy with sentimentalists who weep over the hard treatment of toughs who beat up old women. I don't believe one can attribute all viciousness to insanity. I know a man whom no one considers insane who tied up my former neighbor Alice and then attached her to the back of his car and drove off dragging her over a block. My wife and I saw her bloody face and battered body. What does he deserve? Pine Rest Christian Hospital or forty stripes? He got neither.

On the other hand, to suggest paddling as a disciplinary measure in classrooms, corridors, and playgrounds which exhibit the violence portrayed in the media would be dangerous indeed. Such schools are supported by communities which are writhing under the complex burden of Pandora's box opened in the 1960s: romantic individualism; eroded or nonexistent Christian values; alcoholism and drug abuse among the young; overdue rectification of racial discrimination; parental absenteeism; permissiveness, crookedness, and sexual immorality at every level; raw violence on television and the films; widespread adherence to educational philosophies whose wisdom is alien to Christianity. It is a wonder to me that the problems are not more severe and that so much good survives in purely secular schools. It is a pity that so many teachers are in the eye of the storm, particularly when they have achieved professional competence, prestige, and pay.

The solution to these problems is far beyond my competence to find, but I should like to record a fact and offer a timid suggestion.

First the fact. For the last twenty-five years we lived across the street from the Oakdale Christian School in Grand Rapids, from which our four children were graduated. I saw this neighborhood change from white middle American to half black and half white, now becoming increasingly black. Neither the changing character of the community nor the taut pressures of the late sixties dimmed the vision or witness of this school. Instead of flight there has been adaptation, and a steady evolution into a multi-racial student body. Through love, persistent innovation, competent teaching, fairness, and faith, the initial tensions in the student body were relaxed, so that the student body is simply Oakdale Christian, supported by parents of various races devoted to sound learning and living according to the law of our Lord. This school is to us a witness to the grace of God and the loyalty of his servants. It is a good school and it is a good Christian school.

The suggestion, I fear, may strike the readers who have survived up to this point as simplistic and unpalatable. No schoolroom can function without order; the order may be loosely and creatively structured, but it must be present. The final responsibility for such order rests, I believe, on the parents. Children do not belong to the state; neither are they the final responsibility of the state. Teachers cannot be psychologists, policemen, and servants of the juvenile court as well as masters of subject matter and normally successful methods of teaching it. Persistently disruptive students should be banned from the schools until parents and society make them fit to profit from them.

Do Illiterate A.B.'s Disgrace Us All?

College Composition and Communication (February, 1957)

Though the answer to my title question should be self-evident, not all college teachers accept corporate responsibility. They have to agree to frequent graduate illiteracy; it is a truth as plain as a pyramid. Our A.B.'s can, I agree, read the daily paper after a fashion; they can write an intelligible, incorrect, and dull letter. But literacy conceived as the ability to write a sensible fifteen-hundred-word paper in properly punctuated, clear, and correct English is beyond thousands of current A.B.'s. Literary mediocrity is beyond them, and we are all to blame.

The rapidly mounting evidence that many upperclassmen cannot meet these minimum qualifications of collegiate literacy has caused colleagues to look accusingly and belligerently at the English Departments. The distressing fact must be localized and the locale is easily if speciously identified. The English teacher is not doing his job. But is it his job?

The English teacher grows lean on perplexities. He has inherited and currently bears the full brunt of contemporary educational cross-currents and confusion. Left-wing linguists sabotage him from within by regarding the teaching of formal grammar as a barbarous relic; right-wing classicists blame him for the pathetic grammatical and literary ignorance his pupils frequently display. It is his business to impart a sense of form and structure in a world of "communications courses," telephone conversation exercises in English textbooks, and true-false tests. He is presumably dedicated to teaching the best that has been thought and written to a generation gorging itself on cowboys, ranchers, robbers, and spacemen — most of whom grunt, groan, or recite mathematical formulae. If he teaches in a Christian school, he faces additional problems of selection, perspective, and integration. In the words of A. MacLeish,

> Around, around the sun we go:
> The moon goes round the earth.
> We do not die of death:
> We die of vertigo.

The Freshman English teacher has a particularly difficult task. It is his business to teach writing, and writing like thinking is exacting work. His minimum goal is the attainment of clear, correct expression on the part of every student. He hopes that by June every freshman will be able to write clear, correct sentences, properly organized paragraphs, and unified compositions, without flagrant misspelling and erroneous punctuation. The techniques he emphasizes are standardized and orthodox because he believes that successful original experimentation most frequently grows out of a knowledge of the rules. Joyce, the most radical experimenter in the English language, had a thorough classical education and began his career by writing normal if brilliant English prose. I may add that just getting students to write is an arduous task. Having nothing to say, most of them resent having to say it every week.

That the English teacher does not attain his goal is evident. All of us teachers have read ulcer-breeding upperclassmen papers and tests — the jarring syntax, the doleful spelling, the sprawling participles, the wandering modifiers, the shoddy diction, the vagueness, the occasional unendurable pomposity. If literary competence is our target, we are all misguided missiles.

Why is this so? Although there are, of course, many students who write well, and some who write with distinction, why do so many, and not a few of them intelligent, write so poorly? Why are there students who take 125 semester hours at college and still fail to write respectable English papers, fail to make respectable speeches? I do not refer to color, verve, punch; I am talking about grammar laid waste, diction disheveled, and syntax badly wounded.

There are certain causes pervasively operative before the college teachers even see the students. One such cause is the steady weakening of the classical high school curriculum, a weakening so thoroughgoing that not only has Latin often been abandoned, not only have modern foreign languages often been abandoned, but even formal English grammar has been eliminated. Much too frequently freshmen tell me that they have never studied formal grammar; some have assured me that they have never written a composition. These students have aggravated their already serious literary problems by a steady diet of comic books, a strong devotion to tinny music, and a gluttonous attention to television. They arrive at college plump with ignorance.

What is sometimes even more disconcerting is the fact that students may come from good schools where we know there are good teachers and they still are ignorant of grammar and good writing. That is a minor miracle. There is granite in the soul of the student who for six years survives unscathed the attacks of grammarians. Not even a preposition got by that elemental rock. Some of these students have good minds. There is something in their cultural atmosphere that makes them regard the study of grammar as useless. And that is the pragmatic temper of our time.

We live in a pragmatic, sense society; we are drenched in the values of material things. Things are in the saddle and ride mankind. This spirit, this modern pragmatic mind envelops us like a mist and seeps into the minds of both students and teachers. To many students grammar seems a theoretical detour to something he can do well enough without. Formal English, especially as studied systematically, seems impractical. His father, who speaks with the tongues of the philistines, is a wealthy man. The whole matter of literature seems to him not to matter. Why should he learn to read poems well? Such knowledge is irrelevant to prosperity. In fact, despite the tremendous growth of schools, there is increasingly less interest in the intellectual life. College for many students is not an intellectual challenge; it holds no esthetic charm; it is primarily a social experience. Formal discipline is a yoke to escape as quickly as possible.

A recent best seller was entitled *Why Johnny Can't Read*, and the man who wrote it lost himself in battles about spelling. Possibly a more relevant question would have been, DO JOHNNY'S PARENTS READ?

Mr. G. Gallup in a preliminary report on a two-year study of our national reading habits says that fewer people read and buy books in the United States than in any other democracy, that if we had as many bookshops as the Danes we would have 23,000 instead of 1,450, and that if we were as adequately supplied with libraries as the Swedes we should have 77,000 instead of 7,500. Mr. Dupee, president of the Great Books Foundation, says in an article in the *Saturday Review*, June 2, 1956:

> Today, at any time, only 17 per cent of the adults in the U.S. may be found reading a book — any book, Spinoza or Spillane. [Spillane has sold 25,000,000 copies of his abdominal adventures in artistic mayhem.] In England, where schooling is far from universal 55 per cent of the population at any given time may be found reading a book. . . . Forty-two per cent of the houses in America today are without bookcases or bookshelves of any kind.
>
> [And the most devastating bit of statistics of them all]: . . . if we went to college more than a quarter of us have not read a single book in the last year.

Can English teachers do much about these depressing conditions? They can hardly wage successful battle against the massive forces of a pragmatic culture. They can hardly alter the cultural habits of the American masses. Though they constantly encourage good reading habits, though they battle the study of the classic in the apparatus of the comic, though they resign themselves to a grinding campaign:

> Boots-boots-boots-movin' up and down again
> There's no discharge in the war.

Unless we are agreed that college is open to candidates whose only qualifications are locomotion and respiration, we as English teachers can exert pressure on admissions policies. The colleges can say, and I believe the American people would support the saying — only students of demonstrated mediocrity need apply. High school students with a strong "D" record should not even be admitted unless they have respectably passed entrance examinations. There are, of course many colleges strong enough to do just that. I am pleading for such a policy in every Dean's office. There are hundreds of Deans who would quake for their academic lives, if they were now to pursue it.

What can we as faculties do about the situation? I begin with the English Department. We should try to do better work in Freshman English under good circumstances to do it. The means of achieving better work is largely a technical matter of interest mainly to the department. It may be of interest to note the general conviction that good reading habits and good writing go hand in hand. Therefore we constantly confront freshmen with models of good English for inspiration and imitation. I think hard reading is as important as the formal discussion or practice of good writing. I have yet to find a good reader who was a poor writer. He may have need of grammatical, punctuational, and orthographical polish but the substance is there.

At the risk of being considered a mossback, I recommend increasing attention to formal grammar. I believe a thorough knowledge of syntax is a prerequisite to the discovery and correction of errors. I believe that grammar is more than fortuitous custom but represents a rational structure. Here are two sentences:

> To look well dressed, one's clothes should harmonize.
>
> The apples were got down by striking the tree.

To detect these errors one needs logic and grammar; one has to find out what is wrong before one can correct it. Mastery of grammatical nomenclature facilitates the whole process. Punctuation, too, is based upon a comprehension of syntax. The comma fault is such a bugbear just because students do not understand grammar. Everyone knows that usages change, but everyone should know that language is basically very conservative. Grammatical structure in Chaucer is closely similar to our own; our own will be closely similar to that of 2050, when our generation of gerund-grinders will have left the scene. Sherwood Anderson in his memoirs complains that in grammar school:

> You did a thing called parsing sentences, and what an unjust terrible thing to do to a seemingly innocent sentence.

Yet I am sure the easy, limpid style of Anderson's prose owes something to this training.

We want, as English teachers, to do better work; to do so we need good circumstances under which to do so, and the biggest good circumstance we need is smaller class loads. We suggest as our ideal fifteen students per class in Freshman English; we shall be happy with twenty. We are not aiming at a diminution of work; we are aiming at better work. As some faculty wag has said, it is no harder not to mark four hundred papers than it is not to mark forty papers. This proposal does not then intend, to use the words of T.V. Smith, to provide more leisure for the theory class.

I want to be very concrete about this problem not only to dramatize the need of English departments, but the need of all departments that are understaffed or overburdened. It is easy to judge the fair by our own booth; we can bear our colleagues' burdens lightly. In giving this picture I am illustrating the problems of all colleagues under pressure.

Let us take a look then at Professor Ivy who teaches Freshman English. Since he is a beginner he is stuck with four sections of it; and under our present teacher-pupil ratio of 27 per class this gives him 108 freshmen. For variety and escape from unmitigated hackdom he is also teaching a section of American Literature of 40 students. So he has 150 students in all. Professor Ivy is a conscientious idealist who takes seriously the departmental directive of eight to ten compositions a semester; he decides to order nine. Each theme takes a minimum of fifteen minutes to process (he soon learned to process them). Each batch will therefore consume 1,620 minutes or 27 hours a batch. This will occur nine times during the semester. Part of our departmental program to assure greater literacy involves increased assignment of themes in 200 and 300 courses, so he will assign three themes in American Literature which will consume six hundred minutes or five hours a batch. Furthermore, since English teachers have a congenital and philosophical aversion to true-false tests, he will have two bluebooks of sustained if dismal prose to occupy him for a total of fifty hours a semester. The final examinations will consume thirty hours more. I don't suppose anybody but a mathematics teacher has the totals in mind, so I will inform you that this teacher will have spent 338 hours marking papers by the end of the first semester. But this man must also teach, freshly, provocatively. We will allow him fifteen hours a week preparation; this much because he must teach literature as well as grammar, and in literature courses a lot of reading makes a little saying. He also teaches fifteen hours a week. There are sixteen weeks in the semester (excluding Christmas vacation which we will however use); thus, he is busy fifty-one hours a week. Committee meetings, extracurricular duties, counseling, quizzes, "must" programs will bring his total to about sixty hours a week. Meanwhile he will not have taught anywhere long before he will hear from the community that social helpers are in demand — strong demand. He himself, looking at his galloping budget, wishes he could teach somewhere else for an evening a week to pay for his children's shoes; he looks wistfully at the pulpiteer who combines idealism with income on Sunday and rests on Monday. He may also be working on a higher degree since he has his eye on the ever-receding upper echelons of the faculty pay structure. This chap is going somewhere, and my guess is that he is going neurotic is not psychotic. Is it any wonder we have difficulty in finding suitable candidates? Not everybody is dying to die.

Now this is not hyperbole, rant, or special pleading. Suppose you give the teacher three sections of Freshman English and two of American Literature. He will have more preparation for the latter classes, more tests, and in our suggested program of increased writing for upperclassmen more papers than formerly. The only way to lower the load as it stands is simply not to do it. And that has been the case. The number of themes has been reduced to eight and even six; the more frequent writing of upperclassmen has not materialized. Class sections must be diminished or lower caliber work or ill health will result. You pays your money and you takes your choice.

I would urge, in the next place, that all teachers give as much work in formal writing as possible, that we make form a weighty factor in the determination of grades, that we eliminate true-false tests whose only literary discipline is geometrical. I see no good reason why the humanities generally do not assign more term papers and critical reviews. Such subject matters as history, education, philosophy, foreign literature offer manifold opportunities for supporting our program greatly. If that requires a reduction of class loads, steps can be so taken.

We in the English Department lean heavily upon the teachers of languages and speech. We would, of course, prefer to have it the other way; but many students say they first learn grammar through Latin or German. The reason for that at college is that in these languages the students start with the rudiments which they have never mastered, whereas our course is always conducted as a sort of review of something many have never viewed. We do not in English have students conjugate: I run, you run, he runs; yet there are many freshmen who think runs is a plural form. We don't have students master synopses, or paradigms. The language teachers help us here. We are in a real spot with many students; if we were to give them what they really need, it would be seventh-grade grammar, but even a college teacher reaches a limit of indignity. The people who don't know seventh-grade grammar should, I still believe, be made to take a non-credit three-hour course till they do.

We also look confidently to the teachers of logic. Clear writing and clear thinking are essential in our courses for freshmen. We are not in our freshman course interested in symbolism, suggestion, overtones, fragmentary prose, and experimentation. We want students to know the rules of sound thought and writing. The thinking of many freshmen is as roiled as the swirling waters of Big Muddy. Their thinking is personalistic and misty. Many are most concerned with who goes with whom and why isn't it I? Freshman papers teem with galloping generalizations; they burst with "non-sequiturs"; they dodge issues, and leave gaps in the thought, and the only argument they have really mastered is that of *ad misericordiam*. The teacher of logic is in a magnificent position to help student writing.

I have dealt largely with incompetence and shoddiness in writing. These bulk large in the experience of English teachers, but they are happily not the whole story. If English Departments are largely to be held responsible for poor writers, they should have their accolade for the good. But our time goes into the mediocre. We spend hours on comma faults and abominable syntax and lack the minutes to guide the gifted. The gifted are still our lost generation; they are too often taught below their reach — and that is tragic, or so I think.

We need the gifted. They are not always highly tolerable; opinionated, prickly, a thorn in the flesh, often hypercritical, knifing through our protective folds of padding, they embarrass us as well as spur us on. Yet we need them desperately in our society. Mr. Handlin says in the article quoted above, "No dean or department head ever was criticized by his administration for taking on the safe mediocrity." It should not be our policy towards students. We must beware of taking on mediocrity as our major function.

Under present conditions we are not even assured of mediocrity. As the college halls fill with students, as the platforms continue to groan with graduates, the conscientious teacher knows that unless courageous measures are arduously undertaken, the so-called bachelors of art will be hollow men and women who after four years of schooling cannot write a composition which a generous teacher can mark "C" without unnerving administrative pressure.

11
"Lives of Great Men"
BIOGRAPHY

*I*n the second letter of Paul to his young protégé Timothy, the great apostle warned him against men who would lead the saints astray (II Tim. 3). It was not a matter of pride that Paul proposed to such men the example of his own life: "Now you have observed my teaching, my conduct, my aim in life, my faith, my patience, my love, my steadfastness. . . ." Paul paid the price of great suffering, and eventually his life, for that example.

The lesson endures. We can learn much from the lives of great men. The terms of that greatness, however, must be qualified. We live in an age of stargazers, overwhelmed by the eclipse of stage lights and a genius for self-aggrandizement. The following selections recognize that greatness which endures, long after the luster of media stars has burned out like a fitful candle. There is a greatness which endures in the lives of great men.

On Writing a Life

The Calvin Forum (February-March, 1956)

Biography has been crowding fiction on the shelves of best sellers for some years. Novelists and biographers both deal with the soul of man, that labyrinth of never plumbed curiosities and mysteries. There may be some interest in the questions — What makes a good biography? How does one write a life?

Samuel Johnson said that it was the biographical part of literature that he loved best. It is poetic justice that he is best remembered by his own *Lives of the Poets*, and, above all, by Boswell's incomparable life. It is, indeed, poetic justice that Boswell has given a speaking likeness of that burly, dominating figure, that we hear his "Yes Sir, No Sir, Why, Sir?" over the "dark backward and abysm of time." Through Boswell's magic gift a real man emerges, and when that booming voice settles an argument in the elegant eighteenth-century drawing room concerning the respective merits of poets Derrick and Smart by saying,

"Sir, there is no settling the precedency between a louse and a flea"

we feel the living man among us. That is the art of biography.

The art of biography is closely related to its purposes. As these purposes vary so do the biographies, and some of the purposes result in bad biography.

I suppose the commemorative urge has played a decisive part in most biographies. The wish to keep the memory of greatness green is basic. It is an indispensable motive, but not the most important.

Many biographies have been motivated and vitiated by the edificatory urge, the wish to preach a lesson and a sermon. When that motive predominates we have the whitened angel, the gilded lily, King Arthur "wearing the white flower of the blameless life," Whitman masquerading as the "Good Grey Poet." We get then hagiology, saint-worship, not biography.

On the other hand, biographers may be motivated by dislike, even venom. Then we get Griswold's life of Poe, Woodword's life of Grant, and a biography of the twenties intriguingly entitled *My Grandfather: An Ass.*

But the best biographies have strongly behind them another more fundamental motive: sympathetic curiosity, the desire to understand and interpret human nature. The biographer is then fascinated by the endless variety of the heart of man "the glory, jest, and riddle of the world." What a range that heart has. There are the damaged souls whom Bradford has so penetratingly described. A man like Benedict Arnold, innately heroic, who goes strangely wrong. There are the sinners like Cesar Borgia who served with distinction and poisoned with pride; there are saints like Sister Theresa and Saint Francis; there are the proud braggarts like Cellini and Rousseau; the sufferers from the fever of the bone like Donne and Bunyan, the waspish little great men like Alexander Pope, and the magnanimous men like Lincoln. The range is endless but the problems are basically the same: love and hate, money — how to get it and how to keep it, hope and despair, ambition and disillusion. The folly of mankind is endless, as Wilder says in *Our Town*:

> Wherever you come near the human race, there's layers and layers of nonsense.

There is the pity and sadness of it. That tangled skein of human nature is the biographer's basic interest, and to penetrate for a moment its mystery, and to present a living likeness of a single soul is his basic objective.

I believe that the portrayal of a human soul is a work of art. I am aware that Virginia Woolf maintains that biography is a craft rather than an art because the biographer is tied where the artist is free. The artist can create, the biographer cannot. That is true; the biographer is indeed tied to fact; he cannot create or fabricate; but the imagination implied in adequate recreation, in catching the rhythm of life, the consummate skill involved in a just application of means to ends, the necessity of style and pattern in the portrayal seem to me to justify calling biography an art. It may be a minor art, but it is a real one.

There is another reason why biography may be considered an art. The late Professor Parker of Michigan used to define art as the imaginative satisfaction of desire. Though that is peculiarly true of creative art, I believe it is also partially true of biographical art. The biographer then deeply wants the career and character of the subject for himself, the subject is in a sense a fulfillment of his dreams. In recreating that personality and career, he identifies himself with it, and imbues the treatment with some of the intensity of his own experience. I think Amy Lowell did something like that in her life of Keats; I believe she experienced comfort from the vicious attacks made upon Keats's poems, since something of the same contumely had greeted hers. I am sure Boswell shared the joy of Johnson's thunder, and that Sandburg had a satisfaction in the brooding sympathy of Lincoln.

As an art, biography is the imposition of pattern upon the inchoate details of a life, resulting in a living likeness. How is such a speaking portrait to be created? It is achieved through a happy combination of the right subject, the right biographer, and the right means.

Mr. A. Maurois maintains that granted the right biographer a good biography can be made about anybody from a seller of mousetraps in Kresge's to a sophisticated wit like Oscar Wilde. Possibly, if the biographer has a "God's eye view" of the matter, and can explain the mystery of personality. Otherwise, and that to me means always, the biographer is wise in selecting a subject with great human interest, a subject with dash and color. Assuming the right biographer (Dr. Dryasdust would go wrong with Henry VIII) the right subject makes a difference. One cannot go far wrong with dazzling personalities like Mark Twain or Charles Dickens. Twain's imperturbable showmanship, Disraeli's sinuous brilliance, Dickens' gusto, and Wilde's exhibitionism are sure-fire. The statuesque greatness of a man like Washington is far less effective material than the warm humanity of Lincoln. Select a colorful man, preferably a villain.

Furthermore, a subject is not right unless it is available. Shakespeare is an interesting subject, but there has been no great biography of Shakespeare because the data are sparse and often inferential. The biographer then falls prey to the constant temptation to interpret an author's biography in terms of his publications. Shakespeare thus analyzed results in a Hydra-head, a Romeo, Mercutio, Falstaff, Hamlet, Prospero grotesque. There is as yet no good biography of Matthew Arnold because the family has turned the key on the basic data. Biography is woven from diaries, letters, journals, memoirs, and personal reminiscences. A man's twenty-five volumes may still leave us in the dark as to the essential man. The essential Henry James is still in the shadows.

The right biographer is equally essential. Victorian biography came out every Thursday in two portly volumes called *The Life and Letters*. Heavy-handed, eulogistic, amorphous, a dull, unshapely mass, originating in piety, executed in obtuseness, and soon embalmed in library dust — such it was. Written by a family friend, usually a preacher, with the tearful widow censoring the job over his shoulder, how could the work come alive? A good biographer is not so easily come by.

The right biographer must, of course, generally be a scholar, trained in gathering and evaluating materials; he must have imagination and intelligence; he must have structural sense and style; but he must beyond all these and foremost possess three qualities: sympathy, skepticism, and courageous honesty. He must love human beings, and be able to enter sympathetically into their complexity. He must be largehearted and tolerant, and the master of a kindly irony. Otherwise we get a sermon. Imagine Edwards writing the biography of Franklin.

The right biographer must have a skeptical streak. He must admire greatness, but he must sift it carefully. He can be no hagiologist or hero-worshipper, whitening the angel, suppressing the uncomplimentary, and making a myth of a man. He must debunk, and by that I do not mean belittle, but to remove the bunk, the legends that surround a hero. Sainthood is rare and he must be sure it is present.

He must have courageous honesty. I do not mean that he must deliberately exhume the faults of a man or make a parade of peccadillos, but he must always tell the essential truth, and must suppress nothing essential to it. Tennyson said:

> What business has the public to know of Byron's wildness? He has given them fine work and they ought to be satisfied.

But without the wildnesses one does not have Byron, without the opium one does not have Coleridge, without Wordsworth's illegimate daughter one does not have Wordsworth, without Henry Fielding's disreputable second marriage one does not have Fielding. And even without Tennyson's comment in the picture galleries, "Come on, let's go get some beer," one does not have Tennyson. Boswell refused to make a kitten out of his tiger; neither must a biographer prettify or falsify.

Lytton Strachey once said:

> We do not realize that it is perhaps as difficult to write a good life as to live one.

I should say that it was considerably harder. I single out two major problems. It is extremely difficult to find out the truth about a man, and it is almost as difficult to present that truth artistically.

The child, said Wordsworth, is father of the man, and most people would agree to that, but where is the child? How can he be recovered?

Dare we trust an author's memoirs: his memory falsifies, forgets, and rationalizes. Dare we trust the parents' memoirs? They are subject to the same limitations. Can we hope ever to reconstruct the burning experience of youth? I wonder.

And the mature man is almost as hard to recover. Even with all the available documents in hand, it remains hard to plumb the inner soul. Piecing all the evidence together, the central motive may still elude discovery. Froude, the biographer of Carlyle, with all the evidence of friendship and research concludes that Jane Welsh Carlyle was an unhappy woman, and the victim of Carlyle's selfishness and waspish temper. Mr. Drew, another biographer of Carlyle, calls Jane Welsh a shrew. Carlyle's wife was seen scrubbing the flagstones of their Chelsea place on hands and knees. No one knows for a fact why she did so; yet Froude calls Carlyle a brute for allowing his wife to do so. Was he? The incident is a fact, but the inference as to Carlyle's character is surely unwarranted; too many other considerations enter in.

A second major difficulty of the biographer is the artistic presentation of the truth he finds. A work of art has pattern, form; a good novel has, or used to have, plot; it was formed material. Can one combine the structure of the novel with the stubborn factual material of the biography? Not, of course, in the same way. One can hardly manipulate biographical facts into a thriller. One must be true to fact; yet I believe a biography may attain real structure. It can do that if everything in the biography contributes to its basic end, namely, a lively and convincing portrayal of character. If every detail fills out the portrait, if the life catches the rhythm of the personality it depicts, and if we finish the work with a ripe sense of real acquaintance, then that biography is a work of art.

Granted now the right biographer and the right subject, what is the right means of portrayal? Suppose one has determined to write a life of Henry Ward Beecher; one has then a good subject. Suppose also that all the necessary materials are available. What now are the right means of making that life vivid?

Well, how does one get a vivid impression of any personality? One knows people, first of all, through their bodies; so too the spirit one has studied is not a wraith or spector; he stood so many feet, weighed so many pounds, was an Apollo or a disaster. One's physique affects all of life. If obtainable, there should be good portraits in a biography. The face is an index of the mind. Lincoln's gangling homeliness, Byron's spectacular good looks, Johnson's burly body, and Lamb's stutter are an integral part of their lives. We remember people by their characteristic mannerisms, the characteristic habits of gesture, voice, or action. These, the good biographer collects and uses aptly whenever they reveal character. Johnson's compulsive collecting of orange peels and counting of lamp posts, Cowper's fondness for gentle pets like rabbits and ducks, Rossetti's fondness for exotic pets like armadillos, peacocks, and even an elephant reveal the man. And what a difference health or disease make. What a contrast between Browning's robust health and Carlyle's dyspepsia. For how much did Byron's club foot count or Stevenson's bad lungs? The physical man should be sharply realized and interwoven through the life.

We remember people through their bright sayings, and what a significant role anecdote plays in illuminating a man. It often sends a blinding flash into the dark. Think of Daniel Webster at his death-bed saying to a friend just before he died: "Have I said anything unworthy of Daniel Webster?" Think of Aaron Burr habitually referring to Hamilton as "my friend Hamilton whom I shot." Consider the philosopher Bishop Berkeley who once went to see a man hanged and coming home persuaded his friend Contarin to hang him experimentally. He was cut down nearly senseless and exclaimed: "Bless my heart, Contarin, you have ruffled my band!" Or consider Sidney Smith's priceless remark on gout: "Gout is the only enemy I don't want to have at my feet." Or to change the tone of the anecdotes, look at John Keats when he first coughed a single drop of blood. He said:

> Bring me the candle Burns and let me see the blood. That drop of blood is my death warrant. I shall die.

The good biographer uses the telling anecdote whenever relevant.

In these days we do not generally treasure letters. Many causes have united in the degeneration of that art. Yet letters, especially spontaneous letters, are often revelatory. I would not wholly endorse Leslie Stephen's remark that they are "the one essential to a thoroughly satisfactory life," but their wise use is certainly essential. They afford an intimate acquaintance obtainable nowhere else. Think of doing without the Browning correspondence or the love letters of Mark Twain; the former so urbane and polished, the latter so impromtu and amusing. Letters serve not only in revealing personality, but they give great aid in checking events. When a private letter and a public event clash, the biographer has an interesting problem. Even the letters with an eye to posterity have their value if only as a study of vanity. Of course, we must not, as did the Victorians, include the letters enmasse. Letters should be excerpted or even omitted if need be; they must subserve the biographer's basic aim. How much a letter says at times! Take the letter written to Wilkes by George Farquhar, as Farquhar the dramatist lay dying:

> Dear Bob:
> I have not anything to leave thee to perpetuate my memory but two helpless girls. Look you upon them sometimes and think of him that was to the last moments of his life, thine,
>
> George Farquhar.

Memoirs, diaries, and journals serve a similar purpose, although when elaborate and formal with an eye on the printer and posterity their value is reduced. Apparently artless diaries like Pepys' are invaluable; sophisticated journals like Gamaliel Bradford's have less value. Then they approximate autobiography and run all the hazards of autobiography, the idealizing memory, forgetfullness, vanity, and rationalization. Yet even here the value may be great. An example would be Gibbon's remark when his father sternly forbade his further courtship of a girl in France. Gibbon gave in, for his allowance was at stake, saying "I sighed as a lover, but obeyed as a son."

There remain the public acts of the man: the writings, the business career, the military campaign. That career always involves a culture or a *Zeitgeist*. The cultural background must, of course, come alive, but it should never be developed at the expense of the life. A biography loses its balance when the times swallow up the subject's career. Even the analysis of the public acts should be subservient to the treatment of character. A biography of a literary man should be biography and not literary history or literary criticism. Even so great a biography as Sandburg's *War Years* suffers from the voluminous data concerning the times. The data of the war occasionally dwarf the portrait of the hero. Lincoln is frequently lost under the flood of newspaper quotations. Here, too, incidentally, the writer faces the vexing problem of the man and his age. Did the man produce the time or the time the man? Is genius the molder of events, or is he simply the inevitable outcome of events, the finest flower of a culture rather than its maker? Would Lee have been Lee without the Civil War, would Lincoln? Could Shakespeare have written his plays in the eighteenth century?

In the case of a biography of a writer, the published volumes are immensely significant, but they must be used with great care. Biographers have always been prone to infer biographical fact from fictional representation, and that is a perilous venture. Did Wolfe do everything in *Look Homeward, Angel*; is Joyce Ulysses, is Whitman recording history in the *Sons of Adam*? Thomas Hardy complained bitterly of one biographer who inferred much fact from what was mere fiction. The writings though genuinely revelatory should be used with caution.

Should the biographer judge the life? Is he to evaluate it either in transit or formally at the end? I do not mean that he should deliver a sermon or perpetrate a tract. Earlier lives doubtless erred on the side of tedious moralizing. I am asking whether the biographer should do more than present the facts, or lay bare the history of the soul as a psychiatrist might analyze a case of melancholia.

The biographer does not deal merely with scientific facts; he is inevitably involved in values, with the soul, with the spirit. He handles value-facts. He works in a moral framework. I submit that whatever his pretensions, it is impossible for him to write without a moral bias, and that it will inevitably appear. Lytton Strachey's *Queen Victoria* is a criticism of a life as well as an account of one. In displacing the idealized Widow of Windsor, he substituted a stubborn fat lady who made a sort of grandeur of triviality. Every human life is a judgment upon itself. The biographer has the right to make that judgment explicit. He can estimate that life without disturbing its drama.

The just biographer must escape a linear or horizontal perspective. The naturalistic biographer sees curiosity and tragedy but little meaning in a man's life. The Freudian distorts whatever meaning there is on that basis. The humanist attempts to be universal but remains horizontal. The crucial question always revolves about the nature of man, and the linear perspective misunderstands his nature. Man can neither be understood nor judged except in terms of his relation to the eternal, to God.

Biography is indeed, both in its study and practice, a fascinating occupation. What is more interesting than human beings? To catch the color and mystery of the human heart, to illumine the darkness here and there for a moment, to feel humor and pity, that is a biographer's reward.

Carlyle said:

Human portraits, faithfully drawn, are of all pictured the welcomest on human walls.

That holds for bookshelves as well.

Lives of Great Men

The Banner (October 6, 1961)

Longfellow in a rather pointless stanza once wrote:

> Lives of great men all remind us
> We can make our lives sublime,
> And, departing, leave behind us
> Footprints on the sands of time.

I say this is a rather sentimental stanza because the lives of many great men were often far from sublime, because great men impress us most by their distance, and because footprints in sand are exceedingly perishable. But the lives of great men have something interesting and valuable to tell, and I should like to make a few comments on the memories of great men and the values of good biography. My hope is that some reader may be urged to enjoy the fascinating art of biography.

A study of the lives of great men brings home to us the endless vanity and the fundamental unity of men, "the glory, jest, and riddle of the world." There are the damaged souls like Benedict Arnold, so rarely gifted, so ironically traitorous. There are the imperturbable egoists like Cellini and Rousseau, the spectacular exhibitionists like Lord Byron, versifying the pageant of his bleeding heart and setting all upper England agog. There are the devious politicians like Machiavelli who lie with intention. One gets to know the silent torture of the poet Cowper whose visitations of madness broke a saintly soul. One gets to see the springs behind a man like Theodore Roosevelt, all act and movement. There are the waspish little men like Pope and the large-hearted spirits like Lincoln. The saints shine with the presence of grace. The range is endless, but the problems are always the same: love and hate, money — how to get it, and alas, how to hang on to it, hope and despair, faith and doubt, sadness and mirth, and always layers of nonsense. The pity and sadness; the brief candle gutters in the sweep of time while

> Ever at my back I hear
> Times winged chariot hurrying near.

The greatest hero frets his hour on the stage and after that the dark.

The memories of great men make us sympathetic with the greatly vexed and fumbling human race. In a good biography one discovers the context of error and sin, the cruel dilemmas and pressures that warp and bend. We get behind the curtain which often obscures our judgment in real life. Alexander Pope, the poet, was often a cruel, dishonest man, boiling his enemies in poetic vitriol, taking advantage of his best friends, deceiving many; but if one knows what he calls "this long disease, my life," if one understands the long torture that twisted little body endured from childhood; if one comprehends the prejudicial treatment his religion cost him, one tempers his judgment and indignation without excusing the sins. The memories of great men teach us the expense of greatness, and the towering burdens even the strongest crumble under. Biography develops pity, understanding, and appreciation for courage.

Thinking on the lives of great men makes us realistic about ourselves. Greatness is rare; it cannot be bought or borrowed. Genius is neither self-appointed, democratic, nor predictable. Great men are not made by rhetoric, but by blood, sweat, and tears. I always feel uneasy before the wisdom of the omniscient sophomore who knows all the answers at twenty and who gives regular diagnostic bulletins on the ills of the world. I marvel at the parents whose children always glitter in their eyes. I think of Coleridge who had read the Bible at five, who composed music at four, and of Bryant who knew the alphabet at sixteen months.

How unpredictable genius is! This is the age of the standardized test, the accumulating folders from kindergarten through college, the continuing statistical data. This is the age of human engineering, the interminable counseling programs, the infallible predictions, the casing of careers. This is the age of the PLAN, from planned parenthood to the final social security check. Genius laughs at it. Burns grew up in a Scotch hut, Lincoln in a cabin, Twain in the dull culture of a river town, Stephen Crane flunked composition at Syracuse University, and Daniel Defoe began *Robinson Crusoe* at sixty. All achieved preeminence, and not one would have done well in the College Board Entrance Examinations. Biography reminds us that gifted people can't always be cased and that they shouldn't be.

In reading biography we are always confronted with the image of man. Whose image does man bear? Is the soul of man merely a complex electronic process wholly sunk in nature as the naturalistic biographers assert?

Or is the soul of man simply a plastic medium, exceedingly malleable, neither good nor bad in itself? Then we are in the world of John

Dewey, and we need first to seek adjustment, group-mindedness, to-getherness, and the like.

Or is the soul of man created by God, housed temporarily in nature but always responsible to an order beyond it? Then we have a Christian view of man, and we need to judge his actions by biblical standards.

The lives of great men make concrete the doctrines of common grace. God does wonderful things even through unregenerate man. One thinks of R. L. Stevenson fighting a long and courageous battle with tuberculosis and at the same time leaving us a legacy of sunny books. One thinks of Voltaire saying, "I disagree with you, but I will defend to the death your right to say it." One thinks of Byron dying for Greek freedom at Missolonghi, Darrow fighting for the badgered and the framed, and all the anonymous young men from quiet country lanes and raucous city pavements charging up the rocky slopes of Iwo Jima.

There is also the unforgettable memory of the saints, the transforming power of special grace: cruel men made tender, coarse men made pure, selfish men made generous, mean men made noble, and evil men made good — the spirits of just men made perfect. We all know the grand chapter in Hebrews, what God wrought through faith. But think of Augustine, the lecher made pure; Luther, the coarse and unknown peasant made an heroic leader; Calvin's logical genius turned to the benefit of the church; Kuyper transforming a small group into a power. We linger with these memories to our lasting good.

The good biographer begins in admiration, curiosity, and sympathy, presents the relevant facts with honesty and judgment, and succeeds in creating a living likeness. He does not gild the lily or needlessly rattle the skeletons in the closet. He goes into "the dark backward and abysm" of time and produces not a wraith but a man; the body with its beauty or its homeliness. Browning's robust health and Carlyle's life-long dyspepsia are part of the story. He weaves in the illuminating anecdotes: Webster saying to a friend just before he died, "Have I said anything unworthy of Daniel Webster?"

He quotes from diaries and letters. He brings witnesses to bear and ransacks the newspapers. He quotes the spoken and written word. He tries to relate the man to his age and their mutual effect upon each other. He weaves the countless strands into a design which is drawn from the rhythm of the life portrayed. When one reads the last word, one feels that one knows the subject. Anyone who had read Sandburg's *Lincoln*, or Boswell's *Johnson* has enlarged his life with a new presence.

The biographer if he is worth his salt will not dodge the moral and religious issues mentioned earlier. He will evaluate the life. Was this great man merely the apex of social forces, or was he an original pressure on his time? Was he merely a complex animal? Was he simply human nature at its best, or was he made in the image of God and to be judged by the law of God? He must indeed be explained but he must also be estimated. Johnson and Carlyle make forthright evaluations; many modern biographers do not. It is up to the Christian reader to complete the evaluation. That too is a most rewarding effort. He will relate the finite to the infinite, the life of the man to the law of God, for he knows:

> The Good, the True, the Pure, the
> Just —
> Take the charm 'For ever' from them,
> and they crumble into dust.

The Man Behind the Pen

The Reformed Journal (September, 1966)

Some time ago I attended a conference in which a highly competent panel of college English teachers questioned the demise of the biographical heresy, the intrusion of biographical considerations into literary criticism. The panel and the audience were unanimous in concluding that the heresy was not only still alive, but lively, and that such intrusion was a sorry critical error. There was, in fact, such remarkable unanimity about the latter point that the whole meeting struck one as a plot. It almost seemed as if the panel were brilliantly spurring dead critical horses to the literary pound. I have been wondering ever since whether a heresy so pertinacious were so totally without defense.

The panel did assert at various times that biographical information is important to the teacher in at least two ways: as a ploy or gimmick to arouse interest in the life and work of the writer, and as a source of elucidation and interpretation. This panel assumed that the author had some idea of what he wanted to say, both before and after he said it. I believe these ideas are thoroughly usable as I shall try to show.

The English teacher who lives in the ivory tower, who greets the dawn with the thought of Cleanth Brooks, who burns incense to Henry James in his major phase and patterns his pedagogy on antiseptic formalistic principles has different students than I do. Most of my students are not panting after image clusters in *Epipsychidion*, exchanging deep thoughts on the objective correlative, or tracking down the beast in the jungle. These are all noble activities, but the majority of college students have to be cajoled, tricked, or strong-armed into them. Here, the biographical ploy is of real assistance. People or their fictional shadows interest almost everybody. Interest in the personality of the poet may lead to interest in his art, comment on the origins of the novel to interest in the fiction itself. The ideal, of course, is to fully engage the student with the work of art, but if the teacher fails, or if the student fails, there is always something to be said for an interest in a gifted human being.

How can one use the ploy? William Wordsworth was a great poet with no sense of humor. Here was a man who would recite his poems while the barber cut off his locks. When John Keats visited him and finally shattered the monolog, Mrs. Wordsworth said, "Mr. Wordsworth is never interrupted." Although Coleridge had publicly and marvelously praised Wordsworth's poetry, Wordsworth said of "The Rime of the Ancient Mariner," "The poem of my friend has great faults." Keats refers to his poetry as the "egotistical-sublime." What kind of poems *will* such a man write? To take another case. In 1890 Samuel Clemens was at the peak of fame and fortune. His bank account was burgeoning, his family affectionate and lively, his popularity so amazing that a card with his portrait drawn on for an address reached him from Australia. Then came a series of catastrophes almost in the manner of medieval tragedy. Their crushing impact permanently impaired his image of himself, and guilt feelings lacerated him virulently. How does a man seek to escape such overwhelming psychological pressures? Read *The Mysterious Stranger*. Finally, if one teaches at Calvin, little biographical reminiscence is needed to send students to the library for De Vries and Manfred.

Biography clearly illuminates certain writings. The most rigorous formalistic critics have been cagey about their pieces for explication; yet even Brooks cannot escape the eighteenth-century context of Pope's *The Rape of the Lock*, and he seems to be misinterpreting Wordsworth's famous "Ode" when he considers it apart from the doctrine of pre-existence so elaborately referred to in an author's note. Some critics are indeed highhanded about authorial comment. J. Jerome accuses Coleridge of "nonsense" and "gibberish" in "Kubla Khan," and another critic calls his history of the genesis of the poem "a prose rigamarole" and "characteristic piece of self-deception." For some critics, the author seems the victim instead of creator. Even if the author only thought he knew what he was saying, it would be an interesting thought. But there is more to it than that. Mark Twain's fiction continually reverts to the valley of his youth, and Hannibal remains Hannibal no matter how the moods of his later life distort the village. How much does Hemingway's fiction actually owe to his wounds in World War I? How does this traumatic experience echo through his creations to the end? He fought against the idea of the suicide of his father all his life and ended his own with a shotgun.

Sometimes a poet's own experience is so tyrannously dominant that it colors his portrait of another. Arnold's elegy of Clough in "Thyrsus" is probably a better picture of Arnold than of Clough into whose portrait he unconsciously weaves his own divisions, frustrations, and longings. Unless one knows something extraliterary about both men, one is hardly in a position fully to understand or elucidate the poem. Allen Tate wrote an elaborate analysis of his "Ode to the Confederate Dead," which renders an extremely complex poem more intelligible. In the case of Hart Crane's comments on the imagery in his poem "On Melville's Tomb," I must confess to little illumination. I do not mean to suggest that these works are unintelligible without extraliterary information, but that purely formalistic criticism hardly does them justice.

It was the consensus of the panel and the audience that we have now arrived at the end of biographical usefulness; here the cordon sanitaire must be placed. Biographical data must be rigorously excluded from evaluation. Certain elements in such a position are true. To condemn Edmund Wilson's criticism because *he* was a Marxist at one time; to condemn Whitman's *Leaves of Grass* because *he* was a covert homosexual, of Hart Crane's work because *he* was an open one, is unjust. But the matter seems more complex to me than this. The whole question revolves about what one means by literary criticism. If literary criticism is to be strictly limited to assessing the fusion of matter and form, if the work of the critic is confined to an analysis of the formal cause, or at the most to what the writer forms out of his material, then one can limit criticism to questions of communication. One will ask: How well does the writer organize what he says? Are means and ends well-adjusted? Does each part contribute to an organic whole? Whether the author is systematically blaspheming God or adoring Him really makes no difference. Literary excellence is to be measured by artistic complexity rather than by moral or spiritual criteria. It is here that I have my greatest reservations because I cannot dissever my values in such a matter. Literary art is always a combination of form and human experience, and the human experience whether realistic or imaginative is inextricably woven with a structure of values. I feel that formal criteria are always partial and that in making a critical evaluation of a novel or poem I am always involved in value judgments about the shared experience. One has often to admit that offensive value structures are organized with formal distinction and that to that extent they are art, but they are incomplete and unsatisfying art.

All this may sound like effete Matthew Arnoldism or the rearguard defense of the last puritan, but one gets tired of being pushed around by formalist critics and their disciples. One gets bone-tired of having to admire works whose morality is utterly shoddy, whose religious orientation is impious, and whose reading of life is radically distorted. Why should one be forced to say such corrosive journeys into the repellent are great works of art because they are technically impressive? Art seems to me to become great finally in terms of spiritual and religious perspectives. These are, of course, not universally convincing, but one has to judge in terms of the highest values he knows. That seems to me the most honest and responsible form of criticism, and it will never be satisfied with technical analyses. It will recognize a withered tree when it sees one.

If one grants the validity of non-formal judgments, then biographical data may influence one's final evaluation. Let us look at a few cases. Pope's letters to Swift are usually considered works of art; they are urbane, witty, and interesting, but, if one knows that Pope deliberately revised them before publication, thereby enhancing his own portrait and denigrating Swift's, if one knows they are a brilliant fake, and Pope a sinuous poseur, does not that knowledge have relevance as to their value? Or take Pope's famous portrait of Addison in "The Epistle to Arbuthnot." It is incisive and brilliant, but is it not important to know whether it is true? How can one know that without biographical data? Does it make any difference if one knows that Dreiser is sometimes speaking out of both sides of his mouth at the same time and acting at variance with both? If the study of biography reveals a man to be a fake in his writing, can one still wholeheartedly praise his work? Why do we usually abominate the fulsome syrupy adulations of patrons in poetical effusions? Is sincerity redundant?

Look at Burns' vehement scorn of the selfish rake in "The Cotter's Saturday Night," and then think of Burns' own remarkable career in such activities. Can one really separate all these things?

Let us look at the other side of the coin. All I have read about John Keats or by John Keats seems of one piece. The *Letters* and the poems reflect the same throbbing search for identity and meaning. One may disagree with Keats' final vision, but one is impressed by his consistent, passionate sincerity. Or to take another case, that of Willa Cather, whose world, as she said, broke in half in the year 1922. This was the year in which her simple pre-war world was finally shattered. The simple, primitive values of the frontier which she cherished and the humanistic values of traditional art which she affirmed, were replaced by the glitter and mammonism of the age and the shattering experiments in the new fiction. When Cather's own fiction became popular, her success proved unsatisfying. She was drawn backwards into earlier values, economic, artistic, and spiritual. This experience she gave fictional order in *The Professor's House*.

In *The Professor's House*, the protagonist is Professor St. Peter, an arduous scholar who wrote a magnificent history about an ancient culture. He wrote it in an old study under an aged roof, where he is creative and spiritually whole. His favorite student is Tom Outland, who is interested in the primitive culture of the American cliff dwellers. Tom Outland hates pushers, people who view the ancient pottery as things to be bought. He cannot understand Rodney Blake who sells the priceless pottery and then says to Tom, "I didn't know you valued that stuff any different than anything a fellow might run on to—a gold mine or a pocket of turquoise." Tom Outland is also an inventor; and when he dies his formula, bequeathed to Lilian, St. Peter's daughter to whom he was engaged before he died, is sold for a fortune by her husband, Marcellus. Marcellus buys a gaudy, pompous house, a standing and screaming repudiation of all Tom Outland stood for. The Professor's wife buys a new house from the profits of her husband's scholarly work, and he is moved to a sleek, impersonal apartment, devoid of tradition and meaning, and killing to his spirit. He attempts suicide but he is rescued at the last moment. He never feels at home again. His faith in life is gone and he can only look forward to his last house, the grave:

> For thee a house was built
> Ere thou was born
> For thee a mould was made
> Ere thou of woman camest.

Life's values, exemplified by the repudiated ancient cultures, are destroyed, and he lives with broken wings.

The novel imaginatively reflects with painful honesty Willa Cather's bitter personal experience. Knowing the biographical data not only helps one understand the fiction but proves its authenticity. I would not assert as Thomas Wolfe does in his Purdue speech that "every novel, every piece of creative writing that anyone can do is autobiographical," but I do believe that when fiction and experience are sincerely fused an added dimension of significance and value is achieved. One tends to think less of even a poem like *Lycidas* by Milton if forced to regard it as academic rather than heartfelt. Sincerity is, of course, an ambiguous term, but in its deepest sense of faithfulness to one's vision and to one's art, it seems to me relevant, and a knowledge of biography elucidates this relevance. As Henri Peyre says in his brilliant book *Literature and Sincerity*, "We may be grateful to the champions of sincerity in modern literature. . . . They have recalled to us that craft and artifice and technique are important but secondary."

Biography remains valuable in understanding and evaluating literature. It helps interest the student in good writing. It saves one from such a screamingly false interpretation of poetry as I recently read in an analysis of Keats' "La Belle Dame Sans Merci," where the critic, totally disregarding Keats' hectic and unnerving love affair with Fanny Brawne, engages in a farfetched rigamarole of symbolism and esthetic conjectures. It enables us more effectively to engage in total evaluation. We are all up to the neck in value judgments; we can hardly sidetrack our basic convictions about the relation between a man and his work and then view the work in isolation from the life with a genteel, spectatorial attitude. One is, it seems to me, driven not only to evaluate the artistic vision but its integrity. I admire most "men who live their visions as well as write them."

12

"Beware of the Leaven"

SATIRE

Satire, once the crown jewel of earlier literary periods, is a much diminished art in the modern age. Instead of satire we often have vitriol; instead of humor mere laceration; instead of encouragement a verbal bulldozing. Others may speculate why this is. In its classical tradition satire is one of the healthiest forms of literary expression. It is, of course, critical of certain things, but satire is critical with humor and wit. And satire is not content merely to be critical; it also intends to improve a human situation if not humanity itself. The following selections cast a critical eye on some modern phenomena, but while the judgments adduced may be critical of those phenomena, they are tendered in a spirit of wit, humor, and gentle corrective.

Something Like Little Vermin

The Reformed Journal (September, 1970)

After the magnanimous king of Brobdingnag had heard Gulliver's account of the British armament industry, he says to Gulliver that the bulk of his compatriots are a "most pernicious race of little odious vermin." After I had read Jessica Mitford's article "Let Us Now Appraise Famous Writers" in the July *Atlantic*, I felt a similar disgust and condemnation. I felt that way because these famous writers through their very exalted status guaranteed a ruthless and highly profitable swindle by the Famous Writers School, an unscrupulous correspondence school which cajoles people who can read into thinking that they can also write. There are fifteen of these famous writers, among them Bruce Catton, Bennett Cerf, Paul Engle, Bergen Evans, Clifton Fadiman, and Phyllis McGinley, together with such deceptive names as Faith Baldwin and Mark Wiseman, and such an utterly appropriate name as J. D. Ratcliff. These people are the guiding faculty, and their benevolent faces beam above the announcement: "If you want to write, my colleagues and I would like to test your writing aptitude. We'll help you to find out whether you can become a successful writer." If you do well on this test, which none of the guiders read, they promise to "teach you to write successfully at home." For this professed service the guiders do nothing, although they receive splendid pay. They screen no manuscripts; they guide no writers. They only allow their benign smiles to be photographed in endorsement of a program they have not designed and do nothing to execute.

When Miss Mitford questioned Faith Baldwin about these promised services, stated in the plainest English, her response was, "Oh, that's just one of those things about advertising." None had a stronger defense. Paul Engle said, "I'm so very far away from all that." Bennett Cerf said, "Frankly, if you must know, I'm an awful ham — I love to see my name in the paper." They simply endorse a product which they know nothing about, but it is a scandalous project.

The Writer's Course in the Famous Writers School costs $785 cash and $900 in time payments. Eight hundred salesmen corral the sheep, some of them in the seventies and semi-literate. The manual of instruction as quoted and described by Mitford is uniformly incompetent. Instructional description of student writing is euphorically deceptive. The results have been spectacularly insignificant, and the school makes most of its money out of dropouts who pay the full fee even though the fifteen famous writers no longer look over their shoulders. Famous Writers School is a competent swindle.

The revelation was a shock. The famous writers are or were esteemed and often brilliant. Mr. Engle conducted a nationally known and deservedly prestigious writer's course at the University of Iowa. The famous fifteen are near the core of literary establishment: they make or break reputations of other writers. It is utterly depressing to see important men exchange a fat lie for a fast buck. One can't laugh it off. Their participation dirties our literary life.

I believe one is also enlightened. Possibly, one can now better understand why Cerf publishes some of the work he does, why literary garbage like *Portnoy's Complaint* is praised, why *Couples* receives an enthusiastic reception. Possibly, too, one can understand better the snobbish resistance of the Eastern literary establishment to the idealistic honesty of the best of our western writers. Furthermore, it profoundly reinforces my feelings about the inescapable web of character, sincerity, and literary work. I shall not be able again to read even Catton with the pleasure I did. Finally, I am thankful that the college and university teachers I had in rhetoric were painstakingly devoted to honest criticism and that my colleagues engaged in the same activity are equally so.

Have You Paid Your Uncle?

The Reformed Journal (February, 1974)

Recently I heard of a Pennsylvania judge who excused some Quakers from paying income taxes because it conflicted with their religious beliefs, a tax loophole of magnificent proportions.

Unfortunately, it does not conflict with mine, and so I look enviously at the newly arrived Form 1040 with its annual challenge to intelligence, honesty, and moral sense. To intelligence — because people are often talking about deductions I have the wit neither to find nor exploit. To honesty — because whether I make a mite or a mint, I can easily find ways to cheat. I am unlikely to be audited, and if audited, discovered, and if discovered, fined. To a sense of justice — because I find some elements of the tax decidedly unfair, and some ways in which the government spends my money immoral. Finally, to sour the whole process, there is the knowledge that I can find no legal ways to escape paying three times the tax some rich men with twenty times my income pay.

Preparing tax returns is an annual frustration. In the first place, I find it impossible ever to file a completely accurate report. I know the allowance for sales tax is too low, but squirreling up every sales slip is beyond me. Who has the patience to record every coin or bill put in the collection plates or the Salvation Army buckets? Then there are the knotty little questions. How about the time I traveled forty miles to give a talk, got soaked going from the banquet hall to the car, returned home, got my suit dry-cleaned, and never got a dime? Does that cancel out the twenty dollars I got at another occasion? Should I send for the book *Tax Guide for College Teachers*, which includes "an unbelievable tax trick which you should be able to use." Must I turn tricky and see what my country can do for me? On a deeper level must I protest against immoral use of money by not paying the tax — as Thoreau did with mild consequences or as Edmund Wilson did with unbelievable harassment? In the end I pay the legal dues because this is an imperfect world and after all, most of the unjustices are minor and operational.

Every year, however, I am impressed by the staggering amount of taxes Americans do pay, whatever their reactions. I am greatly encouraged by the fundamental decency of the American public; it is that decency that carries the shirkers, the cheats, the crafty and the plunderers. It is in a sense a gesture of trust and confidence and should have a twofold impact on legislators everywhere. Legislators should feel a solemn obligation to deserve this trust. Furthermore, my hope is that every legislator will resist the power plays of factional interest, will make a real effort to base legality on morality, disenfranchise undeserved benefits, and establish a system in which every citizen bears a fair share of the burden.

In a democracy, where confidence and trust are of crucial importance, those who govern must deserve the trust they expect, and the use of money is a pretty authentic guide to whom you can trust.

Homage to Joggers

The Reformed Journal (February, 1979)

Sometimes I feel rather energetic — until I see a jogger again. When we first moved into our neighborhood, I noticed middle-aged people running down the street and wondered where the fire was. In our old neighborhood middle-aged people never ran around. I soon realized they were joggers, pounding up hilly Saginaw Avenue in sun, rain, heat, and light snow — every day.

Joggers are pacing from Penobscot to Pacific Grove and from Miami to Mackinac Island. They have become a national phenomenon. As they hurtle by while I am driving or sauntering along, they tend to become a moving rebuke and an annoying mortification. Their devotion to health and preventative physical maintenance arouse in me the guilt feelings of a moral drone. Joggers may be fringe faddists, but they are more significant than the flagpole sitters, goldfish eaters, and mini-golf enthusiasts of the 1930s. They are out to build bodies, not to break records.

I am not a jogger. My father, precise, sedate, and immensely dignified, could not have been a jogger. To visualize him in sneakers and shorts blowing up and down the city streets, imperiling and imperiled by traffic, is impossible. When my father bought a new open Chevrolet, for which he paid $800, he equipped himself for driving it by acquiring a duster, gloves, a special cap, goggles, and a muffler. Donning these, he would make the odyssey from Grundy Center to Marshalltown, Iowa, at about twenty miles an hour. Hands tightly on the wheel, eyes unwavering on the rutted dirt road ahead, like Captain Ahab trying to sight a whale, he drove wordlessly, as if his life depended on it. In a real sense it did, but it wasn't good enough. After sideswiping one cow and later driving into the middle of a herd that came suddenly on the road near Wright, Iowa, he sold the car and never bought another. My father was a walking man. In my youth, at the time about which Coleridge said, "What cared this body for wind and weather/ When youth and I dwelt in it together," I could have jogged, but the solitary world of the jogger would never have lured me. The loneliness of the jogger, eyes rigidly ahead, mind focused on physical excellence, does not attract me.

I know I observe joggers from the outside, but I observe many of them. What are they like from the outside? First of all, I have never seen anyone who looks like a happy jogger. Joggers probably enjoy doing their duty; they may be flowing with unappeasable inward happiness, but they don't reflect it on their faces, which are grim, strained, and usually open-mouthed. They pound on as if they were delivering messages to Garcia or hurrying to Thermopylae. A faint shadow of snobbery lurks about their faces.

Secondly, joggers strike me as wholly intent on running, riveted on motion. I do not think they fantasize or reflect. A walker can dream, imagine, reflect. Shelley read the Greek poets as he paced the beach. Wordsworth composed whole works as he sauntered about the Quantock hills; once he returned immediately to transcribe the long poem "Tintern Abbey." The jogger seems just to jog.

The typical jogger, in the third place, exhibits a remarkable insouciance as to what he looks like. Sweat shirts, shorts, and sneakers do not work wonders for everyone. Bald at the top, bare at the gnarled knees, belly bouncing, dripping with sweat, he slogs relentlessly up Saginaw hill and undermines what may be my false pride.

Finally, many joggers are mavericks on the roadway, especially when it is sheathed in snow or ice. I dread hitting anyone, but it would be doubly painful to maim a jogger.

I respect the relentless physical self-improvement of the jogger. Observing them arouses in me faint feelings of guilt. That feeling was heightened by reading a recent issue of *The Banner*, the official denominational paper of the Christian Reformed Church. In it was a sizable number of interesting articles on aging, mostly written by people half my age. Taken together, they almost constituted an activist manifesto. How shall we, the elderly, then live? The answer was — in perpetual motion. Nobody recommended lounging in an armchair reading Cicero on old age; nobody mentioned Browning's Rabbi ben Ezra, who saw it as a period of quiet reflection and assessment; but there were many suggestions about *activities*. Get out of your chair and join, carve and weave, run for elder and run as elder, play: shove at shuffleboard, throw horseshoes, carom croquet balls, play golf mini or major. Unfortunately, no one mentioned umpiring little league baseball games.

I became uncomfortable. Should I pedal furiously on an exercise bike or bounce on the bench at a Baldwin Fun Machine, the new electronic organ (if I could afford one)? Or should one quote Robert

Maynard Hutchens, former President of the University of Chicago? He once attributed his good health to the fact that whenever he had an impulse to exercise he lay down until it passed. I would not question the importance of reasonable exercise or a personal preference for activism; what I dislike is elevating what is something of a fad to a model and a preference into a principle.

I pay a certain homage to the joggers as they file down footpath and pavement toughening their bodies and buoyed, I assume, by the conscious rectitude of Eagle Scouts. I enjoy seeing films of softball stars in their late seventies and reading an account of a rocky Englishman climbing Wordsworth's mountains at ninety. I don't resent activists; what I resent is the idea that I am derelict in not joining them.

Some years before I retired, people were asking me when I was going to retire. Now they are asking me what I am *doing* when retired. Some have the notion that when you are retired from what you can do well, you ecstatically embrace activities that you can't. If retirement means anything, it means that you have paid your dues and that further contributions are voluntary. I sometimes think all activists should remember Franklin's maxim: "Presumption first blinds a man, then sets him running." The presumption involved is that the activist's way is the right way to spend old age, and that there is a certain self-righteousness attached to that judgment. I respect activists, but there is as much to be said for reading in a good life as there is for running in one.

Paradise in Palm Springs?

The Reformed Journal (August, 1980)

If *Sixty Minutes* began sixty minutes later, I could see all of it. Yet even watching only the half of it which does not coincide with the evening church service, I enjoy its ferrets into chicanery, hypocrisy, and occasional noble achievement. The other Sunday evening I saw a spectacular, indelible, and obscene documentary on the voluptuous lifestyle of Palm Springs, California.

Palm Springs, California, is a golden little city, hemmed in by aus-tere mountains and reached only by private planes. Here, in the happy valley, the citizens live in an opulence that makes the magic of Alad-din's lamp look dim. Houses cost $3 million and up. They are fronted by grass knee-deep in Vigoro and hedges clipped as meticulously as Haile Selassie's beard. Down the street glides a gold-plated Rolls Royce, as the man with the big cigar sees Nellie home. Flanking the houses are swimming pools — sometimes two: his and hers. Inside live the millionaires, so rich they never need ask what a thing costs.

These millionaires spend money as if it were endless, which it seems to be. Here are drawing rooms with rugs into which the nabob's shoes (at $500 a pair) sink as if into soft snow. A soused burgher need not worry about spilling a double martini on his $250 tie. A hostess can smile about a salad plate tipped on her $5000 dress. We saw one hostess with a face and a voice like a parrot displaying five deep rows of $2000-$5000 dresses: a row for sports, a row for lunch-eon, a row for cocktail parties, and two rows whose peculiar fitness I have forgotten.

The dogs are pedigreed back to Fafir, and the slinking Persian cats, with golden bells, stare at one with insufferable arrogance. Some of the citizens, when they golf, ride a gold-plated golf cart, and draw a golden putter from a $67,000 set to putt a silver-plated ball on the seventh green. The treasure of continents pours into Happy Valley, delighting the residents, who benefited most from the mad Mr. Jarvis' tax cuts. They live in an exquisitely selfist lifestyle; they live it up on a scale which to a Christian they can never live down.

This lifestyle is simply wicked, a monument of hoggish selfishness, a supreme manifestation of gluttony. Chaucer's Pardoner should have seen it, for it is the very essence of "escesse and glotonyes." Here is the psychology of selfishness, the moral miasma of materialism. Noth-ing justifies it, and even if, like Huntington, Stanford, Carnegie, and Frick, they give money to colleges and libraries, they are without excuse. Sumptuous giving does not exonerate sumptuous living.

For 99 percent of the human race this is an unreal city, the ultimate suburb, arrived at only by plane, as alien to the mass of Americans as the hanging gardens of Babylon. Money and mountains bar the world of welfare, food stamps, seedy houses, and the struggle of or-dinary people to make a decent living. How can a woman with hundreds of dresses understand a mother who shops for her children at garage sales? How can a man who swings a golden driver understand what it feels like to be fifty-five and suddenly permanently unemployed?

They will say, as they did in the Great Depression, "Any man who wants to can find a job." I lived through that depression. I was twenty-one when it began and over thirty when it began to end. I know what a lie that was. They may characterize the welfare system as a public trough patronized by chiselers. I lived next to a black lady with five children, and I know what a geyser of baloney such a generalization is. How can people who dine on caviar and lamb understand a family that buys bread at the Butternut Thrift Shop? I know that many on welfare cheat; that some use food stamps for luxuries, but that is not the peculiar ethic of the poor. I daresay that for everyone who cheats on welfare there is a counterpart who cheats in government, business, income tax returns, and the subterranean barter system. Let us not patronize the poor because of their petty thievery.

F. Scott Fitzgerald once said to Hemingway, "The rich are different from us," and Hemingway replied, "Yes, they have more money." That is the difference — not desires, but opportunity. Greed is not limited to class. Thoreau pointed out that a poor man can go to his crusts with the same greediness that a rich man approaches his sumptuous fare. There is something of Palm Springs in us all.

We can escape neither our sinful nature, nor the selfist, materialistic culture that urges us to give ourselves what we so richly deserve. Self-expression and self-realization, operating in a world where other selves become means and objects, influence us all.

The true selfist sees no face but his own; he never, as Lewis remarks somewhere, sees that other face. To him that other kingdom is a myth. The selfist lives in style far more luxurious than he needs to do the work God wants him to do in the world. He dines richly on fare that gives him gout. Without being an alcoholic he drinks enough in a year to clothe a dozen children. He takes vacations, expensive and frequent, far beyond the need for refreshment to do his tasks. The selfist fumbles about in his purse and fishes out a dime for the poor. The selfist works for money and lets others work for nothing. The selfist never gave a twenty dollar bill to a poor man in his life.

I have never heard a minister preach on the text "*Again* I tell you it is easier for a camel to go through the eye of a needle than for a rich man to enter the kingdom of God." I have read explanations of the text which enlarge the needle and shrink the camel, so that if he really crunches down and throws off baggage, he can just squeeze through. At best, then, the rich man is going to have to be squeezed! Is your lifestyle ever really squeezed by your Christian faith, or do you think you will get through the needle without giving up a single pleasure? Or is this a truth like the one I once heard a minister comment on by saying, "This is a truth which we do not accept."

The American Way of Life

The Reformed Journal (September, 1953)

The American has always been something of a paradox; he has from the beginning worshiped God with a glance to Mammon, or worshiped Mammon with a regretful awareness of God. In recent years, however, the traditional idealisms have become dimmer, and the pride and satisfaction in things more intense, so much dimmer that the Vice-President of General Motors could in a speech at the industrial cavalcade "The Parade of Progress" identify the American way with the booster's paradise, an endless profusion of things. Mammon towered above the rows of gleaming cars.

The calvalcade was interesting. The film showed arrestingly beautiful industrial designs. The cars and planes had the hard glamor of superb craftsmanship in steel and color. Here was creative industry, a fruitful wedding of natural form and the dream of man, no mere imitation of nature but rather a fusion of the geometrical lines and balance of the bird with beaten metal. As the fact for the form, said Emerson; here it was bird become jet plane. But most interesting of all was the keynoter's speech in which he undertook to define the American way of life. And that way consisted of a geometrical ratio in the increase of things: more and better cars, more and better planes, more machines in a paradise of instruments. The hope of the exhibition, said the speaker, was to set a boy dreaming — of things. This is the American way of life, then; the American in charge of an Aladdin's lamp of technology calling up the industrial jinn to bring into being an ever-growing flood of machines. Having achieved this we can sing with Sandburg's woman, named Tomorrow:

> We are the greatest city
> The greatest nation:
> Nothing like us ever was. . . .

Was the speaker right in identifying the American way of life with the abundance of things? Then the "past is a bucket of ashes," and then the great voices of the American past are no longer even echoes.

For the Puritan put the city of God before the city of man. As Edward Taylor said:

> Make me Thy loom then, knit therein
> This twine
> And make Thy Holy Spirit, Lord,
>   wind quills.

Despite the sordid branches, the main road of the American revolution was called *Freedom*. Emerson and the Romantics said things must not be allowed to vault into the saddle and control mankind. Whitman's hope of democracy rested upon ideal values — brotherhood not social security. The great reformers from Garrison to Bryan, the countless ordinary Americans who have been Christian, the late humanists have all recognized a law above the law of the thing. If the speaker was right, these voices have had their day. But it seems to me that he was misreading both our past and our present. Nobody would deny that the pioneer gouging out the continent, that Franklin, predatory capitalism, manifest destiny, pragmatism, and instrumentalism are American. They are peculiarly American, but they are part not the whole or central trait of our paradoxical American character and way of life. The speaker was then both right and wrong. My fret was that he never mentioned the end for which the means exist, and my worry is that he may be more right than I think.

I did not expect the speaker to quote Emerson on the danger of too many possessions; I have no quarrel with technology as such. I am no agrarian, and I don't care to move to Walden Pond to study the emerald pickerel. I would like to drive any new General Motors car. I am fully aware of the crucial importance of automobiles in the American economy. What distresses me is the careless confusion of ends and means, the resting in the materials of civilization, the sacrifice of ends to means. What is the paradise of machines for? Of that there was not a word, and I believe, without being naive, that there should have been such a comment. If we rest in the machines, we will eventually become machines. We will resemble the traveler who runs his car six hundred miles a day. Instead of landscape he has seen green lights, filling stations, and license plates. He has become a living joint between wheel and pedal. He is part of the Ford he drives. My point is that the real American sees beyond the means to the goals which he should serve. He has the "vision of latitudes unknown," and the vision goes beyond the dizzy thrust of the jet plane. It penetrates to the pattern of the ideal man, and at its best finds the ideal man in the Word of the Lord.

Since America has always had plenty, and since Americans have always had craft and energy, she has always been threatened by things. Mammon has always stood by with his hands full of gold. The astute Puritan traders, the canny Dutch, the solid Jersey farmers, the prosperous Quakers, the lavish Virginia planters merely begin a list of the exploiters of the fathomless resources of America. And only too often the Puritan found his heart in the counting houses of Boston. The pressure of things reached its unsavory peaks in the Gilded Age of Grant and the scandals of the Harding Administration. And the circle came full in the twenties when a descendant of the Puritans occupied the White House in Washington and said that the business of America was business.

The materialism of modern America needs no proof. One needs but to compare the revenue raised for the church and for cocktails. One need but to scan one's own budget to see where the money goes, and then to realize that most Americans contribute little or nothing to churches or Christian schools. Superficially considered, the speaker seemed sadly right. Furthermore, his remarks synchronized with the popular philosophy of our time — instrumentalism. Instrumentalism reduces the mind itself to a thing, and defines the good life as the successful integration of the mind, a thing, with the other shapes of things we call society.

Even though materialism may be the dominant trend in American life, it can not yet, I believe, be called the American way of life. The essential American tradition is still alive in many places. Dissent is still with us. The Puritan and Christian speaks in the noble verse and prose of Eliot, the humanist is alive in Frost, and even the American satirists like Wolfe and Lewis, whom we so often belabor, score heavily. There is alive yet the residual Puritanism in the social reformers and humanitarians. There are many believers who hold to a Christian ideal that always determines the use of things, that regards them as valuable only in relation to men, and man as valuable only in relation to God.

But the candle may be guttering at times, even among us. We need to be on guard; we need to check the use of our energies. Do we preserve for spiritual activity a wide margin of the leisure which machines provide? Is our leisure creative as well as recreative? Do we value freedom as we ought? Most men, said Thoreau, lead lives of quiet desperation. They will always do that if they live in things. Absorption in things can only satisfy a society of adolescents. Americans need a peptalk like *Life Begins at Forty* because they have by that time neither mastered things nor acquired enough of them. If one does not master things one can never acquire enough of them. Success is measured by the bank account, and that is never big enough, for the person caught by the lure of material success would rather drive a Cadillac on time than a Ford paid up. Life begins when one becomes aware of the central meaning of spiritual values, when it is God-centered. If the American way of life is to be in things, most adult Americans will lead lives in quiet desperation.

Bibliography

Student Writings at Calvin College

1929

"To You" (poem), *Chimes* (May, 1929), p. 158.

"A College Paper and College Ideals" (editorial), *Chimes* (October, 1929), pp. 249, 251.

"The Bluebird" (poem), *Chimes* (December, 1929), p. 326.

"Satire on the Prowl" (editorial), *Chimes* (December, 1929), pp. 351-352.

1930

"The Incredible Occurs: A Collegian Appreciates" (editorial), *Chimes* (March, 1930), pp. 103, 106.

"John Galsworthy" (editorial), *Chimes* (April, 1930), pp. 136-138.

"The Violet" (poem), *Chimes* (May, 1930), p. 182.

"A Rolled Stone" (editorial), *Chimes* (May, 1930), p. 192.

"Philistines" (editorial), *Chimes* (September 19, 1930), p. 2.

"A Sunbeam" (poem), *Chimes* (September 19, 1930), p. 3.

"Images" (poem), *Chimes* (September 19, 1930), p. 3.

"The Campus and What to Do with It" (editorial), *Chimes* (October 17, 1930), p. 2.

"Deeds Not Breath" (editorial), *Chimes* (November 24, 1930), p. 2.

"George Gissing" (editorial), *Chimes* (November 28, 1930), p. 2.

"Oratory" (editorial), *Chimes* (December 18, 1930), p. 2.

"So This Is College" (article), *Prism* (1930), pp. 104-105

"The Ray" (poem), *Prism* (1930), p. 111

1931

"Chapel" (editorial), *Chimes* (February 9, 1931), p. 2.

291

"Extra-Curricular Activities" (editorial), *Chimes* (May 20, 1931), p. 2.

"The Spirit of Transition" (editorial), *Chimes* (May 22, 1931), p. 2.

Articles and Book Reviews

1935

"An American Novel," Review of *Lucy Gayheart* by Willa Cather, *Calvin Forum*, I (September, 1935), p. 47.

"Pieter Brueghel Novelized," Review of *Droll Peter* by Felix Timmermans, *Calvin Forum*, I (October, 1935), p. 71.

1938

"Jeremiah Come to Life," Review of *Hearken unto the Voice* by Franz Werfel, *Calvin Forum*, IV (August, 1938), pp. 21-22.

1939

Review of *Old Haven* by David Cornel DeJong, *Calvin Forum*, IV (January, 1939), pp. 134-135.

"The Road from Xanadu," *Calvin Forum*, IV (February, 1939), pp. 159-160.

"Passengers of Infinity," *Calvin Forum*, IV (March, 1939), pp. 183-184.

"Pupils Paint Their Ideal Teacher," *The Journal of Education*, CXXII (March, 1939), pp. 89-91.

"Siegfried Sassoon's 'Old Century,'" *Calvin Forum*, IV (May, 1939), p. 232.

"Not a Blue Flower," *Calvin Forum*, V (November, 1939), pp. 71-72.

1940

Review of *But Who Wakes the Bugler* by Peter DeVries, *Calvin Forum*, VI (October, 1940), pp. 54-55.

"Poetry and The Commonplace," *Calvin Forum*, VI (November, 1940), pp. 69-71.

1941

"A Saga of Matunska Valley," Review of *Another Morning* by Wessell Smitter, *Calvin Forum*, VII (August-September, 1941), pp. 31-32.

1946

"Dreiser's Latest Novel," Review of *The Bulwark* by Theodore Dreiser, *Calvin Forum*, XI (June-July, 1946), p. 252.

1947

"Sinclair Lewis on Racial Prejudice," Review of *Kingsblood Royal* by Sinclair Lewis, *Calvin Forum*, XII (June-July, 1947), pp. 251-252.

1948

"Our Own Grub Street," *Calvin Forum*, XIII (January, 1948), pp. 114-115.

"Experiment in Tolerance," Review of *The Metaphysical Society* by Alan Brown, *Calvin Forum*, XIII (April, 1948), pp. 196-197.

"An A. J. Cronin Entertainment," Review of *Shannon's Way* by A. J. Cronin, *Calvin Forum*, XIV (November, 1948), p. 79.

1949

"The Criticism of Fiction," Review of *Forms of Modern Fiction* by William Van O'Connor, ed., *Calvin Forum*, XIV (January, 1949), p. 127.

"Plain Talks on Calvinism," Review of *The High Points of Calvinism* by Bastian Kruithof, *Calvin Forum*, XV (August-September, 1949), p. 29.

"Tennyson, Man and Poet," Review of *Alfred Tennyson* by Charles Tennyson, *Calvin Forum*, XV (October, 1949), pp. 54-55.

1950

"Fiction with Catholic Propaganda," Review of *The Cardinal* by Henry Morton Robinson, *Calvin Forum*, XV (June-July, 1950), pp. 247-248.

1951

"Sinclair Lewis and F. Scott Fitzgerald," *Calvin Forum*, XVI (April, 1951), pp. 186-187.

1952

"Something of the Shorter Catechist," Review of *Voyage to Windward* by J. C. Furness, *Calvin Forum*, XVII (February, 1952), pp. 138-139.

"On Guidance and Counseling," *The Reformed Journal*, II (May, 1952), pp. 3-4.

"Is *Pilgrim's Progress* Still Readable?" *The Reformed Journal*, II (August, 1952), pp. 7-8.

"The Fish, the Man, the Sea, and the Sky," *The Reformed Journal*, II (October, 1952), p. 2.

1953

"America Unlimited," Review of *The Course of Empire* by Bernard DeVoto and *The Big Change* by Frederick Lewis Allen, *Calvin Forum*, XVIII (March, 1953), pp. 167-168.

"The American Way of Life," *The Reformed Journal*, III (September, 1953), pp. 1-2.

"Two Worlds," Review of *The Bounty Lands* by William D. Ellis and *Two Worlds for Memory* by Alfred Noyes, *Calvin Forum*, XIX (November, 1953), p. 67.

1954

"The Crowded Intellectual," Review of *Company Manner* by Louis Kronenberger and *America and the Intellectual*, *Calvin Forum*, XIX (May, 1954), pp. 210-211.

"Love Thou the Land," *The Reformed Journal*, IV (July-August, 1954), pp. 2-4.

1955

Review of *My Several Worlds* by Pearl S. Buck, *Calvin Forum*, XX (March, 1955), pp. 164-165.

"The Popular Book," *The Reformed Journal*, V (December, 1955), pp. 12-13.

1956

"Cecil De Boer: 1898-1955," *Calvin Forum*, XXI (January, 1956), p. 65.

"On Writing a Life," *Calvin Forum*, XXI (February-March, 1956), pp. 84-88.

"Five Travelers," *The Reformed Journal*, VI (May, 1956), pp. 7-10.

"Dr. Henry Zylstra," *Chimes*, LI (December 7, 1956), p. 1

1957

"Henry Zylstra: In Memoriam," *The Reformed Journal*, VII (January, 1957), p. 4.

"Do Illiterate A.B.'s Disgrace Us All?" *College Composition and Communication*, VIII (February, 1957), pp. 50-55.

"Pens, Pennies, Patrons," *The Reformed Journal*, VII (November, 1957), pp. 8-10.

"Writing the Christian Novel," *The Reformed Journal*, VII (December, 1957), pp. 14-17.

1958

"Henry Zylstra: The Man and His Work," Preface in *Testament of Vision* by Henry Zylstra. Grand Rapids: Eerdmans, 1958.

1959

"Teaching the Great Books," *The C.E.A. Critic*, XXI (January, 1959).

"Calvinism and Literary Criticism," *The Banner*, XCIV (June 26, 1959), pp. 9, 24.

"Siouxland and Suburbia," *The Reformed Journal*, IX (October, 1959), pp. 9-11.

"Then Jesus Came," *The Banner*, XCIV (December 11, 1959), p. 6.

1960

"A Lion Without," *The Reformed Journal*, X (January, 1960), p. 10.

"No Exit," *The Banner*, XCV (April 1, 1960), pp. 6-7.

"The American Dream," *The Banner*, XCV (August 12, 1960), pp. 6-7.

"The Colors of Fall," *The Banner*, XCV (November 18, 1960), pp. 6-7.

1961

"Seven Pitfalls in Reading," *The Reformed Journal*, XI (January, 1961), pp. 5-6.

"Lincoln as an American Hero," *The Banner*, XCVI (February 10, 1961), pp. 4-5.

"Literature in the Calvin Classroom," *The Banner*, XCVI (June 9, 1961), pp. 16, 29.

"The Unextinguished Hearth," *The Reformed Journal*, XI (September, 1961), pp. 9-12.

"Lives of Great Men," *The Banner*, XCVI (October 6, 1961), pp. 6-7.

1963

"Robert Frost: 1875-1963," *The Reformed Journal*, XIII (February, 1963), p. 5.

"Alien Fruit," *The Reformed Journal*, XIII (April, 1963), pp. 6-8.

1966

"The Man Behind the Pen," *The Reformed Journal*, XVI (September, 1966), pp. 12-14.

1969

"The Intentional 'Intentional Fallacy,'" *The Reformed Journal*, XIX (January, 1969), pp. 20-21.

"The Writer's Side of the Story," *The Reformed Journal*, XIX (May-June, 1969), pp. 12-13.

1970

"Why 'Bottle-Up' the Author," *Dialogue*, II (January, 1970), p. 4.

"You Must Know Everything," Review of *You Must Know Everything* by Isaac Babel, *The Reformed Journal*, XX (March, 1970), pp. 24-25.

"Something Like Little Vermin," *The Reformed Journal*, XX (September, 1970), pp. 2-3.

"Emerson and Our Permissive Society," *The Banner*, CV (October 23, 1970), pp. 16-17.

"The Beginning and the End," *The Banner*, CV (December 25, 1970), pp. 12-13.

1971

"The Dimensions of a Home," *The Banner*, CVI (February 26, 1971), pp. 4-5.

"A Book for All Seasons," *The Banner*, CVI (April 23, 1971), pp. 4-6.

"The Schoolmaker," *Christian Home and School*, L (September, 1971), p. 27.

"Dr. Johnson's Thorn," *The Banner*, CVI (September 3, 1971), pp. 16-17.

"The Drummer at Walden Pond," *The Banner*, CVI (December 31, 1971), pp. 4-5.

1972

"The Sermon in Disrepute," *The Reformed Journal*, XXII (April, 1972), pp. 5-6.

"Religious Perspectives in Faulkner's Fiction," Review of *Yokna-Patawpha and Beyond* by J. Robert Barth, ed., *Christianity and Literature*, XXII (Fall, 1972), pp. 23-24.

"Do Not Let These Stories Die," *Spark*, XIX (September, 1972) pp. 4-6.

"Alice and the Deacon," *The Reformed Journal*, XXII (September, 1972), pp. 5-6.

"Antiques and Our Heritage," *The Banner*, CVII (September 29, 1972), pp. 6-7.

"In Praise of the Sermon," *The Outlook*, XXII (December, 1972), pp. 6-7.

"The Never-Ending Journey of the Wise Men," *The Banner*, CVII (December 15, 1972), p. 9.

1973

Review of *Trousered Apes* by Duncan Williams, *The Banner*, CVIII (February 16, 1973).

"Prudes and Savages," *The Reformed Journal*, XXIII (March, 1973), pp. 5-6.

Review of *Poems '67 to '72* by E.W. Oldenberg, *The Reformed Journal*, XXIII (September, 1973), p. 47.

"Greed or Grain," *The Reformed Journal*, XXIII (September, 1973), p. 3.

"The Books in a Boy's Life," *The Banner*, CVIII (October 5, 1973), pp. 16-17.

1974

"Have You Paid Your Uncle?" *The Reformed Journal*, XXIV (February, 1974), p. 3.

Review of *The Honorary Consul* by Graham Greene, *The Reformed Journal* XXIV (April, 1974), pp. 21-22.

"Thirty and Out," *The Reformed Journal*, XXIV (September, 1974), pp. 5-6.

"Big Words and Long Articles," *The Banner*, CIX (September 13, 1974), p. 12.

Book Review of *Conversations with Frederick Manfred* by Frederick Manfred, *The Reformed Journal*, XXIV (October, 1974), pp. 22-23.

1975

"As I Knew Them," *Dialogue*, (April, 1975), pp. 20-22.

"Babe Ruth and the National Pastime," *The Reformed Journal*, XXV (July-August, 1975), pp. 6-7.

"Modern Communications and the Sermon," *Outlook*, XXV (September, 1975), pp. 5-6.

"This Land Is Whose Land?, Review of *The Massacre at Fall Creek* by Jessamyn West, *The Reformed Journal*, XXV (September, 1975), pp. 27-28.

"The Odds Are on Objects," Review of *Here at the New Yorker* by Brendan Gill, *The Reformed Journal*, XXV (November, 1975), pp. 29-30.

"Two Who Won: Mr. and Mrs. George Kamp," *The Banner*, CX (November 14, 1975), pp. 10-11.

1976

"Centennial Reflections: Rev. Mr. J. J. Hiemenga: Calvin's First President" *The Banner*, CXI (January 30, 1976), p. 12.

"Centennial Reflections: President Broene Makes a Prophecy," *The Banner*, CXI (February 13, 1976), p. 13.

"Centennial Reflections: Veterans — Among the Finest Group Ever Taught at Calvin," *The Banner*, CXI (February 20, 1976), p. 9.

"Whatever Happened to Alice?" *The Reformed Journal*, XXVII (March, 1976), pp. 6-7.

"Paul DeKoekkoek: Much Praise, But. . . ," *The Banner*, CXI (June 25, 1976), pp. 20-21.

"The Real Thing," Review of *The Manly-Hearted Women* by Frederick Manfred, *The Reformed Journal*, XXVI (May-June, 1976), pp. 36-37.

"Ellis Island and the American Dream," *The Reformed Journal*, XXVI (July-August, 1976), pp. 3-4.

"Monuments and Myths in Temple Square," *The Reformed Journal*, XXVI (October, 1976), pp. 3-4.

"But How Did He Do It?" Review of *How It Was* by Mary Welsh Hemmingway, *The Reformed Journal*, XXVI (December, 1976), pp. 27-29.

1977

"Karate at 70-Plus," *The Reformed Journal*, XXVII (March, 1977), pp. 5-6.

"A Gem of a Story," Review of *The Shepherd* by Frederick Forsyth, *The Reformed Journal*, XXVII (March, 1977), p. 31.

"Darkness on the Diamond," *The Reformed Journal*, XXVII (August, 1977), pp. 4-5.

"The Past in Your Future," *The Banner*, CXII (September 30, 1977), pp. 6-8.

"Mr. Chips Couldn't Make It Today," *The Reformed Journal*, XXVII (November, 1977), pp. 3-5.

"Old Year's 1926," *The Reformed Journal*, XXVII (December, 1977), pp. 2-3.

"Mr. Chips Couldn't Make It Today," *The Reformed Journal*, XXVII (November, 1977), pp. 3-5.

"Old Year's, 1926," *The Reformed Journal*, XXVII (December, 1977), pp. 2-3.

1978

"Safe in the Eye of the Storm," *The Reformed Journal*, XXVIII (April, 1978), pp. 17-18.

"Dragonflies Draw Flame," Review of *Brother to a Dragonfly* by Will D. Campbell, *The Reformed Journal*, XXVIII (May, 1978), pp. 24-25.

"Christians and Free Speech," *The Reformed Journal*, XXVIII (October, 1978), pp. 2-3.

"Hard Times for a Best Seller," *The Banner*, CXIII (October 27, 1978), pp. 5-7.

1979

"A High-Class Gentleman," Review of *Max Perkins* by A. Scott Berg, *The Reformed Journal*, XXIX (January, 1979), pp. 25-26.

"Homage to Joggers," *The Reformed Journal*, XXIX (February, 1979), pp. 5-6.

"Professor John H. Tuls, 1907-1978," *The Banner*, CXIV (March 16, 1979), p. 23.

"Reflections on Sabbath Observance," *The Banner*, CXIV (March 30, 1979), pp. 23-24.

"Presents to the Lord," *The Banner*, CXIV (May 25, 1979), pp. 6-7.

"Some Notes on Magnanimity," *The Reformed Journal*, XXIX (August, 1979), pp. 2-4.

"A Magnanimous Exchange," *The Reformed Journal*, XXIX (November, 1979), p. 6.

"Christian Civility on the Frontier," Review of *The Sign of a Promise* by James Schaap, *The Reformed Journal*, XXIX (November, 1979), pp. 21-22.

"The Reluctant Angel," *The Reformed Journal*, XXIX (December, 1979), p. 9.

"Biography as Art," Review of *The Nature of Biography* by Robert Gittings, *The Reformed Journal*, XXIX (December, 1979), pp. 22-23.

1980

"In Debt to Alma Mater?" *The Calvin Spark*, XXVI (February, 1980), pp. 6-7

"The Man Who Dared to Criticize Harvard," Review of *The Harvard Mystique* by Enrique Lopez, *The Reformed Journal*, XXX (February, 1980), p. 34.

"Communicating the Incommunicable," Review of *The Wind Blows Free* by Frederick Manfred, *The Reformed Journal*, XXX (March, 1980), pp. 26-27.

"Paradise in Palm Springs," *The Reformed Journal*, XXX (August, 1980), pp. 2-3.

"A Joyful Critic," *The Reformed Journal*, XXX (November, 1980), pp. 5-6.

1981

"Whatever Happened to Sunday?" *The Reformed Journal*, XXXI (February, 1981), pp. 13-15.

"Diamond Greed," *The Reformed Journal*, XXXI (July, 1981), pp. 6-7.

"Eschatological Fiction," Review of *The Clowns of God* by Morris West, *The Reformed Journal*, XXXI (August, 1981), pp. 25-26.

"A Noble Profession," *The Reformed Journal*, XXXI (September, 1981), pp. 4-5.

1982

"Recreating Nero," Review of *The Flames of Rome* by Paul L. Maier, *The Reformed Journal*, XXXII (March, 1982), pp. 24-25.

"Bears, Raspberries, and Mr. Watt," *The Reformed Journal*, XXXII (May, 1982), pp. 3-4.

Books

Leslie Stephen as a Biographer. Dissertation, Northwestern University, 1940.

Promises to Keep: A Centennial History of Calvin College. Grand Rapids: William B. Eerdmans, 1975.

Reviews of *Promises to Keep*

James Daane, *The Reformed Journal*, XXVI (March, 1976), p. 32.

Neal Plantinga, *The Banner*, CXI (June 18, 1976), pp. 24-25.
Nelvin Vos, *Christian Scholars Review*, VIII (No. 3, 1978), pp. 268-271.

Grand Rapids Press Portraits

Bruce Buursma, "A Professor Who Made His Mark," *Grand Rapids Press*, June 8, 1975, pp. 2B-3B.

Gerald Elliott, "John J. Timmerman: Books, the Essence of Life," *Grand Rapids Press*, October 10, 1978, p. 15A.